PRIMARY ENGLISH
FOR TRAINEE TEACHERS

Sara Miller McCune founded SAGE Publishing in 1965 to support the dissemination of usable knowledge and educate a global community. SAGE publishes more than 1000 journals and over 800 new books each year, spanning a wide range of subject areas. Our growing selection of library products includes archives, data, case studies and video. SAGE remains majority owned by our founder and after her lifetime will become owned by a charitable trust that secures the company's continued independence.

Los Angeles | London | New Delhi | Singapore | Washington DC | Melbourne

PRIMARY ENGLISH
FOR TRAINEE TEACHERS

2ND EDITION
(REVISED & UPDATED)

DAVID WAUGH,
WENDY JOLLIFFE and
KATE ALLOTT

 |

Learning Matters
An imprint of SAGE Publications Ltd
1 Oliver's Yard
55 City Road
London EC1Y 1SP

SAGE Publications Inc.
2455 Teller Road
Thousand Oaks, California 91320

SAGE Publications India Pvt Ltd
B 1/I 1 Mohan Cooperative Industrial Area
Mathura Road
New Delhi 110 044

SAGE Publications Asia-Pacific Pte Ltd
3 Church Street
#10-04 Samsung Hub
Singapore 049483

Editor: Amy Thornton
Development Editor: Jennifer Clark
Production Controller: Chris Marke
Project Management: Deer Park Productions
Marketing Manager: Catherine Slinn
Cover Design: Wendy Scott
Typeset by: C&M Digitals (P) Ltd, Chennai, India
Printed and bound by
CPI Group (UK) Ltd, Croydon, CR0 4YY

Library of Congress Control Number: 2016960203

British Library Cataloguing in Publication data

A catalogue record for this book is available from
the British Library

ISBN 978-1-4739-7340-4 (pbk)
ISBN 978-1-4739-7339-8

At SAGE we take sustainability seriously. Most of our products are printed in the UK using FSC papers and boards.
When we print overseas we ensure sustainable papers are used as measured by the PREPS grading system.
We undertake an annual audit to monitor our sustainability.

Contents

Acknowledgements

We are grateful to all the teachers and trainee teachers who contributed ideas and experiences for case studies for this book. In particular, we would like to thank Chris Carr, who wrote about his drama work during placement at St Joseph's Catholic Primary School, Stanley, and Alex Callaghan of Durham University, who wrote about his drama work at Holmwood School in Middlesbrough. Thanks also to Emma Anwar, a trainee teacher from Edge Hill University who shared her multimodal text work from her final professional practice, and Sarah Wright, a senior lecturer at Edge Hill University, for sharing her experience of using digital texts. We would also like to thank Samantha Jane Twentyman, Debbie Myers's former NQT, for the Paper-bag Princess Case Study.

About the editors, contributors and series editor

Editors

Kate Allott

Kate is a lecturer in primary English at York St John University. She has also worked as a literacy consultant for North Yorkshire County Council, and as a regional adviser for the National Strategies Communication, Language and Literacy Development programme.

Wendy Jolliffe

Wendy is Professor of Education and was, until recently, Head of Teacher Education at the University of Hull. She has worked as a Regional Adviser for ITT for the National Strategies and advised ITT providers on effective provision for literacy. Wendy is a former deputy head teacher in a primary school in Hull and she has published extensively on teaching English and implementing Cooperative Learning.

David Waugh

David is the subject leader for primary English at Durham University. He has published extensively in primary English. David is a former deputy head teacher, was Head of the Education Department at the University of Hull, and was Regional Adviser for ITT for the National Strategies from 2008 to 2010. As well as his educational writing, David also writes children's novels, including *The Wishing Room*, which was written with 44 children from 16 East Durham schools.

Contributors

Kirsty Anderson

Kirsty is a former deputy head teacher, worked as a literacy consultant in Newcastle Upon Tyne and is now a Teaching Fellow in English and Art for Primary Education at Durham University. She is a member of the HEA.

Jane Carter

Jane is a former deputy head teacher and is now a senior lecturer in primary education at the University of the West of England. She has been seconded as the manager of the Bristol Primary Teaching School Alliance for the past two years. Jane is also a National Teaching Fellow of the Higher Education Academy.

Eve English

Eve, a former head teacher, is a lecturer in English on the PGCE (Primary) and BA (QTS) courses at Durham University. She has published extensively on primary English.

Holly Dyer

Holly teaches at East Farleigh Primary School in Kent.

Ruth Harrison-Palmer

Ruth is a former acting head teacher. She has worked for the National Strategies and Cumbria Local Authority as a literacy consultant. Currently, Ruth is Head of Department for Postgraduate Programmes and Partnership in Education at the University of Cumbria.

Debbie Myers

Debbie is a Senior Lecturer in Primary Education at Canterbury Christ Church University, specialising in English, science and professional studies. She is a former head teacher and Literacy Consultant who developed a whole-school programme of role-play supported writing resulting in the achievement of Excellence in Cities Awards (2004–2006).

Claire Norcott

Claire, a former primary school teacher, is now a senior lecturer in primary English at Edge Hill University. Claire teaches English on Undergraduate and Postgraduate Programmes.

Claire Warner

Claire has worked as a senior adviser for literacy with the National Strategies and as a senior lecturer and leader of undergraduate ITE programmes at Chester University. She is now an independent consultant for primary English, working with universities and schools on a wide range of literacy initiatives.

Series Editor

Alice Hansen

Alice is the Director of Children Count Ltd, an education consultancy company that provides continuing professional development for teachers in primary mathematics education and primary schools in curriculum development in England and abroad. Prior to her current role, she was a primary school teacher and senior lecturer in primary education before becoming a programme leader of a teacher-training programme. Alice is an active researcher and her research interests include primary mathematics, technology-enhanced learning and teacher professional development.

Introduction

This book is linked closely to the latest *National Curriculum in England* (DfE, 2013), the English section of which you will find in Appendix 3. In it, we have explored key elements of the English curriculum and have shown, through reference to established research and case studies of classroom practice, ways in which the challenges of implementing the new curriculum may be met.

The curriculum is not compulsory for academies, free schools and independent (private) schools, but it is likely that it will be followed, at least in part, by most of these, given that the Standard Attainment Tests (SATs) and Spelling, Punctuation and Grammar (SPAG) tests will be linked to its content. The curriculum is a response to perceived shortcomings in education and yet the United Kingdom ranks highly in international educational performance tables. In May 2014, Pearson Education produced rankings based on an amalgamation of international tests and education data, including the OECD's Programme for International Student Assessment (PISA) tests, and two major US-based studies, Trends in International Mathematics and Science Study (TIMSS) and Progress in International Reading Literacy Study (PIRLS). The rankings placed the UK in second place among European countries and sixth overall in a global education league table (**http://thelearningcurve.pearson.com/index/index-ranking**).

Nevertheless, some of the studies, such as PIRLS (2011), which were drawn on to compile the global rankings show that there are aspects of primary English performance which should concern teachers in the UK. For example, although most 11-year-olds read well, there is still a long tail of underachievement and too many children leave primary school unable to read at a level which will equip them for secondary education. Worryingly, English children appear less enthusiastic about reading than in many other countries and this may hamper their future progress.

This book begins with a chapter which outlines key elements of the National Curriculum for English. This is followed by a chapter in which Wendy Jolliffe examines the place of speaking and listening in the curriculum – a key aspect of language which many felt continues to be neglected in the curriculum. Jane Carter explores vocabulary development in Chapter 3, and this is followed in Chapter 4 by Kate Allott's examination of spelling and how it can be taught effectively. Together with spelling, grammar and punctuation are key features of the curriculum, with a considerable proportion of the publication devoted to these areas. In Chapter 5, David Waugh looks at ways of teaching grammar and punctuation effectively. At the heart of government policy on literacy is an emphasis on systematic synthetic phonics (SSP), and in Chapter 6 Ruth Harrison-Palmer discusses the role of SSP within the teaching of reading.

Many English specialists were relieved to note the attention given to fiction and poetry in the new curriculum, and these are explored by Debbie Myers and Holly Dyer in Chapters 7 and 8 respectively. In Chapter 9, Kirsty Anderson examines the place of non-fiction in primary schools, including exploring the role of digital texts. Claire Warner's Chapter 10 on writing stresses the need to balance the technical and compositional aspects of writing, and the importance of talk for writing, while in Chapter 11 Claire Norcott explores the use of multimodal texts and their growing importance in schools.

In Chapter 12 Eve English asks whether there a place for drama and concludes that there certainly is.

In Chapter 13, Kate Allott provides guidance on planning to deliver the curriculum. In Chapter 14 Kirsty Anderson discusses how assessment is an invaluable classroom resource. The book concludes with Kate Allott's chapter on Mastery in English.

Throughout the book you will find activities and self-assessments which will support your growing subject knowledge. At the end you will find an appendix which provides simple definitions of some key terminology and answers to self-assessment questions which are provided in the chapters.

Primary English has been written by people with expertise in primary English, most of whom have published widely in the field, and all of whom teach the subject in schools or universities. We hope that it will help you to gain a strong insight into the English curriculum and will support your development as an informed and enthusiastic practitioner.

David Waugh, Kate Allott, Wendy Jolliffe
January 2017

Reference

DfE (2013) *The National Curriculum in England: Key Stages 1 and 2 Framework Document.* London: DfE.

1 The National Curriculum

David Waugh

Learning outcomes

By reading this chapter you will develop your understanding of:

- what you need to know as primary teachers in order to teach the 2014 English National Curriculum;
- some of the challenges you face when you teach the 2014 English National Curriculum;
- approaches to teaching the 2014 English National Curriculum.

Teachers' Standards
3. Demonstrate good subject and curriculum knowledge:

- have a secure knowledge of the relevant subject(s) and curriculum areas, foster and maintain pupils' interest in the subject, and address misunderstandings;
- demonstrate a critical understanding of developments in the subject and curriculum areas, and promote the value of scholarship;
- demonstrate an understanding of, and take responsibility for, promoting high standards of literacy, articulacy and the correct use of standard English, whatever the teacher's specialist subject.

Introduction

In a book about primary English, you might expect authors to maintain that English is the most important subject in the curriculum. However, this view is reinforced by government in the Key Stage 1 and Key Stage 2 National Curriculum for England, which is dominated by three areas and by English in particular, in the number of pages devoted to different subjects, as you can see below.

English	87	Computing	2
Maths	45	Art and design	2
Science	32	Music	2
History	4	Physical education	2
Geography	3	Languages	2
Design and technology	3		

In this chapter, an overview of the English curriculum will be provided in order to set other chapters in the book in context. It is interesting to analyse the emphases in the English National Curriculum by looking at the number of times different aspects of English are mentioned:

Writing	140
Reading	115
Spelling	101
Books	60
Grammar	50
Punctuation	33
Listening	19
Poems	14
Poetry	11
Drama	8
Speaking	6
Literacy	2
Literature	2

The curriculum is only statutory for maintained schools, so academies and free schools do not have to adopt it. However, given that pupils in these schools will still take the Year 1 phonics screening check and the Year 2 spelling, punctuation test, as well as SATs tests and the Year 6 spelling, grammar and punctuation test, it is likely that all state schools will at least pay lip service to the content of the curriculum.

In some ways, the latest curriculum is less detailed than its predecessors, but it does include considerably greater attention to spelling and grammar, as well as having a lengthy glossary which defines the terminology that pupils will be expected to know and understand. A key element in the then Secretary of State's mantra for education is subject knowledge and this is reflected across subject areas. For English, there is a wealth of subject knowledge required by both pupils and teachers, particularly given the strong emphasis upon grammar and grammatical knowledge. As Michael Gove stated: *Our new national curriculum affirms – at every point – the critical importance of knowledge acquisition* (Michael Gove, BBC News, 6 February 2013).

This is reflected in the English curriculum as a whole with its two statutory appendices on Spelling and on Vocabulary, Grammar and Punctuation, which provide *an overview of the specific features that should be included in teaching the programmes of study* (DfE, 2013a, p16). Indeed, the curriculum states the following:

Throughout the programmes of study, teachers should teach pupils the vocabulary they need to discuss their reading, writing and spoken language. It is important that pupils learn the correct grammatical terms in English and that these terms are integrated within teaching.

(DfE, 2013a, p16)

Activity: grammatical terminology

The National Curriculum requires children to know and understand the following terms:

- noun, noun phrase;
- statement, question, exclamation, command;
- compound, adjective, verb;
- suffix;
- tense (past, present);
- apostrophe, comma.

Are you confident that you know and understand the terms?

For which age group do you think this knowledge and understanding is required?

(You will find the answer at the end of the chapter and definitions in the glossary (Appendix 1) of the English National Curriculum.)

How does the 2014 National Curriculum differ from its predecessor?

In this section you can see examples of some of the key ways in which the 2014 curriculum differs from its predecessor.

General

- Instead of Key Stage 1 and Key Stage 2 objectives, there are now year-by-year objectives for Year 1 and Year 2, then Lower Key Stage 2 (Years 3–4) and Upper Key Stage 2 (Years 5–6).
- The spelling and grammar objectives are very specific and there are word lists which must be learnt for different age groups.
- Phonics is given strong emphasis in both key stages and phonics is expected to be taught systematically.

- There is a focus on reading for pleasure and children should be encouraged to *read widely across both fiction and non-fiction ... to establish an appreciation and love of reading, and to gain knowledge across the curriculum. This is important to increase pupils' vocabulary.* The introductory section on language and literacy states that schools *should provide library facilities* and set ambitious expectations for reading at home (DfE, 2013a, p11).

- Children are expected to be able to memorise and recite poetry.

- There are clearer expectations about transcription in writing.

- There is less focus on specific text types and genres than in previous national curricula and the Literacy Framework.

- There is greater flexibility about what to teach in many areas.

- Spoken English, which was neglected in earlier drafts, acquires greater status in the final version, with children expected to recite poetry, take part in debates, discussions, presentations, performances, role play and improvisations. Indeed, there is an emphasis upon spoken language across the curriculum:

  > Teachers should develop pupils' spoken language, reading, writing and vocabulary as integral aspects of the teaching of every subject ... . Fluency in the English language is an essential foundation for success in all subjects.

  > (DfE, 2013a, p10)

- Drama is given greater emphasis in the final version of the curriculum, which states that *All pupils should be enabled to participate in and gain knowledge, skills and understanding associated with the artistic practice of drama* (DfE, 2013a, p15).

- There is also increased emphasis on handwriting, which is expected to be fluent, legible and speedy.

- Reading is given high priority and the curriculum is quite prescriptive about actions schools should be taking:

  > Pupils should be taught to read fluently, understand extended prose (both fiction and non-fiction) and be encouraged to read for pleasure. Schools should do everything to promote wider reading. They should provide library facilities and set ambitious expectations for reading at home.

  > (DfE, 2013a, p10)

Key Stage 1

- There is more emphasis on re-reading books and reading aloud.

- There is greater focus on engaging with and interpreting texts.

- Some aspects of language are now introduced earlier – for example, *prefixes* and *suffixes*.

- There is an increased focus on composition and more detail is included on grammar and punctuation.

- Writing has been made more challenging, with children expected to develop 'stamina' for writing longer compositions.

- Children will be expected to write from memory simple sentences dictated by the teacher that include words they have learned.

- Handwriting is emphasised and non-statutory guidance is quite prescriptive as, for example, the instructions for Year 1:

> Handwriting requires frequent and discrete, direct teaching. Pupils should be able to form letters correctly and confidently. The size of the writing implement (pencil, pen) should not be too large for a young pupil's hand. Whatever is being used should allow the pupil to hold it easily and correctly so that bad habits are avoided.
>
> Left-handed pupils should receive specific teaching to meet their needs.
>
> (DfE, 2013a, p24)

Years 3 to 6

- At Key Stage 2, the National Curriculum continues to refer to word reading, with pupils expected to use the skills they have acquired in Key Stage 1 to help them to read unfamiliar words.

- As with Key Stage 1, there is more detail on handwriting. For example, non-statutory guidance for Years 3–4 states the following:

> Pupils should be using joined handwriting throughout their independent writing. Handwriting should continue to be taught, with the aim of increasing the fluency with which pupils are able to write down what they want to say. This, in turn, will support their composition and spelling.
>
> (DfE, 2013a, p38)

The non-statutory guidance for Years 5–6 states the following:

> Pupils should continue to practise handwriting and be encouraged to increase the speed of it, so that problems with forming letters do not get in the way of their writing down what they want to say. They should be clear about what standard of handwriting is appropriate for a particular task, for example, quick notes or a final handwritten version. They should also be taught to use an unjoined style, for example, for labelling a diagram or data, writing an email address, or for algebra and capital letters, for example, for filling in a form.
>
> (DfE, 2013a, p47)

Although pupils are expected to continue to read books with a range of different structures, the curriculum gives far less attention to different genres and text types than its predecessors, including in particular the 1998 National Literacy Strategy (NLS).

There is a strong emphasis on spelling, grammar and punctuation, which includes lists of words that must be learned at different stages. The lists were modified during the consultation stages, with some rather odd choices which scarcely figure in children's reading or their lexicons, such as haughty, hearty, lawyer and quench, being removed along with, interestingly, Europe and European. In fact, the Years 5–6 spelling list was reduced from 235 words to 100, with only 45 of the words in the draft appearing in the final version: all of which suggests that the consultation genuinely listened to and acted upon feedback.

Reaction to the 2014 curriculum has been mixed, with some organisations welcoming changes in the final version in response to lobbying and consultations, while others lamented the emphasis upon transcription, phonics and grammar. Below you can read three responses to curricular change. Note how the authors tend to see opportunities rather than problems arising from the 2014 curriculum.

The Cultural Learning Alliance particularly welcomed the increased emphasis upon drama.

Research focus: drama

Drama is now represented on the National Curriculum

We are extremely heartened to see that our suggested paragraph on Drama has been included within the Aims section of the English Curriculum. Up to this point Drama was not included in the statutory section of the document. The Spoken Language section now reads as follows.

> All pupils should be enabled to participate in and gain knowledge, skills and understanding associated with the artistic practice of drama. Pupils should be able to adopt, create and sustain a range of roles, responding appropriately to others in role. They should have opportunities to improvise, devise and script drama for one another and a range of audiences, as well as to rehearse, refine, share and respond thoughtfully to drama and theatre performances.

There is still not enough Drama within the curriculum and the document lacks the structured drama learning framework we would like to see, but this paragraph represents a real step forward. It makes a clear statement that *all* children should learn through and about drama; describes drama as an artistic practice; and makes it clear that young people should be enabled to respond to theatre and performance. It is a first building block for teachers, drama and theatre professionals on which to base great teaching and learning.

→

CLA colleagues were involved in delegations to the DfE, Roundtables and submission drafting throughout the consultation process; and all our partners, particularly National Drama, should feel proud that their tenacity has led to tangible change, even though there are further battles to be joined in order to give drama the parity and status it deserves.

Cultural Learning Alliance (2013), 'The New National Curriculum – a quick guide', 13 September, www.culturallearningalliance.org.uk/news.aspx?id=115 (accessed 31 March 2014).

The limited attention given to exploring different genres might be seen as providing opportunities for teachers rather than restricting them, as The Literacy Tree Learning Consultancy argues below.

Research focus: different genres

There is no real mention of writing genres within the 2014 curriculum, which is of no surprise as it is not a framework or a strategy, so this gives schools some freedom with their delivery of the programme of study for writing. This is split into two sections: transcription (spelling and handwriting) and composition (articulating ideas and structuring them in speech and writing). While the existing framework was useful in many ways for supporting schools to plan units of work where the children would be immersed within a genre for two or three weeks, there were sometimes tenuous choices of texts or extracts chosen to support a particular genre. This gives us the opportunity to pick a text which can really excite and engage a class and maybe use it to support the writing for one or two genres. Indeed, the document itself states that *This is not intended to constrain or restrict teachers' creativity, but simply to provide the structure on which they can* construct exciting lessons.

The Literacy Tree Learning Consultancy, Planning with the new primary English curriculum, available at: **http://theliteracytree.co.uk/newcurriculum/** (accessed 13 June 2014).

James Clements, a senior leader at an outstanding inner-city primary, looked closely at what is expected in comprehension.

Research focus: aspects of comprehension

'The expectations for comprehension in the 2014 curriculum are demanding. Right from the start, children are expected to practise and develop higher order comprehension skills. Rather than be restricted to simple recall of information, Year 1 children should have the opportunity to infer information about characters and make predictions based on what they know from

$\longrightarrow$

the text. As children become older and more sophisticated as readers, it isn't the complexity of the aspect of comprehension, it is the level of challenge provided by the text. Key Stage 1 teachers know that a Year 1 child is just as able to make inferences about how the characters are feeling in *Owl Babies* as a Year 6 child can in *Treasure Island*.

Language comprehension

In the 2014 curriculum the focus is on language comprehension, rather than reading comprehension, so reading lessons are not limited to texts that children can read for themselves. Instead, hearing a book or poem read aloud and then discussing it as a class has a key part to play in supporting children's understanding. As the 2014 curriculum states, children should:

> Listen to and discuss a wide range of poems, stories and non-fiction at a level beyond that at which they can read independently.

> (DfE, 2013, p21)

We know that children's word-reading skills and comprehension often develop at different rates and by focusing on language comprehension, children will be able to engage with texts that will challenge their understanding, develop their vocabulary and support them in becoming stronger readers. By regularly listening to and discussing books beyond their current reading level, children will have the opportunity to hear books that are exciting and motivating, supporting them to develop a love of books and reading.

Teaching comprehension

Teachers know that the best way to develop children's comprehension skills probably won't be to give them an extract from a text followed by ten questions to answer. While this may be a legitimate strategy for assessment occasionally, the expectations within the 2014 National Curriculum lend themselves to a much more dynamic way of teaching comprehension. Instead, the teaching sequence might be something much more like the following.

The teacher reads a challenging text aloud to the class, stopping to clarify meaning and draw children's attention to certain features, be they specific language features, unfamiliar words or phrases or interesting ideas.

The children discuss the text, both with the teacher and in groups or as a class, the teacher leading the discussion through careful questioning and interventions.

The class can then demonstrate what they have learnt in another context, whether that's through a written outcome or a discussion or debate.

Clements, J (2013) English in the national curriculum, 10 October, available at : **http://community.tes.co.uk/national_curriculum_2014/b/english/archive/2013/12/05/english-in-the-national-curriculum-by-james-clements.aspx** (accessed 13 June 2014).

The DfE has removed levels from the curriculum

The Government accepted the Expert Panel's recommendation to omit level descriptors from the National Curriculum and not replace them, stating the following:

> This is because we agreed that levels have become too abstract, do not give parents meaningful information about how their child is performing, nor give pupils information about how to improve. Levels have detracted from real feedback and schools have found it difficult to apply them consistently – the criteria are ambiguous and require teachers to decide how to weight a huge array of factors. Beyond the tests at key stage 2 and GCSEs at key stage 4, it will be for schools to decide how they assess pupils' progress.

(DfE, 2013b, p2)

What does the curriculum mean for the way we teach?

Does the curriculum dictate how we should teach?

The programmes of study outline what should be taught, but do not provide guidance or instruction about how things should be taught. This contrasts with the first version of the National Literacy Strategy Framework for Teaching (DfEE, 1998), which provided highly structured guidance on the literacy hour, even to the extent of stating how much time should be devoted to shared work, whole-class work, group and independent work, and a plenary session.

Is there scope for teachers to focus on some areas more than others?

Schools have to cover the programmes of study, but teachers can decide which aspects they wish to emphasise. They may, for example, decide to cover some things in a day or a week, but spend half a term on others. It is up to schools to decide how to plan and deliver the curriculum.

Planning for teaching

Subjects do not have to be taught discretely, so there may be opportunities to develop literacy and oracy through different subjects and topics. However, because the content of subjects needs to be covered, it will be important to ensure this happens while developing children's knowledge and skills.

Do children have to work at the level appropriate for their age?

Some children's needs will be better met if they work from programmes of study from earlier or later key stages. The curriculum states the following:

> Schools are, however, only required to teach the relevant programme of study by the end of the key stage. Within each key stage, schools therefore have the flexibility to introduce content earlier or later than set out in the programme of study. In addition, schools can introduce key stage content during an earlier key stage if appropriate. All schools are also required to set out their school curriculum for English on a year-by-year basis and make this information available online.
>
> (DfE, 2013a, p17)

So while there is flexibility in how schools decide to deliver the curriculum and when, they do need to plan carefully and make their plans available to the public.

Do teachers have sufficient subject knowledge to teach the National Curriculum?

Many trainee teachers will have been taught English with a curriculum which included the National Literacy Strategy (NLS) Framework (DfEE, 1998). It is interesting to compare the content of the NLS with the 2014 National Curriculum (NC) by comparing the glossaries which each document provides. Both glossaries include a preamble which states that they are designed for teachers, but both are made up of terms which feature in the curriculum and which children are expected to know and understand.

The biggest difference is in the size of the glossaries, with the NLS defining 195 terms while the NC defines only 76. Both include a large number of grammatical terms, and the NC states that it *includes all the grammatical terms used in the programmes of study, as well as others that might be useful.* The NLS, however, also focuses on terms connected with text types, something which is not a feature of the NC, but both include several terms associated with phonics.

There are 38 terms which are defined in both glossaries:

> *adjective, adverb, antonym, apostrophe, article, clause, compound word, conjunction, consonant, digraph, ellipsis, etymology, grapheme, homonym, homophone, inflection, morpheme (morphology in NC), noun, object, participle, passive, phoneme, phrase, plural, prefix, preposition, pronoun, punctuation, root word, sentence, Standard English, subject, suffix, syllable, synonym, tense, verb, vowel.*

It might be expected, then, that teachers who were taught using the NLS would be familiar with a good proportion of the metalanguage of the 2014 curriculum, as well as being aware of a range of text types. However, it is worth looking at the terms which appear in the NC but not in the NLS to check that these are also understood:

active voice, adverbial, auxiliary verb, cohesion, cohesive device, complement, continuous, co-ordinate/co-ordination, determiner, finite verb, fronting/fronted, future, grapheme-phoneme correspondences, infinitive, intransitive verb, main clause, modal verb, modify/modifier, noun phrase, past tense, perfect, possessive, preposition phrase, progressive, received pronunciation, register, relative clause, schwa, stress, subjunctive, subordinate/subordination, subordinate clause, transitive verb, trigraph, word, word class, word family.

Close inspection of the NLS shows that many of the above are subsumed within other definitions in the NLS, so those teachers who acquired and understood the terminology of the NLS are unlikely to find the terminology of the NC particularly challenging.

Activity: more terminology

Look at the lists of terms above and consider which you will need to find out more about and which you feel confident about. You can find the National Curriculum glossary at the back of the English National Curriculum and at: **www. gov.uk/government/publications/national-curriculum-in-england-primary-curriculum**

Use the glossary to check your subject knowledge.

It is worth considering what informed recent developments in education and the National Curriculum. The former Secretary of State for Education, Michael Gove, looked at other countries which outperformed England in international tests. Finland, in particular, seemed to impress Mr Gove, but there are some important things to consider when looking for the reasons for Finland's strong performance.

Research focus: Finnish lessons

In 1970, Finland was near the bottom of international educational rankings, so its government decided to take radical steps in a bid to improve performance. These are described in Pasi Sahlberg's (2011) book, *Finnish Lessons*. Sahlberg, a Finnish educator and visiting

$\longrightarrow$

Professor of Practice at Harvard University's Graduate School of Education, describes the key reforms as including:

- abolishing private education in Finland – it became illegal to charge for education;

- an emphasis on equality, and not excellence;

- no standardised testing until 16;

- competition being frowned upon;

- children being encouraged to follow their interests, and develop their skills, rather than a government curriculum;

- increases in teachers' pay and status, with a requirement that all are university-trained and have master's degrees, so that they become respected in the community.

Although local planning is guided by the regulations of the National Framework Curricula, curriculum planning varies from school to school and is the responsibility of teachers, schools and municipalities rather than the state. As Ravitch (2012, p1) states:

> Finland's national curriculum in the arts and sciences describes what is to be learned but is not prescriptive about the details of what to teach or how to teach it. The national curriculum requires the teaching of a mother tongue (Finnish or Swedish), mathematics, foreign languages, history, biology, environmental science, religion, ethics, geography, chemistry, physics, music, visual arts, crafts, physical education, health, and other studies.

The outcomes have been significant. For many years after 1970, Finland did not take part in international tests, but when it did from 2000 it consistently appeared at or near to the top. Interestingly, PISA 2009 data for 29 OECD nations showed that Finland had the lowest variation between schools in reading performance (about 7 per cent). Between-school variance for the US was about 45 per cent; the highest between-school variance was in Italy, where it is over 75 per cent. In the 2011 PIRLS reading tests (Mullis *et al.*, 2012) Finland was ranked third compared with England's eleventh. It is worth noting, however, that Finnish is much easier to learn than English due to its highly regular alphabetic system, as Jolliffe *et al.* (2014, p28) discovered.

> Venezky (1973) studied 240 Finnish children in grades 1 to 3 and found how easy it was to learn to read and write a transparent alphabet. Children begin reading in Finland at age seven. After one year of tuition, in a reading test of nonsense words denoting the complete Finnish orthography, the children scored 80 per cent and the same test administered to college students showed 90 per cent correct. This showed that it takes only about a year to gain proficiency in Finnish spelling.

It is important, then, that we are aware of other countries' approaches to the curriculum and that we see our own in perspective. Since the first National Curriculum in England and Wales in 1988, there have been many changes and revisions. Each time a new curriculum is introduced, a consultation process takes place and, as can be seen in the latest incarnation, cognisance is taken of people's views. If you are to be able to make a contribution to curricula of the future, it is important that you develop your knowledge of what is possible by finding out how other countries work. You should also use the Internet to find out how schools are responding to the 2014 National Curriculum, as many share their plans and ideas.

The 2014 English National Curriculum makes some new demands upon teachers and pupils, but close inspection reveals that there is little content that is significantly different from previous curricula and the literacy frameworks. There is, however, a stronger emphasis upon some aspects of literacy such as spelling, punctuation, grammar and handwriting, and this may make demands upon teachers' subject knowledge.

Despite the fears expressed by many educators when draft versions were released for consultation, the final curriculum continues to emphasise the importance of speaking and listening and drama, and of children listening to experienced readers. In the Year 3–4 non-statutory guidance, for example, it is stated that:

> Pupils should continue to have opportunities to listen frequently to stories, poems, non-fiction and other writing, including whole books and not just extracts, so that they build on what was taught previously.

(DfE, 2013a, p36)

The flexibility that schools have in timing their delivery of the curriculum contrasts sharply with the NLS, which prescribed which term in which year different elements of English were to be taught. However, the NLS was not a statutory document and schools could decide whether or not they wished to adopt it. The National Curriculum is statutory for maintained local authority schools, but academies, which have increased in number significantly since the curriculum appeared, free schools and independent schools do not have to adopt it. It will be interesting to see how many of the schools which are not required to follow the curriculum actually do so, given that their pupils will ultimately sit tests which are based on its content.

In other chapters in this book, the different aspects of the curriculum will be explored in more detail and you will find case studies which show how teachers and trainee teachers have approached the English curriculum.

Learning outcomes review

You should now know:

- what you need to know as primary teachers in order to teach the 2014 English National Curriculum;
- some of the challenges you face when teaching the 2014 English National Curriculum;
- some approaches to teaching the 2014 English National Curriculum.

Self-assessment questions
1. Which types of school do not have to implement the 2014 National Curriculum?
2. How does the 2014 National Curriculum differ from the National Literacy Framework in its approach to text genres?
3. Do children have to work at the appropriate stage of the curriculum for their age?

Answers to activity

Grammatical terminology

You were asked to state in which year group the following terms were to be known and understood:

- noun, noun phrase;
- statement, question, exclamation, command;
- compound, adjective, verb;
- suffix;
- tense (past, present);
- apostrophe, comma.

The answer is Year 3.

Note

Please see Appendix 3 on page 289 for National Curriculum Programmes of Study.

Further reading

For a very useful planning tool which can be downloaded as a PDF file see the following.

The National Literacy Trust: *The English Curriculum Review and Planning Tool*, available at: www.literacytrust.org.uk/schools_teaching/curriculum

To help you develop your subject knowledge about language the following may prove useful.

For phonics:

Jolliffe, W and Waugh, D with Carss, A (2015) *Teaching Systematic Synthetic Phonics in Primary Schools*. London: Learning Matters/SAGE.

Waugh, D and Harrison-Palmer, R (2013) *Auditing Phonic Knowledge and Understanding*. London: SAGE.

For spelling, punctuation and grammar:

Medwell, J, and Wray, D with Moore, G and Griffiths, V (2014) *Primary English Knowledge and Understanding*. London: Learning Matters SAGE.

Waugh, D, Warner, C and Waugh, R (2016) *Teaching Grammar, Punctuation and Spelling in Primary Schools*. London: SAGE.

Wilson, A (2005) *Language Knowledge for Primary Teachers*. London: David Fulton.

If you have access to a tablet computer or digital phone, you might wish to use an app. designed to develop your subject knowledge and provide ideas for teaching:

Waugh, D, English, E, Bulmer, E, Allott, K and Waugh, R (2014) *Spelling, Punctuation and Grammar*. Morecambe: Children Count.

References

Clements, J (2013) 'English in the National Curriculum', 10 October, available at: **http://community.tes.co.uk/national_curriculum_2014/b/english/archive/2013/12/05/english-in-the-national-curriculum-by-james-clements.aspx** (13 June 2014).

Cultural Learning Alliance (2013) The New National Curriculum – a quick guide, 13 September, available at: **www.culturallearningalliance.org.uk/news.aspx?id=115** (accessed 31 March 2014).

Department for Education (DfE) (2013a) *The National Curriculum in England: Key Stages 1 and 2 Framework Document*. London: DfE.

Department for Education (DfE) (2013b) *National Curriculum and Assessment from September 2014: Information for Schools*. London: DfE.

Department for Education and Employment (DfEE) (1998) *National Literacy Strategy Framework for Teaching*. London: DfEE.

Jolliffe, W, Waugh, D, Beverton, S and Stead, J (2014) *Supporting Readers in Secondary Schools*. London: Learning Matters SAGE.

The Literacy Tree Learning Consultancy Planning with the New Primary English Curriculum, available at: **http://theliteracytree.co.uk/newcurriculum/** (13 June 2014).

Mullis, IVS, Martin, MO, Foy, P and Drucker, KT (2012) *Progress in International Reading Literacy Study (PIRLS)*. Chestnut Hill, MA: TIMSS & PIRLS International Study Center, Boston College.

Ravitch, D (2012) Schools we can envy. *The New York Review of Books*, March, available at: **www.nybooks.com/articles/archives/2012/mar/08/schools-we-can-envy/** (13 June 2014).

Sahlberg, P (2011) *Finnish Lessons: What Can the World Learn from Educational Change in Finland?* (The Series on School Reform). New York and London: Teachers College Press.

Venezky, RL (1973) Letter-sound generalizations of first, second, and third-grade Finnish children. *Journal of Educational Psychology*, 64: 288–92.

2 Speaking and Listening: Spoken Language

Wendy Jolliffe

Learning outcomes

By reading this chapter you will develop your understanding of:

- the role of spoken language as a tool for learning;
- the importance of developing proficient spoken language skills as an essential life-long skill;
- how spoken language supports the development of reading and writing skills;
- a range of teaching strategies to enhance spoken language;
- planning and assessing spoken language.

Teachers' Standards
3. Demonstrate good subject and curriculum knowledge:

- have a secure knowledge of the relevant subject(s) and curriculum areas, foster and maintain pupils' interest in the subject, and address misunderstandings;
- demonstrate a critical understanding of developments in the subject and curriculum areas, and promote the value of scholarship;
- demonstrate an understanding of, and take responsibility for, promoting high standards of literacy, articulacy and the correct use of standard English, whatever the teacher's specialist subject.

Introduction

There is a wealth of research, which dates from the Bullock Report (DES, 1975) and from the National Oracy Project (Norman, 1992), to show that speaking and listening not only supports literacy development, but also enhances learning. Yet the inclusion of speaking and listening in the curriculum has been erratic. The National Oracy Project in the late 1980s demonstrated its importance and coined the word 'oracy': a more comprehensive term than 'speaking and listening'. Howe (1993) provides four linked dimensions to help in understanding the meaning of the term 'oracy':

1. to enhance learning;

2. the ability to use the resource of language (such as vocabulary);

3. the reciprocal social nature of talk;

4. the ability to reflect on learning through talk.

The impact of the National Oracy Project was demonstrated by the 1988 National Curriculum which gave speaking and listening equal importance to reading and writing in the English curriculum. Some ten years later, however, its importance received a setback when the Primary National Strategy omitted it from its Literacy Framework (DfEE, 1998), which Corden (2000, p4) described as a 'shameful neglect'. This was compounded when, in spite of continued research which added weight to the premise that talk is crucial to learning (Alexander, 2000, 2009; Mercer, 2000), the draft 2014 National Curriculum omitted any mention of speaking and listening. Following a considerable outcry, statutory requirements were included for 'spoken language'. These are not age-differentiated, unlike other areas of the curriculum, and a single brief programme of study covers the whole of the primary age range, which, yet again, creates a possibility of undervaluing this key aspect. There is also a danger that the term 'spoken language' used in the 2014 curriculum leads teachers to the misconception that this refers to speaking clearly in Standard English. This would be a narrow interpretation of the need to develop proficiency for talk as the foundation for learning and literacy. Nevertheless, the National Curriculum does state:

> The national curriculum for English reflects the importance of spoken language in pupils' development across the whole curriculum – cognitively, socially and linguistically.
>
> (DfE, 2013, p14)

This chapter will provide a clear rationale of the importance of talk, with links to the underpinning research. It will examine a progression in developing the skills of speaking and listening in order to support teachers' understanding when assessing children's development. It will also provide a range of effective teaching strategies for what has historically often been an area that has received insufficient emphasis. The chapter will conclude with guidance on methods of assessment.

Talk for learning

Mounting research demonstrates that talk is a key ingredient in the learning process (Barnes and Todd, 1977; Corson, 1988; Johnson *et al.*, 1988; Mercer, 2000; Slavin, 1983; Wells, 1990). It is important to understand why and what Halliday (1993) has termed 'a language-based theory of learning'. Its roots can be traced to Dewey in the 1930s who acknowledged the role of language and referred to the need for human beings to learn by *doing*. It was the Russian psychologist, Lev Vygotsky, who saw our use of language as serving two purposes: first, as a 'cultural tool' for sharing and developing knowledge, supporting social interactions, and second, as a 'psychological tool' to help organise our individual thoughts. Vygotsky emphasised that thought is not merely expressed in words but exists because of them. He also developed the concept of the *zone of proximal development* (ZPD) which is defined as:

> the distance between the actual development level as determined by independent problem solving and the level of potential development as determined through problem solving under adult guidance or in collaboration with more capable peers.

> (Vygotsky, 1978, p86)

Bruner (1985) built on this concept and suggested that the learner passes through mental developmental phases, which are supported by structured learning experiences. In addition, Bruner concurs that speech is a primary mechanism for thought, and therefore it is vitally important for children to have the opportunity to talk through their ideas. Bruner's term for the support that adults provide in the learning process is 'scaffolding', whereby an adult varies the level of support, gradually withdrawing it as the child gains in competency.

The development of pedagogy that exploits this methodology has been termed 'dialogic teaching' where effective questioning promotes and extends learning. Dating back to Socrates and what is termed 'Socratic questioning', the importance of dialogue is highlighted by Bakhtin (1986, p168): *if an answer does not give rise to a new question from itself, it falls out of the dialogue.* The value of this process, as Nystrand *et al.* (1997, p72) emphasise, is: *the extent to which instruction requires students to think, not just report someone else's thinking.*

Alexander's (2000) fascinating cross-cultural research into classrooms across five countries found that French and Russian classrooms have a much stronger emphasis on oral language for learning than in England. Alexander (2008) developed the concept of dialogic teaching, defined as 'reasoned discussion' which can take place in whole-class forums as well as in small groups, to support the use of talk. This teaching approach aims to harness the power of talk to stimulate and extend pupils' thinking and understanding. Dialogic teaching has been used and researched in a range of schools, demonstrating that it can have a real impact on interactions in the classroom. However, it requires considerable time and effort to be effective as it is *in effect a transformation of the culture of talk and the attendant assumptions about the relationship of teacher and taught* (Alexander, 2005, p16). Dialogic teaching consists of the following five elements:

- It is collective: children work together on tasks, as a group or class.

- It is reciprocal: teachers and children listen to each other and comment/share ideas.

- It is supportive: children are supported to discuss their views freely.

- It is cumulative: teachers and children build on each other's ideas to create coherent lines of thinking.

- It is purposeful: teachers plan and steer classroom talk with specific purposes.

Simpson (2016) notes the importance of supporting trainee teachers to develop a deep understanding of dialogic teaching and cites a research study where this was successful, in which both pre-service and in-service teachers experienced dialogic teaching during professional development sessions. She notes that:

> Giving pre-service teachers the chance to experience dialogic teaching through a structured discussion tool such as Literature Circles provides them with valuable insights to how learning may occur through well-scaffolded interaction.
>
> (2016, p91)

The Cambridge Primary Review made a powerful case for talk to underpin the revised curriculum. It recommended that:

> In addition to the programmes of study for English there should be a clear statement on language across the curriculum which requires attention in all subjects to the character, quality and uses of reading, writing, talk and ICT, and to the development of pupils' understanding of the distinct registers, vocabularies and modes of discourse of each subject.
>
> (Alexander, 2011, p305)

The National Curriculum does acknowledge that: *Spoken language underpins the development of reading and writing* (DfE, 2013, p14); however, there is no detail provided through programmes of study of how teachers should plan for this. The Statutory Requirements for spoken language for all year groups state that pupils should be taught to:

- listen and respond appropriately to adults and their peers;

- ask relevant questions to extend their understanding and knowledge;

- use relevant strategies to build their vocabulary;

- articulate and justify answers, arguments and opinions;

- give well-structured descriptions, explanations and narratives for different purposes, including for expressing feelings;

- maintain attention and participate actively in collaborative conversations, staying on topic and initiating and responding to comments;
- use spoken language to develop understanding through speculating, hypothesising, imagining and exploring ideas;
- speak audibly and fluently with an increasing command of Standard English;
- participate in discussions, presentations, performances, role play, improvisations and debates;
- gain, maintain and monitor the interest of the listener(s);
- consider and evaluate different viewpoints, attending to and building on the contributions of others;
- select and use appropriate registers for effective communication.

(DfE, 2013, p18)

Activity: examining a language-based theory of learning

1. Vygotsky considered two aspects of language as crucial to learning – what are these?
2. Why does Bruner uphold that scaffolding by peers or adults is crucial?
3. What is distinctive about Socratic questioning?
4. In what ways does dialogic teaching support effective learning?

(Answers can be found at the end of the chapter.)

Research focus: talk for learning

Pierce and Gilles (2008) have researched the powerful way exploratory talk can deepen understanding of literature with children aged 9–10 years. They found that it can move beyond support for understanding texts and note:

> We have moved from considering how we can use literature and talk to help students understand the text and themselves, to using literature and talk to tackle broad social issues – such as discrimination, equality and justice.

(p52)

Pierce and Gilles summarise a number of ways in which talk supports learning as follows.

- As social talk which can bind a learning community together so that when pupils know each other well they can recognise each other's differences and strengths and use these effectively;

$\longrightarrow$

- As exploratory talk to challenge each other's thinking and revise their own thinking and questioning of each other;

- As presentational talk to share understandings with others often in the form of presentations;

- As meta-talk to explore the nature of talk itself and its power and to make talking 'visible'.

- As critical talk where pupils critique each other's views through critical conversations to raise questions about key issues and consider new possibilities.

Mercer (2000) focused on understanding the quality of teaching and learning as an 'intermental' or 'interthinking' process.

> For a teacher to teach and a learner to learn, they must use talk and joint activity to create a shared communicative space, an 'intermental development zone' (IDZ) on the contextual foundations of their common knowledge and aims.

(p141)

This is facilitated by dialogue.

> If the dialogue fails to keep minds mutually attuned, the IDZ collapses and the scaffolded learning grinds to a halt.

(p141)

Mercer (1995) also presents three ways of talking and thinking.

- *Disputational talk*: this is characterised by disagreement, short exchanges that consist of assertions or challenges and decisions being reached by individuals, not collaboratively.

- *Cumulative talk*: here pupils work together, often in pairs, to construct 'common knowledge' by accumulation.

- *Exploratory talk*: here pupils work collaboratively and engage critically but constructively with each other's ideas. Challenges are justified and alternatives offered and progress is made towards a joint agreement. In exploratory talk 'knowledge is made more publicly accountable and reasoning is more visible in the talk'.

(p104)

Mercer built on the work of Douglas Barnes, who first developed the concept of exploratory talk. Barnes (2008) has revised his earlier ideas and focused on the role of the teacher in providing the climate for learning, including providing small group work. Nevertheless, supporting effective group work has been described as particularly challenging for teachers to do successfully (Sutherland, 2006). Coultas (2007) examined these problems with challenging classes and found the appropriateness of the task was the key and that this should incorporate real problem-solving as well as being carefully structured. A framework for collaborative talk produced by Newman (2016) has also been shown to help in developing collaborative talk in the classroom. In particular, this study emphasised the importance of 'meta-talk' in developing students' awareness of the interpersonal processes of collaborative talk.

Language for life

Language is not only a tool for learning, but also supports skills for life. The Communication Trust 'I Can' publication, *Speech, Language and Communication Needs and the Early Years* (2007), highlights the impact of poor speech, language and communication skills on children's lives. The report states that:

> COMMUNICATION IS FUNDAMENTAL ... for learning and development.
>
> Children and young people with a communication disability cannot express themselves, understand others or build relationships because of problems in one or more of these areas: ... understanding and finding the right words ... producing, ordering and discriminating between speech sounds ... using rules about how words, phrases and sentences are formed to convey meaning ... using and understanding language in different social contexts. One in ten children and young people struggle with this invisible disability. Without the right help, at the right time, they will be left out and left behind.

(p1)

Good speaking and listening skills are therefore fundamental to every aspect of life and work.

Developing spoken language skills

The 2014 National Curriculum provides no guidance on progression for the development of spoken language. However, if teachers are to support this crucial area of development, it is important they have an understanding of what features to look for.

Speaking, Listening, Learning (DfES, 2003) examined the features of progression for Years 1–6 for the areas of speaking, listening, group interaction and drama, which provides useful guidance of the features of progression.

Another very useful resource for supporting progression in oral language development is the 'First Steps' *Oral Language: Developmental Continuum* (Evans, 1999). This resource links assessment to teaching to help teachers examine what children can do, in order to inform planning for further development. The following phases of development are indicated and the resource provides indicators of each, together with the major teaching strategies to support next steps for a child:

Phase 1 – beginning language.

Phase 2 – early language.

Phase 3 – exploratory language.

Phase 4 – emergent language for learning.

Phase 5 – consolidated language for learning.

Phase 6 – extended language for learning.

A further resource to support understanding of early language development in young children entitled *Communicating Matters* (DfES, 2005) presents *key learning principles* within each phase (or strand of development). The four strands are:

1. **Knowing and using sounds and signs** Having the ability to recognise, comprehend and produce the distinct sounds critical for oral language behaviour.

2. **Knowing and using words** The ability to recognise, comprehend and produce the particular units of language, in particular words or phrases, which carry independent meanings.

3. **Structuring language** The ability to recognise, comprehend and produce longer units of language that are organised in systematic ways.

4. **Making language work** The ability to recognise, comprehend and produce language appropriate for a range of different social interactions.

For some children, this developmental process is not straightforward and they experience difficulties. The Bercow Report (DCSF, 2008a) reinforced the need for developing effective communication skills and examined the services for supporting children and young people with language difficulties. The report found patchy services across the country and recommended better training for professionals in this area. One programme that resulted was *Every Child a Talker* (DCSF, 2008b), a national programme to develop language and communication for children from birth to five years. The case study below shows an example of the type of work carried out in schools and nurseries.

Case study: developing early language

John, a trainee teacher, helped to set up a 'language library' in one school. The aim was just like a toy library for parents to borrow items for use at home. The resources were especially chosen to help language and included storybooks with character toys, CDs of songs and rhymes and interactive toys such as puppets. They also had a range of puzzles, which were also used in nursery sessions, to encourage talk. Having similar resources at home and school meant familiarity for the children and encouraged both children and parents to have a go with them. Both parents and children really enjoyed the range of resources they could take home.

The project had a positive impact on the children and importantly supported parents and carers.

Curriculum link

The use of a range of resources linked to a storybook provides useful support for developing early reading and particularly comprehension skills.

For Year 1, the statutory requirement states that pupils should:

develop pleasure in reading, motivation to read, vocabulary and understanding by:

- listening to and discussing a wide range of poems, stories and non-fiction at a level beyond that at which they can read independently.

(DfE, 2013, p22)

Talk and literacy

The National Curriculum acknowledges that requirements for spoken language are *contextualised within the reading and writing domains* (DfE, 2013, p15). In relation to reading, the curriculum notes that *high-quality discussion* is the means of developing comprehension skills.

There is a strong focus on the development of vocabulary in the curriculum. However, the detailed Appendix 2 places vocabulary alongside grammar and punctuation with detail of the content to be taught. The vocabulary is focused here on the terminology associated with grammar, although elsewhere in the aims of the curriculum it is asserted that pupils should acquire a wide vocabulary: *Pupils' acquisition and command of vocabulary are the key to their learning and progress across the whole curriculum* (DfE, 2013, p12).

For further details of developing children's vocabulary, see Chapter 3.

The impact of building vocabulary is seen clearly in children's reading skills. The Rose Review of the teaching of early reading (Rose, 2006) emphasised the key importance of speaking and listening:

> The indications are that far more attention needs to be given, right from the start, to promoting speaking and listening skills to make sure that children build a good stock of words, learn to listen attentively and speak clearly and confidently. Speaking and listening, together with reading and writing, are prime communication skills that are central to children's intellectual, social and emotional development.

> (p3)

The Rose Review highlighted the two key strands in effective reading: word recognition and language comprehension. This is based on a model known as the Simple View of Reading (Gough and Tunmer, 1986). Language comprehension is defined by Gough and Tunmer as the process by which words, sentences and discourse are interpreted. Both interrelated process need to be developed for children to become efficient readers. The area of language comprehension is complex. Hoover and Gough (1990) explored this in more detail and particularly the two domains of linguistic knowledge, or knowledge of the formal structures such as syntax, and knowledge of the context of the subject being read.

Dialogue is a critical tool in developing language comprehension as Palinscar and Brown (1984) have shown. The method they suggest involves the reciprocal teaching of comprehension strategies, which was designed to provide a simple introduction to group discussion. The basic procedure is that a teacher and a group of pupils take turns leading a discussion on the content of a section of text they are jointly attempting to understand. Four strategies are practised: *questioning*, *clarifying*, *summarising* and *predicting*. Skidmore (2003) also argues that where pupils are allowed to take on a wider range of speaking roles, it can support deeper understanding of texts.

Activity: book talk

Review the questions below adapted from the work of Aidan Chambers (1993) to prompt more extensive talk about texts with Key Stage 2 pupils and identify those that are particularly helpful.

- Was there anything you liked about this book?
- Was there anything you disliked about this book?
- Was there anything that puzzled you?

- Were there any patterns – any connections – that you noticed?
- How long did the story take to happen?
- Where did the story happen?
- Which character interested you the most?
- When you were reading, did you 'see' the story happening in your imagination?
- Who was telling the story? Do we know? And how do we know?
- Did we ever get to know what the characters were thinking about?
- If you had written this book, how would you have made it better?
- Which parts in the book seem to you to be most true to life?

Consider what other questions you could ask and how this would vary according to the book and according to the age of the pupils.

Talk for writing

Not only does talk support language comprehension skills, it is also a key tool in becoming an effective writer. Perhaps one of the most notable projects in recent years has been the work done by Pie Corbett, based on Chambers's work on book talk, which highlights the need for oral work before, during and after a specific writing project.

The Talk for Writing programme, developed for the National Strategies by Corbett, aimed to demonstrate that talk should be incorporated in each of the key stages of the writing process. These stages include:

1. Familiarisation with the text type.

2. Capturing ideas and oral rehearsal.

3. Teacher demonstration.

4. Teacher scribing, supported writing and guided writing.

5. Independent writing.

This process encourages 'writer-talk' – i.e. the articulation of the thinking and creative processes involved in all stages of the act of writing: talk that helps children to think and behave like a writer (and indeed consider themselves to be one). It supports the thinking behind the process of *reading like a writer* and *writing as a reader* (DCSF, 2008c, p6). The process involves the learning and repeating of oral stories in order to build up children's confidence so they move through a process of imitation of stories, to innovation of elements of stories, and finally invention in devising their own stories.

Research focus: talk and writing

Corden (2000) demonstrated that writing is enhanced through fostering group and whole-class talk. Fisher *et al.* (2010) built on this work particularly to use response partners to generate ideas as oral rehearsal or 'writing aloud', as well as a reflection on the process of writing. Other research has highlighted the need for reflective talk on the process of writing and children's conceptions of being writers (Cremin, 2006; Feigenbaum, 2010). Research has also shown that working with a partner encourages children to become readers of their own writing and therefore helps to develop an inner voice that is a feature of an effective writer. Talk can extend the working memory for writing (Latham, 2002), as through talk the memory of the composition element is helped rather than focusing on the secretarial aspects. Latham (2002, p40) argues that *spoken language forms a constraint, a ceiling not only on the ability to comprehend, but also on the ability to write, beyond which literacy cannot progress*, and that speech supports and propels writing ability forward.

Teaching strategies

According to Mercer (2000), language is our most significant pedagogical tool. Studies of teaching in England show that the teacher's practice in the classroom of questioning that consists of initiation, response and feedback (IRF), where the teacher initiates talk in the classroom through a question, a learner responds and the teacher gives feedback, is still common (Myhill, 2002). The Talk Project (Burns and Myhill, 2004) found that there was little constructive meaning making taking place in classrooms and limited opportunities for pupil participation. The following examples demonstrate how spoken language can be harnessed productively as an effective teaching tool.

Philosophy for Children

One strategy that helps encourage children to be critical, creative and collaborative in their thinking is Philosophy for Children. It focuses on enquiry, where children are encouraged to think and reason as a group. Fisher (2006) claims this supports children's thinking skills and that children as young as five years can engage in philosophical questioning. It does not simply provide opportunities for free-flowing discussion, but research shows that it impacts on academic achievement (Fisher, 2005; Trickey and Topping, 2004). The common lesson format is as follows:

1. Focusing exercise: sharing the learning objectives, reminding children of the agreed rules and using a game to ensure attention.

2. Sharing a stimulus: present a story, poem or picture or other stimulus for thinking.

3. Thinking time: children consider what is unusual or interesting about the stimulus and sharing with a partner.

4. Questioning: children ask their own or partner's questions which are written down, discussed and then one is chosen to investigate.

5. Discussion: children are asked to respond, and the teacher responds and supports the children to build on each other's ideas.

6. Plenary: review the discussion often using a graphic organiser or map, invite summary comments from the children and make links to real situations.

For a range of teaching resources, see: **www.P4C.com**

Developing questioning skills

One clear way to promote effective talk to is to review the use of teachers' questioning. Research (Galton *et al.*, 1999) shows that teachers usually ask closed questions, such as the 'guess what I am thinking?' type, where the teacher has a clear idea of the answer and the children have to guess it, rather than open questions that genuinely seek to explore children's understanding and views. Myhill *et al.* (2006, p68) argue that *when a teacher asks a question, it is well understood by children, she already knows the answer or a range of possible answers.* In order to progress beyond this and enhance the potential of talk for learning, it is important to develop a range of questioning.

Activity: questioning techniques

Review the following strategies to support better questioning and consider the effectiveness of each.

1. Use a 'no-hands up' rule. This tactic directs questions at particular pupils (rather than a general question and all pupils put their hands up) and has the potential to differentiate the question according to the ability of the pupil.

2. Build in wait time. Research shows that if a teacher waits at least three seconds for the pupil to think and before answering, there are substantial benefits leading to a greater number of responses, more confidence and 'risk-taking' and encourages pupils to ask questions in return.

3. Carefully plan one or two open-ended questions and considering publishing a challenging question in advance and display. Try to answer these questions yourself to test out whether they are appropriate.

(Continued)

(Continued)

4. Allow time for collaboration before answering.
5. Do not assume that the question will elicit the response you expect – be prepared for the unexpected.
6. Ask more 'How do you know that?' or 'Why do you think that?' questions.
7. Probe – when a pupil responds to a question, use a range of questions to get the pupil to clarify and extend their response.
8. Try to stop and think before you ask a question and consider that different types of questions will provide different responses. Factual questions will elicit recall of facts etc.; procedural questions will be appropriate for classroom management and explanations of tasks; speculative questions will encourage different ideas and hypotheses.
9. If you want to convey key information or facts, consider if questioning is the best method to do this and whether some other form of activity would be more appropriate.
10. When children answer a question, ensure that their answers are listened to before moving on.

Using drama

As Chapter 12 explores in more depth, drama is a powerful pedagogical tool and particularly supports spoken language. The National Curriculum states that: *All pupils should be enabled to participate in and gain knowledge, skills and understanding associated with the artistic practice of drama* (DfE, 2013, p15). Johnson (2006) provides some excellent examples of the use of drama with both Key Stages 1 and 2, illustrating that *drama can be the most dynamic talk in the classroom* (p100). Using techniques such as providing an authentic stimulus that children can clearly relate to such as bullying, she uses techniques of group discussion, group improvisation, still image, thought tracking, teacher and children in role and the mantle of the expert. The last named gives the children the role of the expert with greater expertise than the teacher. This technique can empower children to have a real voice, in this case to develop an anti-bullying policy. For more information on drama techniques, see Chapter 12 and the Primary National Strategy *Speaking, Listening Learning: Handbook* available from: **www.teachfind.com/national-strategies/speaking-listening-learning-working-children-key-stages-1-and-2-%E2%80%93-handbook**

The case study below cites an example of a drama technique to promote real engagement of the class in spoken language.

Case study: forum theatre – the people who hugged trees

A trainee teacher working in a Year 6 class had been reading the Hindu folk tale 'The people who hugged trees', an environmental story about a village that objected to a large number of trees in the surrounding forest being felled for timber and resin. The villages first tied a thread around the trees, a Hindu symbol of a sacred bond, to prevent this and finally, when armed police came, groups of three or four villagers formed a physical ring around each marked tree. Seeing the peaceful but determined protest, the police eventually withdrew their threat to cut down the trees.

The class discussed the story and the themes of protecting the environment versus the need for resources. With the rest of the class in a circle and different pairs of pupils taking turns at directing the action, groups improvised being the villagers, as well as the timber company and the police. At times, the directors stopped the action and the rest of the class made suggestions of things the villagers could say or do. Working over several sessions, a range of alternative interpretations were explored providing opportunities for pupils to work in role and others to direct the action.

The activity culminated in an interactive e-book with groups providing different accounts of the day the villagers hugged trees. Written and recorded verbal accounts together with still photographs of enacted scenes, maps and pictures of the region of Rajasthan in India provided a rich record of the work stimulated by this drama.

(See *The People Who Hugged the Trees* by Deborah Rose (2001) for a version of the story.)

Curriculum link

This drama activity and the other related tasks encouraged a curriculum link with geography: finding out about Rajasthan in India. In particular, it supported pupils to *use maps, atlases, globes and digital/computer mapping to locate countries and describe features studied* (DfE, 2003, p216).

Cooperative learning

Cooperative learning requires pupils to work together in pairs and small groups to support each other to improve their learning. It is not just 'group work' and requires certain factors to be present for it to be genuinely 'cooperative'. Group work is certainly not new; indeed, putting children together to work in groups is a common occurrence in England. But putting children together and then assuming they will interact and support each other's learning is another matter altogether. However, when implemented properly, cooperative learning presents an ideal method of supporting not only children's learning, but also the effective use of talk. The first step is to ensure that pupils are supported with the necessary interpersonal and small group skills to cooperate. The second step is to structure the tasks to maximise the potential to cooperate. This process needs developing in a staged and structured way with teachers requiring ongoing support. For comprehensive details of how to implement this staged process, see Jolliffe (2007).

Certain key ingredients need to be in place for the learning to be cooperative. Johnson and Johnson's (1999) extensive work in this field set out five basic elements that are needed for cooperative learning to be effective:

- Positive interdependence: students must feel that they need each other in order to complete the group's task; they 'sink or swim' together.

- Individual accountability: cooperative learning groups are successful only when every member has learned the material or has helped with and understood the assignment.

- Group processing: this involves giving students time and procedures to analyse how well their groups are functioning, and how well they are using the necessary skills. The processing helps all group members achieve while maintaining effective working relationships among members.

- Small group skills: students do not necessarily come to school with the social skills they need to collaborate effectively with others; teachers need to teach the appropriate communication, decision-making and conflict management skills to students and provide the motivation to use these skills, in order for groups to function effectively.

- Face-to-face interaction: the interaction patterns and verbal exchanges that take place among students in carefully structured cooperative learning groups benefit their learning.

A range of structures, principally derived from Spencer Kagan (1994), to facilitate paired and/ or group work can be applied to different activities across the curriculum. Some of these include: think, pair, share; rally table; line up; three-step interview; two stay and two stray; and jigsaw groups. For further guidance on these structures and others, see Kagan (1994) and Jolliffe (2007).

Case study: cooperative group work

Angela, a newly qualified teacher, describes how she introduces her Year 4 class to cooperative learning.

At the beginning of term I help children to create cooperative learning teams using a numbers game that helps develop teams of four or five children of mixed ability. I first spend some time doing team-building activities, such as a three-step interview, where pairs take turns

$\longrightarrow$

to tell each other something about themselves (one favourite is to tell each other their 'scar story' – how they got a scar). Their partner listens carefully and then relays it to others in the team. Further work in developing a team identity such as a team name or logo is also important. This is supported further when each team member takes on a responsibility or 'role' (such as timekeeper, scribe or resource manager) for an activity which has a shared goal. The more able pupils assist other team members, but are stretched to employ higher-order thinking skills to help the team achieve a common goal. Groups are called 'teams' and activities are called 'challenges' which are distributed in envelopes, the contents of which must be kept secret from the other teams. I do try to make the learning fun and rewards (such as laminated medals), given to the team and not the individual, play a huge part in this.

Children all enjoy this way of working which is inclusive and fun.

Planning for spoken language

Opportunities for speaking and listening need to be planned carefully. Clear objectives from the Early Years Foundation Stage to Key Stage 2 and links into Year 7 were provided by the *Speaking, Listening, Learning: Handbook* (DfES, 2003) which built on the earlier work from the Qualifications and Curriculum Authority (1999) to ensure a range of activities for supporting children's progression in speaking, listening, group discussion and drama. These can be accessed from: **webarchive.nationalarchives.gov. uk/20110202093118/http:/nationalstrategies.standards.dcsf.gov.uk/node/84856**. This includes example units of work to show the integration of speaking and listening with reading and writing.

In considering opportunities for spoken language, it is important to first encourage a range of activities that will support the following:

- Narrative – e.g. through modelling and developing storytelling skills. For powerful examples of this, see Grainger (1997, 2001).

- Explanations – this may be linked to different areas of the curriculum, e.g. science or geography.

- Instructions – e.g. children work in pairs with one pupil creating a simple picture, for which he or she has to relay instructions for the other pupil to reproduce.

- Problem-solving activities – groups of pupils are given a challenge or problem to solve.

- Discussion and debate – different groups are given a contentious issue and have to argue for a particular viewpoint.

- Presentation – developing presentation skills using video recording of groups or pairs of pupils acting as a news or weather reporter.

For all these types of activities, it is important to consider the audience and purpose of the activities carefully in order to make them authentic. It is also necessary to consider different ways of organising the class that will facilitate opportunities for talk, including whole-class teaching, cooperative group work, paired work, and one-to-one opportunities for the pupil and teacher or other adult.

Assessing spoken language

It is important to have a clear focus for assessment with specific criteria and for teachers to find efficient ways to note children's achievements. You should try to collect evidence when:

- specific activities have been devised to teach spoken language and assessments made against the criteria;
- activities across the curriculum provide opportunities to assess spoken language;
- a significant contribution is made by a child.

Where possible, encouraging children to be involved in self-assessment of their spoken language skills can be powerful and give them control over their own learning. This is facilitated by sharing the learning intentions with children and ensuring they understand the related success criteria. Children can also be involved in setting targets. They can be supported by working with a partner and by encouraging peer assessment.

This chapter has provided a rationale of the importance of talk both for learning and literacy development. It has examined a progression in developing the skills of spoken language to support effective teaching. Different case studies have demonstrated effective teaching strategies with details of a range of teaching methods. A focus on manageable ways of planning and assessing spoken language has also been included. While spoken language receives less focus than teaching the skills of reading and writing in the 2014 National Curriculum, this chapter has demonstrated its vital importance as a skill for life as well as underpinning the development of literacy skills.

Learning outcomes review

You should now know:

- the role of spoken language as a tool for learning;
- the importance of developing proficient spoken language skills as an essential life-long skill;

- how spoken language supports the development of reading and writing skills;
- a range of teaching strategies to enhance spoken language;
- planning for opportunities for spoken language and assessing children's development.

Self-assessment questions

1. What are the major ways in which spoken language supports learning?
2. How does spoken language support reading and writing skills?
3. How can teachers provide authentic opportunities for spoken language?

Answers to activity

Examining a language-based theory of learning

1. Vygotsky considered two aspects of language as crucial to learning – what are these?

   - A 'cultural tool' for sharing and developing knowledge and supporting social interactions.
   - A 'psychological tool' to help organise our individual thoughts.

2. Why does Bruner uphold that scaffolding by peers or adults is crucial?

   The adult provides support or 'scaffolding', gradually withdrawing it as the child gains in competency.

3. What is distinctive about Socratic questioning?

   Socratic questioning uses a series of questions to progressively engage higher levels of thinking, including literal, analytical and conceptual levels of thinking.

4. In what ways does dialogic teaching support effective learning?

   Dialogic teaching involves 'reasoned discussion' that helps collective, cumulative and supportive discussion to clarify thinking.

Further reading

For background research into the value of talk to support learning and literacy:

Corden, R (2000) *Literacy and Learning through Talk: Strategies for the Primary Classroom.* Buckingham: Open University Press.

For a range of examples of effective talk in the classroom:

Goodwin, P (ed.) (2002) *The Articulate Classroom: Talking and Learning in the Primary Classroom.* London: David Fulton.

Jones, D and Hodson, P (eds) *Unlocking Speaking and Listening*. London: David Fulton.

For information on implementing cooperative learning:

Jolliffe, W (2007) *Cooperative Learning in the Classroom: Putting it into Practice*. London: Paul Chapman.

References

Alexander, RJ (2000). *Culture and Pedagogy: International Comparisons in Primary Education*. Oxford: Blackwell.

Alexander, R (2005) Culture, dialogue and learning: notes on an emerging pedagogy. Education, culture and cognition: intervening for growth. International Association for Cognitive Education and Psychology (IACEP) 10th International Conference, University of Durham, 10–14 July.

Alexander, RJ (2008) *Towards Dialogic Teaching: Rethinking Classroom Talk* (4th edn). York: Dialogos.

Alexander, RJ (ed.) (2009) *Children, Their World, Their Education: Final Report and Recommendations of the Cambridge Primary Review*. London: Routledge.

Alexander, RJ (ed.) (2011) *Children, Their World, Their Education: Final Report and Recommendations of the Cambridge Primary Review*. Abingdon: Routledge.

Bakhtin, M (1986) *Speech Genres and Other Late Essays*. Austin, TX: University of Texas Press.

Barnes, D and Todd, F (1977) *Communicating and Learning in Small Groups*. London: Routledge & Kegan Paul.

Barnes, D (2008) Exploratory talk for learning, in N Mercer and S Hodgkinson (eds) *Exploring Talk in School*. London: SAGE, pp1–15.

Bruner, JS (1985) Vygotsky: a historical and conceptual perspective, in J Wertsch (ed.) *Culture, Communication and Cognition: Vygotskian perspectives*. Cambridge: Cambridge University Press. pp.21–34.

Burns, C and Myhill, D (2004) Interactive or inactive? A consideration of the nature of interaction in whole class teaching. *Cambridge Journal of Education Studies*, 34(1): 35–49.

Chambers, A (1993) *Tell Me: Children, Reading and Talk*. Stroud: Thimble Press.

Communication Trust (2007) *Speech, Language and Communication Needs and the Early Years*. London: Communication Trust. Available at: **www.ican.org.uk/~/media/Ican2/Whats%20 the%20Issue/Evidence/7%20Speech%20Language%20and%20Communication%20 Needs%20and%20the%20Early%20Years.ashx** (accessed 8 March 2014).

Corden, R (2000) *Literacy and Learning through Talk: Strategies for the Primary Classroom*. Buckingham: Open University Press.

Corson, D (1988) *Oral Language Across the Curriculum*. Clevedon: Multilingual Matters.

Coultas, V (2007) *Constructive Talk in Challenging Classrooms: Strategies for Behaviour Management and Talk-based Tasks*. London: Routledge.

Cremin, T (2006) Creativity, uncertainty and discomfort: teachers as writers. *Cambridge Journal of Education*, 36: 415–33.

Department for Children, Schools and Children (DCSF) (2008a) *The Bercow Report: A Review of Services for Children and Young People (0–19) with Speech, Language and Communication Needs*. Nottingham: DCSF Publications.

DCSF (2008b) *Every Child a Talker*. Nottingham: DCSF.

DCSF (2008c) *Talk for Writing*. Nottingham: DCSF.

Department of Education and Science (DES) (1975) *A Language for Life (Bullock Report)*. London: HM Stationery Office.

Department for Education (DfE) (2013) *The National Curriculum in England: Key Stages 1 and 2 Framework Document*. London: DfE Publications, available at: **www.gov.uk/dfe/nationalcurriculum** (accessed 2 January 2014).

Department for Education and Employment (DfEE) (1998) *National Literacy Strategy Framework for Teaching*. London: DfEE.

Department for Education and Skills (DfES) (2003) *Speaking, Listening, Learning: Working with Children in Key Stages 1 and 2 – Handbook*. Nottingham: DfES. Available at: **http://webarchive.nationalarchives.gov.uk/20110202093118/http:/nationalstrategies.standards.dcsf.gov.uk/node/84856** (accessed 26.06.16)

DfES (2005) *Communicating Matters: The Strands of Communication and Language*. Nottingham: DfES.

Evans, J (1999) *Oral Language: Developmental Continuum*. Sydney: Rigby Heinemann.

Feigenbaum, F (2010) Development of communicative competence through private and inner speech, in A Winsler, C Fernyhough and I Montero (eds), *Private Speech, Executive Functioning, and the Development of Verbal Self-regulation*. Cambridge: Cambridge University Press, pp102–20.

Fisher, R (2005) *Teaching Children to Think and Learn* (2nd edn). Cheltenham: Nelson Thornes.

Fisher, R (2006) Talking to think: why children need philosophical discussion, in D Jones and P Hodson (eds), *Unlocking Speaking and Listening*. London: David Fulton, pp33–47.

Fisher, R, Myhill, D, Jones, S and Larkin, S (2010) *Using Talk to Support Writing*. London: SAGE.

Galton, M, Hargreaves, L, Comber, C, Wall, D and Pell, A (1999) *Inside the Primary Classroom 20 Years On*. London: Routledge.

Gough, PB and Tunmer, WE (1986) Decoding, reading and reading disability. *Remedial and Special Education*, 7: 6–10.

Grainger, T (1997) *Traditional Storytelling in the Primary Classroom*. Leamington Spa: Scholastic.

Grainger, T (2001) Drama and writing: imagination on the page: one. *Primary English Magazine*, April: 6–10.

Halliday, MAK (1993) Towards a language-based theory of learning. *Linguistics and Education*, 5: 93–116.

Hoover, WA and Gough, PB (1990) The simple view of reading. *Reading and Writing: An Interdisciplinary Journal*, 2: 127–60.

Howe, A (1993) Perspectives on oracy, in S Brindley (ed.) *Teaching English*. London: Routledge, pp38–47.

Johnson, C (2006) Dynamic talk: speaking and listening and learning through drama, in D Jones and P Hodson (eds) *Unlocking Speaking and Listening*. London: David Fulton, pp100–11.

Johnson, D Johnson, R and Holubec, E (1988) *Circles of Learning: Cooperation in the Classroom* (revised edn). Edina, MN: Interaction Book Company.

Johnson, DW and Johnson, RT (1999) *Learning Together and Alone: Cooperation, Competitive and Individualistic Learning* (5th edn). Boston, MA: Allyn & Bacon.

Jolliffe, W (2007) *Cooperative Learning in the Classroom: Putting it into Practice*. London: Paul Chapman.

Kagan, S (1994) *Cooperative Learning*. San Juan Capistrano, CA: Kagan Cooperative Learning.

Latham, D (2002) *How Children Learn to Write: Supporting and Developing Children's Writing in Schools*. London: Paul Chapman.

Mercer, N (1995) *The Guided Construction of Knowledge: Talk Amongst Teachers and Learners*. Clevedon: Multilingual Matters.

Mercer, N (2000) *Words and Minds: How we use Language to Think Together*. London: Routledge.

Myhill, DA (2002) Bad boys and good girls? Patterns of interaction and response in whole class teaching. *British Educational Research Journal*, 28(3): 339–52.

Myhill, F, Jones, S and Hopper, R (2006) *Talking, Listening, Learning: Effective Talk in the Primary Classroom*. Maidenhead: Open University Press.

Newman, R (2016) Working talk: developing a framework for the teaching of collaborative talk. *Research Papers in Education*, 31(10): 107–31.

Norman, K (ed.) (1992) *Thinking Voices: The Work of the National Oracy Project*. London: Hodder & Stoughton.

Nystrand, M, Gamoran, A, Kachur, R and Prendergast, C (1997) *Opening Dialogue: Understanding the Dynamics of Learning and Teaching in the English Classroom*. New York: Teachers College Press.

Palinscar, AS and Brown, AL (1984) Reciprocal teaching of comprehension monitoring activities. *Cognition and Instruction*, 1: 117–75.

Pierce, KM and Gilles, C (2008) From exploratory talk to critical conversations, in S Hodgkinson and N Mercer (eds) *Exploring Talk in School*. London: SAGE. pp37–54.

Rose, D (2001) *The People Who Hugged the Trees*. Niwot, CO: Roberts Rinehart.

Rose, J (2006) *Independent Review of the Teaching of Early Reading: Final Report*. Nottingham: DfES.

Simpson, A (2016) Dialogic teaching in the initial teacher education classroom: 'Everyone's Voice will be Heard'. *Research Papers in Education*, 31(1): 89–106.

Skidmore, D (2003) From pedagogical dialogue to dialogic pedagogy. *Language and Education*, 14(4): 283–96.

Slavin, RE (1983) *Cooperative Learning*. New York: Longman.

Sutherland, J (2006) Improving the quality of pupils' talk and thinking during group work. *Literacy*, 40(2): 106–13.

Trickey, S and Topping, KJ (2004) Philosophy for children: a systematic review. *Research Papers in Education*, 19(3): 365–80.

Vygotsky, LV (1978) *Mind in Society: The Development of Higher Psychological Processes*. Cambridge, MA: Harvard University Press.

Wells, G (1990) *The Meaning Makers*. London: Hodder & Stoughton.

3 Vocabulary Development

Jane Carter

Learning outcomes

By reading this chapter you will develop your understanding of:

- what children need to know and understand about vocabulary – for language and reading comprehension and as a support for spelling;
- what you need to know as a primary teacher in order to teach the 2014 English National Curriculum;
- the breadth of study of vocabulary teaching and learning;
- approaches to teaching vocabulary within the different areas of vocabulary teaching.

Teachers' Standards
3. Demonstrate good subject and curriculum knowledge:

- have a secure knowledge of the relevant subject(s) and curriculum areas, foster and maintain pupils' interest in the subject, and address misunderstandings;
- demonstrate a critical understanding of developments in the subject and curriculum areas, and promote the value of scholarship;
- demonstrate an understanding of, and take responsibility for, promoting high standards of literacy, articulacy and the correct use of standard English, whatever the teacher's specialist subject.

Introduction

What is the difference between great and grate; between soul and sole; or the difference between 'A blanket of cloud covered the land' and 'The cloud was like a blanket that covered the land'; or happy, happier and happiest; or bad and atrocious; or your understanding of the word operation – in a maths lesson and when your doctor tells you one is necessary to save your life?

These are all questions of vocabulary. Vocabulary could be described as the often forgotten and unmentioned foundation of literacy teaching and learning. Somehow, there appears to be an assumption that because we all use vocabulary as we talk, read and write, teachers do not need to teach it, that children learn it just by being exposed to it. Perhaps if we were to pause a moment and consider the role of vocabulary in learning, and literacy learning in particular, we might realise why consideration of how children learn vocabulary and the teacher's role in developing vocabulary should be an essential part of teacher education. The work of Snow *et al.* (2005) demonstrates the essential place vocabulary has in all learning. They identify that vocabulary plays a central role in understanding concepts and also in the way we remember them. Significant for literacy learning is the link between vocabulary knowledge and reading success (Biemiller, 2003) and in particular the links between vocabulary knowledge and reading comprehension (Cain, 2010).

This chapter will explore the different elements of vocabulary teaching across the English curriculum and research-based approaches to its teaching.

The importance of vocabulary development

Children are developing vocabulary knowledge from the moment they are born; they learn from the language in their home environments and in the experiences of the world they are introduced to, and specifically from their parents and carers. There are, however, considerable differences in the rate of vocabulary growth in the early years as well as differences in the range of vocabulary a child acquires. Hart and Risley (2003) identified the gap between the vocabulary knowledge of pre-school children from economically advantaged and economically disadvantaged families. Typically, a high-performing child on entry to school may have a receptive and expressive vocabulary of 7,100 root words in contrast to a lower performing child, with a vocabulary of 3,000 words. This is of significance because being able to communicate is the basis for social interaction, for making friends and for learning. Vocabulary knowledge in the early years is a predictor of a child's developing phonemic awareness (Goswami, 2001) and so later reading success (Block and Mangieri, 2006). Children who begin their school life with low levels of vocabulary knowledge can become trapped in a vicious circle: the lower the levels of vocabulary the less success a child has with reading, and the less success the child has with reading, the less likely they are to read, and the less likely they are to read the slower their vocabulary growth (Cunningham and Stanovich, 1998). Having difficulties communicating in the school environment can affect children's behaviour as well as their learning. It is hard to find a more significant component of learning.

Because this is rather a vast subject area, for the purposes of this chapter, vocabulary development will be considered in three main areas:

- vocabulary development to support communication and language development;
- vocabulary development to support reading comprehension;
- vocabulary development to support spelling and word investigation – morphology and etymology.

It is important, however, to see each area above as interlinked and interdependent aspects of learning. For example, investigating morphology as part of teaching spelling can support reading comprehension as it explores word meanings. In the same way, word play, as part of developing communication and language development, can be an important element of teaching spelling. It is also worth noting that all of these areas combine to support the teaching of writing – where careful vocabulary choice is influenced by what the writer wishes to communicate (language development); knowledge of how other writers use words (reading comprehension); and how to spell the words the writer has chosen to use (morphological and etymological influences).

Overview of vocabulary development in the National Curriculum

Vocabulary is mentioned in different parts of the National Curriculum. The 'Purpose of Study: Spoken Language' section states *The quality and variety of language that pupils hear and speak are vital for developing vocabulary and grammar and their understanding of reading and writing* (DfE, 2013, p13). It is identified again in the 'Purposes of Study for Reading': *Good comprehension draws from linguistic knowledge (in particular of vocabulary and grammar)* and later in the 'Purposes of Study' when outlining the importance of *reading widely and often* as it *increases pupils' vocabulary because they encounter words they would rarely hear or use in everyday speech* (p14). Vocabulary is identified again in the 'Writing Purposes of Study': *Effective composition ... requires ... an increasingly wide knowledge of vocabulary* (p15). Vocabulary also appears in the 'Spelling, Vocabulary, Grammar, Punctuation' section, which states:

> Opportunities for teachers to enhance pupils' vocabulary arise naturally from their reading and writing. As vocabulary increases, teachers should show pupils how to understand relationships between words, how to understand nuances in meaning and how to develop their understanding of, and ability to use, figurative language. They should also teach pupils how to work out and clarify the meanings of unknown words and words with more than one meaning.

> (p15)

In 2016, children in Year 2 and 6 took the first SATs (Standard Assessment Tests) based on the new curriculum. Outcomes for reading nationally against these new standards indicated that many children were not meeting the increased demands of the new curriculum standards. One reason for this, which many schools I have been working with identified in their analysis of the returned test papers in Year 6, was the increased demands on children's vocabulary knowledge. This included children's vocabulary knowledge linked to their knowledge of the world and life experiences as well as children's ability to make inferences about vocabulary when they meet new or unusual vocabulary or vocabulary used in a new context.

The specific programmes of study relating to vocabulary will be further explored in the sections below along with approaches to teaching that can enable children to extend their vocabulary knowledge and so prepare them for the demands of SATs but, more significantly, enable them to engage with the world around them and so embrace life.

Vocabulary development to support communication and language development

The National Curriculum

The statutory requirements for Spoken Language require pupils in Years 1 to 6 to be taught to:

- ask relevant questions to extend their understanding and build vocabulary and knowledge;
- use relevant strategies to build their vocabulary.

Research focus

When identifying in research the range of strategies that support the development of children's expressive and receptive vocabulary, the need to create language-rich learning environments that foster 'word consciousness' (Graves, 2006) is evident. This entails creating spaces in classrooms where purposeful talk is encouraged and facilitated as well as ensuring that the classroom is rich in environmental print that engages children in the environment. A language-rich environment also requires the conscious planning for the introduction of new vocabulary that accompanies learning opportunities across the curriculum. Reading aloud for pleasure and purpose is also a regular feature of a language-rich environment. The Ofsted report *Reading for Pleasure and Purpose* (2004) warns against the reading aloud of texts if the focus is purely the mining of a text for its vocabulary – the interesting adjective or the well-placed adverb – but reminds teachers that a language-rich environment is about developing children's love of reading, interest in the words authors choose and how these words can make us laugh and cry, think and question. Cremin *et al.*'s (2009) study, *Teachers as Readers*, explores the ways that teachers need to extend their knowledge of and pleasure in reading children's literature so their enthusiasm for the words of fiction and non-fiction can excite and motivate. Margaret Meek (2010) outlines an understanding of reading that considers the range of ways that *texts teach* and how they provide a framework for our thinking about

$\longrightarrow$

ourselves and others. Reading aloud introduces children to the vocabulary of these different ideas and situations, and importantly provides a context for the vocabulary. However, it is the teacher who is the key to unlocking the word-rich environment, encouraging interest in words, learning new words, playing with words and developing a growing love of language from wherever that language stems.

In addition to reading aloud, the language-rich environment is one that motivates and engages children to be independent readers. Cunningham and Stanovich (1998) used the term 'The Matthew Effect', referring to the Bible passage in the Gospel of Matthew that says *For unto everyone that hath shall be given, and he shall have abundance: but from him that hath not shall be taken away even that which he hath* (Matt.25: 29, KJV), to explain how the more widely and frequently a child reads, the better she becomes at reading and the larger her vocabulary knowledge. Conversely, the less a child reads, the further behind she becomes in terms of her general and vocabulary knowledge, and her skills as a reader. The amount of reading a child does is also a predictor of vocabulary knowledge and subject knowledge, and explained the difference between the vocabulary knowledge of children who read and those who chose not to or who could not read. Other studies have demonstrated similar findings: that wide reading is the *hallmark of word learning that occurs normally and incidentally during reading* (Blachowicz et al., 2006, p528).

With these studies in mind, it is helpful to plan for the learning environment as well as planning specific vocabulary teaching. The environment includes the nature of the displays, the spaces and opportunities created in the classroom for purposeful interactions and the pedagogic choices made to teach language and literacy. The case studies below, taken from very different schools and year groups, explore how a trainee and teacher planned to create a word-conscious, language-rich learning environment.

Case study: using the environment

Marianna, a PGCE student on her final placement, began her planning in a reception classroom in an area of high socioeconomic disadvantage by considering how the environment could support the language development, and in particular the vocabulary development of her class. She selected a version of *Jack and the Beanstalk* to read to the class as the context for learning. She practised reading the story aloud to a friend with a focus on how she would read words she had identified for explicit vocabulary teaching. The text included a range of words about the size of different characters and objects within the story: the beans were 'tiny'; the giant was 'enormous' and the beanstalk grew until it 'towered over Jack's little house'. When the words appeared in the text, Marianna used her voice as well as actions to give meaning to the words; she asked

→

questions about how the enormous giant would make the children feel if they met him; she encouraged role play of climbing the 'towering' beanstalk; she planned for the other adults to use the words in the role play area and she presented the words as a synonym web and then a 'word-cline' (see the word-cline in Figure 3.1) to help children consider the words' 'shades of meaning'. She encouraged children and practitioners to add to the 'word-cline' and used these words on the story map the children had created. She linked the vocabulary to other areas of the curriculum. She modelled, along with other adults in the classroom, using these words across the curriculum – even using the words at fruit time and play time.

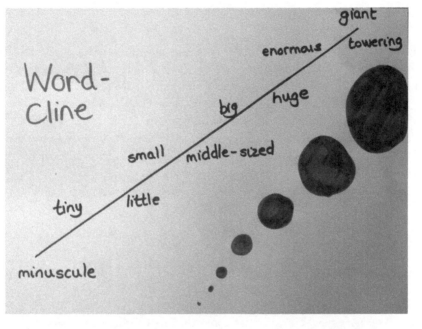

Figure 3.1 Example of a word-cline

Kathryn is a Year 5 teacher in an inner-city school. Her class has large numbers of children for whom English is not their first language. Teaching vocabulary through reading aloud and related word play has been a feature of her teaching for some time. Her school uses the Centre for Literacy in Primary Education (CLPE) 'Book Power' and 'Power of Reading' resources to support planning, and Kathryn chose Siobhan Dowd's book, *The London Eye Mystery*, as the text to read aloud to the class. The main character, Ted, is autistic and sees the world in a slightly different way from his family. The story demonstrates, through the eyes of the character, some of the idiosyncrasies of the English language and this enabled Kathryn to focus on word play with her class, and in particular idioms ('It's raining cats and dogs') and puns ('What did the letter say to the stamp?' 'Stick with me and we'll go places'). The classroom walls became an exploration of idioms, which often cause difficulties in spoken and written language for children who are not English first-language speakers. The children told a 'joke a day' exploring the vocabulary of the pun, although sometimes it took a while for the laughs to come as a discussion was needed about the vocabulary before the jokes made sense.

These examples come from different key stages, but demonstrate the centrality of vocabulary development in the pedagogic approaches of the student and teacher, and a commitment to enriching the spoken language of the children they teach.

Curriculum link

Puns are often created because the words in question are homophones. Homophones are words that sound the same but are spelt differently – e.g. hear and here; some and sum. The programmes of study for spelling in Years 2 to 6 include reference to the teaching of homophones. The objective in Years 5 and 6 requires children to 'continue to distinguish between homophones and other words which are often confused'. Jokes and games can be an effective and engaging way to teach this sort of language knowledge. There are good resources available on line, or Richard Lederer's book *Pun and Games* (1996) is a useful resource.

Activity

Audit the Classroom in which you work: is the classroom a rich literature environment? Consider the following:

- Are there spaces in your classroom that are conducive to 'book talk'?
- Are books and digital media accessible?
- Are there displays that encourage children to leave comments about and express preferences about books they have read?
- Is new vocabulary linked to classroom reading displayed and explored?
- Are there opportunities for children to deliberately and purposefully use the vocabulary investigated in texts?
- Are children involved in selecting the book that is chosen as the 'read aloud' text – perhaps through hearing snippets of different books before expressing preferences?
- Is poetry visible in the classroom (a really rich source of language used for different effects on the reader)?
- Are jokes, puns and 'words of the day' activities available?

The National Literacy Trust website (**www.literacytrust.org.uk/**) provides useful audit documents to support the development of rich, literate environments.

Vocabulary development to support reading comprehension

The National Curriculum

The statutory requirements for reading – comprehension require pupils to be taught the following:

Year 1
Develop pleasure in reading, motivation to read, vocabulary and understanding by:

- listening to and discussing a wide range of poems, stories and non-fiction at a level beyond that at which they can read independently;

- being encouraged to link what they read or hear read to their own experiences;

- becoming very familiar with key stories, fairy stories and traditional tales, retelling them and considering their particular characteristics;

- recognising and joining in with predictable phrases;

- learning to appreciate rhymes and poems, and to recite some by heart;

- discussing word meanings, linking new meanings to those already known.

Year 2
Develop pleasure in reading, motivation to read, vocabulary and understanding by:

- listening to, discussing and expressing views about a wide range of contemporary and classic poetry, stories and non-fiction at a level beyond that at which they can read independently;

- discussing the sequence of events in books and how items of information are related;

- becoming increasingly familiar with and retelling a wider range of stories, fairy stories and traditional tale;

- being introduced to non-fiction books that are structured in different ways;

- recognising simple, recurring literary language in stories and poetry;

- discussing and clarifying the meanings of words, linking new meanings to known vocabulary;

- discussing their favourite words and phrases;

- continuing to build up a repertoire of poems learnt by heart, appreciating these and reciting some, with appropriate intonation to make the meaning clear.

Years 3 and 4

Develop positive attitudes to reading and understanding of what they read by:

- using dictionaries to check the meaning of words they have read;
- discussing words and phrases that capture the reader's interest and imagination.

Key Stage 2 (so across all year groups)

Understand what they read, in books they can read independently, by:

- checking that the text makes sense to them, discussing their understanding and explaining the meaning of words in context.

As you can see, across all year groups the role of vocabulary is highlighted in the 'Programmes of Study' and seen as integral to the teaching of reading comprehension. It is often an area overlooked when teaching reading comprehension but research demonstrates that vocabulary development is an essential component.

Research focus

Vocabulary knowledge plays a role in language comprehension and language comprehension is a component of reading comprehension ('The Simple View of Reading'). When a child decodes a word and knows the meaning of the word she/he has what is known as a semantic representation of that word (Primary National Strategy, 2006) and based on this, when they encounter similar words, they will use this knowledge to work out the meanings of the new word. This knowledge also provides children with some contextual information about what they are reading and supports the child in the development of a 'situation model' (Kintsch and Rawson, 2005). This model is built, often subconsciously, in the mind as we read. It is almost like a picture being painted, or a film being created, or a mind map being written in the mind of the reader, based on the inferences they are making as the words in the text are read. As the reader reads, they continually add to or take away elements of their developing model, building as they read their understanding of the text. Yuill and Oakhill's (1988, 1991) inference training demonstrated that children could be supported in developing reading comprehension through the explicit and deliberate teaching of inference, including the teaching of vocabulary within texts. Inference training is now used as an intervention programme for children with weaker comprehension skills as part of the Reading Recovery suite of programmes.

The vocabulary focus as part of reading comprehension can be taught by the intentional teaching of strategies. Pressley (2000), along with many other researchers, identified these strategies as *prediction, questioning, clarifying, imagining* and *summarisation*. These strategies can be used, therefore, to teach vocabulary. Children need to be taught that they should expect what they are reading to make sense, and part of this is understanding what the vocabulary decoded means. It is easy to assume that it is the more unusual and complex words that need to be taught as part

$\longrightarrow$

of reading comprehension, but Cain (1996) identified that poor comprehension was often due to lack of knowledge of 'local cohesive devices', which means that a reader does not understand the meaning of grammatical function words. So when reading 'Tom walked down the road. He was in a hurry because he was late', the reader needs to infer that 'he' in the second sentence refers to 'Tom' in the first sentence and that the word 'because' is telling the reader that a reason for Tom being in a hurry is about to be given.

This level of vocabulary knowledge enables the reader to make sense of the text as a whole. Deliberately noticing, discussing and mapping words, including those with similar grammatical functions, can support all children, and particularly those where English is not their first language, to develop their use and understanding of vocabulary as well as support their reading comprehension (Conteh, 2012).

Useful strategies

Before reading

1. Encourage children to predict what the story or non-fiction text might be about with a focus on predicting vocabulary. By activating prior knowledge, children are able to share their knowledge of possible technical vocabulary that might occur in the text as well as language structures and patterns they might expect from a particular genre e.g. 'Once upon a time ...'. Record these predictions on post-it notes and return to them as you encounter the words or synonyms for these words in the text.

2. Teach specific vocabulary that you have identified as possibly causing difficulties in terms of decoding or that you know is new for the children. Select words carefully. It is helpful to look at the work of Isobel Beck (2005), who grouped words into three tiers. The first tier is made up of basic words and they rarely need instruction – e.g. chair, happy, pencil. The second tier of words are often synonyms for the first tier words, and words that are common in academic learning and general communication – e.g. discuss, miserable. These words are most useful for teaching as they are words that children will encounter more frequently in spoken and written language and, if known, enable comprehension. Third-tier words include technical and subject-specific vocabulary – e.g. peninsula – and so are interesting in terms of word study, but are not the most effective words to teach for comprehension.

During reading

1. Model using the 'Think Aloud' strategy (Israel and Massey, 2005) how you pause having read a word that is new or unusual (or one of the second-tier words you have selected to teach) and share your thoughts with children about how you go about working out what this word means. Model how you can: rerun the sentence; read on in the text and

then return to the word; draw on prior knowledge, looking at the word structure and considering words that share the structure as well as making inferences based on your prior knowledge of the subject area; refer to other sources – a friend, a dictionary or another text and using any illustrations, diagrams, charts or photographs to search for the meaning of the vocabulary. It is important to model this process *after* the word has been read, demonstrating the active construction of meaning and not as the approach to the decoding itself.

2. The 'Talk for Writing' approach, as described in the *Transforming Writing Evaluation Report* (Rooke, 2013), involves children 'imitating' the text through oral retellings, using story maps or other organisational devices as well as physical actions to accompany grammatical function words. This supports the study of vocabulary within the context of the text and enables children to use the vocabulary repeatedly as they imitate the text in reading and writing.

After reading

1. Returning to the text following reading to discuss, respond to and explore vocabulary meanings enables children to embed vocabulary learning through active engagement with the text. Using drama, 'Readers Theatre', creating synonym banks, creating 'magpie' word displays and raising questions provides children with multiple exposures to new vocabulary as well as offering opportunities for multiple uses of the new vocabulary.

An active approach to reading comprehension enables children to engage with and respond to a text and, in particular, to explore and make sense of the vocabulary. Opportunities to reflect on an author's language choices are important so that children discuss and analyse as they read. Reading comprehension worksheets and exercises rarely motivate children and lack real purpose: not surprisingly, they are also not very effective in the teaching of vocabulary. The following case study illustrates how reading comprehension can be both active and purposeful.

Case study: poetry

Fazana planned a unit of work reading and writing poetry with a class of Year 4 children. She wanted to combine poetry performance with a focus on vocabulary development. She used the poem 'The Sea' by James Reeves. The poem did not present many vocabulary challenges for children and so enabled Fazana to teach the 'Readers Theatre' approach. Fazana modelled how she created a mental model of the poem. She did this by 'thinking aloud' about the vocabulary. This included modelling how she used her prior knowledge of the sea and of dogs (the metaphor used in the poem) to make connections between the vocabulary. Part of the 'thinking aloud' process highlighted the onomatopoeic words, considering what they meant and how they could be spoken to emphasise both the sound and meaning of the word. She recorded her thoughts on the poem - annotating it with drawings and her ideas. She then

→

used these to reread the poem to the children, using her voice to emphasise the meanings of the words, repeating some and changing her tone and volume. The children then worked in groups to annotate the poem and performed the poem. Following this, Fazana introduced another poem about the sea, 'Dover Beach' by Matthew Arnold. This poem had more challenging vocabulary and ideas, but the children were able to use the model from the poem 'The Sea' to investigate the vocabulary, to explore meanings and so perform the poem.

What was particularly effective about this teaching episode was the clear model given to the children before they began to work on a poem of their own. The strategies they could use to support comprehension were demonstrated explicitly and they were then able to use this scaffold to structure their investigation of the second poem. It is important that children are given the opportunity to apply their learning independently across the curriculum, using their learning for purpose and pleasure.

Curriculum link

Cross-curricular opportunities provide a real purpose and context for vocabulary exploration. It is important that strategies to support vocabulary development are used and applied in other areas of the curriculum. Consider the vocabulary demands of a mathematics word problem, the technical vocabulary in a science investigation and the particular range of conjunctions and adverbials used in historical writing.

Activity: teaching strategies

Look at the following sentences taken from different subject areas. Which words would you teach and which strategies could you use to teach them?

1. There were 7 more girls than boys in the class. There were 33 children in the class. How many were boys and how many were girls?
2. The first settlers landed in Jamestown under the watchful eye of the Native Americans.
3. Penguins are rather cleverly camouflaged and have adapted to the harsh, cold conditions they live in.
4. 'The two executioners stalk along over the knolls,
   Bearing two axes with heavy heads shining and wide'
   (taken from Thomas Hardy's poem, 'Throwing a Tree').

(Possible answers can be found at the end of the chapter.)

Getting to grips with some of these words is about having an understanding of how each word has been built – what the root word is, the prefix and suffix, or where a word originates from. This brings us to the third element of vocabulary development.

Vocabulary development to support spelling – morphology and etymology

The National Curriculum

Years 3 and 4
- use further prefixes and suffixes and understand how to add them;
- spell further homophones.

Years 5 and 6
- use knowledge of morphology and etymology in spelling;
- use dictionaries to check the spelling and meaning of words.

You will find further details and a fuller account of how to support children develop as spellers in Chapter 4, but encouraging curiosity about words has benefits for both vocabulary development and spelling.

Research focus

Knowledge of prefixes, suffixes and root words, and an interest in the origins of words characterises the child who has an extensive vocabulary. It is often thought that the teaching of morphology (the study and description of how words are formed) and etymology (the study of the historical origins of words) are confined to the teaching of spelling, but knowledge of how words work can unlock meaning for children, particularly when it is taught alongside comprehension instruction (Baumann *et al.*, 2003). Mann and Singson (2003) suggest that children are naturally curious about words and will hypothesise about morphemes even before any literacy teaching. Word building, where children build words from their constituent morphemes, has been shown to improve spelling and also increase children's vocabulary knowledge (Adoniou, 2013). Adoniou gives the example of the compound word 'breakfast', suggesting that 'if you understand that it means to break a fast after a night of not eating, then you are less likely to spell it as "brekfast"'. She goes on to explore how an understanding of morphemes can help with widening vocabulary, understanding the way that words work enables a transfer of knowledge from one word to another. Adding *-ian* to a word can change *magic* into *magician* and so change an object to a person. This can then be transferred to *electric* (*electrician*).

$\longrightarrow$

In the same way, an awareness of the history of a word, of its origins, can excite and motivate children to explore vocabulary. Different languages favoured different combinations of letters; so Norse spelling used *sk* while *sc* is more often used in the French or Greek. The letters *gh* were introduced by the Dutch – think about Vincent Van Gogh.

English is a rich and diverse language, which also means there is always more to learn. Morphology and etymology, in particular, can challenge a student teacher's subject knowledge.

Case study: morphology

Dean, a PGCE student, on placement in a Year 5 class was aware that his own knowledge of morphology and etymology was weak. He decided to use 'word work' as starter activities during register time every day for a few weeks. Each morning he prepared a 'word web' as a model for children and provided a range of words for children to investigate in the same way. In the first week, he used words that were familiar to children, as in the 'word webs' in Figure 3.2 below.

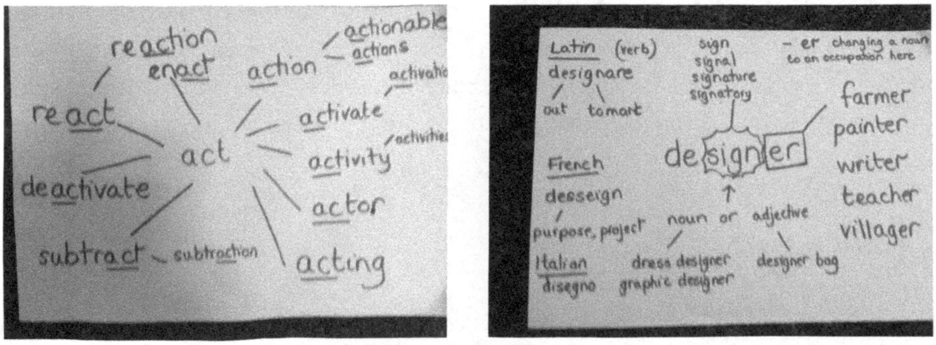

Figure 3.2 Examples of 'word webs'

In the second week, Dean showed children the programme *Call my Bluff* on which unusual words were defined by a panel of three different people, with only one definition being correct. He gave children the correct definition of some words but challenged them to make up plausible alternative definitions based on their knowledge of morphology and etymology. One child made up a definition of 'morphology': 'Morphology is the study of plasticine. Plasticine is able to be moulded and changed or morphed, which means the making of smooth changes. "ology" means the study of a subject and so morphology is the scientific study of the changing shapes of plasticine figures and can be seen in films such as *Wallace and Gromit* with the filmmakers being experts in the area of morphology.' Not a bad definition when considering the meanings of the morphemes in the word – albeit an inaccurate one.

In order to develop your subject knowledge, pause every now and again when you read and consider the words you are reading in relation to morphology and etymology; a good dictionary will give you some analysis of words, and there are many online etymological dictionaries that can be very helpful.

Activity: etymology

Can you identify the country of origin for each of these words? What clues did you use?

skirt	buffet	fjord	sky	cello
soprano	rhythm	rhetoric	maisonette	crescendo

(Answers can be found at the end of the chapter.)

Vocabulary development touches all aspects of teaching English and more significantly has implications for the way we teach in other subject areas. Vocabulary development needs to take place in a language-rich environment that encourages children's natural curiosity in the words that surround them. Alongside this, teachers need to provide structured exploration of vocabulary in context through the deliberate teaching of word comprehension strategies and investigation of morphology and etymology.

And finally . . .

There is perhaps one missing section in this chapter: the National Curriculum has a whole section for each year group in which vocabulary is clearly relevant, in the section titled 'Vocabulary, Grammar and Punctuation'. The vocabulary highlighted here addresses two distinct areas. It refers to terminology – so the specific vocabulary that names, defines and categorises the English language – e.g. the noun, verb and adverb – and also the content vocabulary that can be identified in a grammatical 'category' – e.g. dog, bottle and paper – are nouns. This later area is further expanded in the details of the programmes of study where it outlines how, when teaching writing, teachers should highlight vocabulary choice in relation to structure, organisation and content. It identifies the need to discuss vocabulary choice, considering clarity and cohesion, so drawing children's attention to the need to consider the purpose and audience of the writing.

This is a vast, varied and interesting aspect of vocabulary teaching and so has been addressed in Chapter 5 (Grammar and Punctuation), Chapter 8 (Poetry) and Chapter 10 (Writing), but it inevitably comes into many of the other chapters as well.

Learning outcomes review

You should now know:

- what children need to know and understand about vocabulary – for language and reading comprehension and as a support for spelling;
- what you need to know as a primary teacher in order to teach the 2014 English National Curriculum;
- the breadth of study of vocabulary teaching and learning;
- approaches to teaching vocabulary within the different areas of vocabulary teaching.

Self-assessment question
1. What is meant by a language-rich classroom environment?
2. What is the link between reading comprehension and vocabulary development?
3. Why are the spelling objectives in the National Curriculum important as part of vocabulary teaching?

Answers to activities

Teaching strategies: possible answers

1. There were 7 more girls than boys in the class. There were 33 children in the class. How many were boys and how many were girls?

Vocabulary to teach: 'more than', 'how many more?'.

Strategies for teaching: highlighting or underlining the key words in the problem; using the words in another sentence linked to a different context.

2. The first settlers landed in Jamestown under the watchful eye of the Native Americans.

Vocabulary to teach: 'settlers', 'landed', 'watchful eye', 'Native Americans'.

Strategies for teaching: reading on in the sentence to infer the meaning of 'landed'; referring to prior knowledge, perhaps to learning about Vikings or other invaders and settlers; investigating the word 'settlers': settling, settle, the suffix -er; 'watchful eye': considering times in children's lives where they have watched something, thinking about why they were watching and linking this to why the Native Americans might have wanted or needed to 'watch' the settlers. Refer to other

(Continued)

(Continued)

sources to consider the relationship between settlers and Native Americans, and use this to infer what 'watchful eye' might mean.

It is also interesting to look at place names – 'Jamestown': King James was on the throne when the settlers arrived in America, hence the naming of the town they established as 'Jamestown'.

3. Penguins are rather cleverly camouflaged and have adapted to the harsh, cold conditions they live in.

Vocabulary to teach: 'rather cleverly camouflaged', 'adapted', 'harsh', 'conditions'.

Strategies for teaching: exploring the phrase 'rather cleverly camouflaged', referring to prior knowledge of the word 'camouflage' and, where appropriate, a dictionary. The word 'cleverly' suggests there may be something unusual about the camouflage and referring to another source will tell the reader that penguins are black on top so that when in the sea they are camouflaged against the dark waters when viewed from above and white underneath so that when viewed from below the sea they are hard to see against the light when looking up.

4. The two executioners stalk along over the knolls,
   Bearing two axes with heavy heads shining and wide

Vocabulary to teach: 'executioners', 'stalk', 'knolls'.

Strategies for teaching: 'executioners' – referring to children's prior knowledge about executions, perhaps thinking about learning about the Tudors, for example. Returning to the title of the poem and reading on to the end of the verse to infer what sort of executioners the two people in the poem might be and what they have come to execute.

'Stalk' – inferring that the word here is probably talking about the way the executioners are walking, using the grammatical construction of the sentence to work out that this word is a verb. Referring to prior knowledge: we talk about a cat stalking a bird and a lion stalking its prey – how can this help us infer what the word stalk means?

'Knolls' – rereading the sentence and studying the words before the word 'knolls'. 'Stalk along' and 'over' suggest the executioners are walking over undulating land, 'along' and 'over' suggest possibly walking over hills. A 'knoll', we might infer, is a hill. It might be a good word to look up in a dictionary to confirm the inference.

Etymology

Skirt Scandinavian – the clue is in the *sk*	Buffet French – the clue is in the pronunciation of the *et*	Fjord Scandinavian – the clue is in the *fj* together	Sky Scandinavian – the clue is in the *sk*	Cello Italian – the clue is the *-o* ending
Soprano Italian – the clue is the *-o* ending	Rhythm Greek – the clue is in the *rh*	Rhetoric Greek – the clue is in the *rh*	Maisonette French – the clue is in the *ai* sound and the *-ette* ending	Crescendo Italian – the clue is the *-o* ending

Further reading

For a helpful overview of strategies and some background research read:

DCSF (2008) *Teaching Effective Vocabulary: What Can Teachers do to Increase the Vocabulary of Children who start Education with a Limited Vocabulary?* Nottingham: DCSF Publications. Available at: **http://webarchive.nationalarchives.gov.uk/20130401151715/https://www.education.gov.uk/publications/**eOrderingDownload/TEV_A4.pdf (accessed 17 January 2014).

For a practical handbook (although be aware that it is an American publication) with a focus on strategies particularly helpful for children learning English as an additional language read:

Sinney, R and Velasc, R (2011) *Connecting Content and Academic Language for English Learners and Struggling Students*. Thousand Oaks, CA: Corwin Sage.

References

Adoniou, M (2013) What should teachers know about spelling? *Literacy*. doi: 10.1111/lit.12017. Available at: **http://onlinelibrary.wiley.com/doi/10.1111/lit.12017/abstract** (accessed 13 June 2014).

Baumann, JF, Edwards, EC, Bolland, E, Olenjnil, S and Kame'enui, EJ (2003) Vocabulary tricks: effects of instruction in morphology and context on fifth grade students' ability to derive and infer word meaning. *American Educational Research Journal*, 40: 447–94.

Beck, I (2005) *Bringing Words to Life*. New York: Guilford.

Biemiller, A (2003) Vocabulary: needed if more children are to read well. *Reading Psychology*, 24: 323–35.

Blachowicz, C, Fischer, P and Ogle, D (2006) Vocabulary: questions from the classroom. *Reading Research Quarterly*, 41(4): 524–39.

Block, CC and Mangieri, JN (2006) *The Vocabulary Enriched Classroom.* New York: Scholastic.

Cain, K (1996) Story knowledge and comprehension skill, in C Cornoldi and J Oakhill (eds) *Reading Comprehension Difficulties, Processes and Intervention.* Mahwah, NJ: Lawrence Erlbaum.

Cain, K (2010) Skills for reading comprehension, in K Hall, U Goswami and C Harrison, S Ellis and J Soler (eds) *Interdisciplinary Perspectives on Learning to Read.* London: Routledge, pp74–87.

Conteh, J (2012) *Teaching Bilingual and EAL Learners in Primary Schools.* London: Sage.

Cremin, T, Mottram, M, Collins, F, Powell, S and Safford, K (2009) Teachers as readers: building communities of readers. *Literacy*, 43(1): 11–19.

Cunningham, AE and Stanovich, KE (1998) What reading does for the mind. *American Educator*, 2: 8–17.

Department for Education (DfE) (2013) *The National Curriculum in England: Key Stages 1 and 2 Framework Document.* London: DfE.

Goswami, U (2001) Early phonological development and the acquisition of language, in SB Neuman and DK Dickenson (eds) *Handbook of Early Literacy Research.* New York: Guilford Press, pp111–25.

Graves, MF (2006) *The Vocabulary Book.* New York: Teachers College Press.

Hart, B and Risley, TR (2003) The early catastrophe: the 30 million word gap by age 3. *American Educator*, 27(1): 4–9.

Israel, SE and Massey, D (2005) Metacognitive think-alouds: using a gradual release model with middle school students, in SE Israel, CC Block, KL Bausermann and KK Kinnucan-Welsh (eds) *Metacognition in Literacy Learning: Theory, Assessment, Instruction and Professional Development.* Mahwah, NJ: Lawrence Erlbaum.

Kintsch, W and Rawson, K (2005) Comprehension, in M Snowling and C Hulme (eds) *The Science of Reading: A Handbook.* Oxford: Blackwell, pp209–65.

Lederer, R (1996) *Pun and Games.* Chicago: Chicago Review Press.

Mann, V and Singson, M (2003) Linking morphological knowledge to English decoding ability: large effects of little suffixes, in E Assink and D Sandra (eds) *Reading Complex Words.* New York: Kluwer Academic, pp1–25.

Meek, M (2010) Readings about reading. *Changing English: Studies in Culture and Education*, 11(2): 307–17.

Ofsted (2004) *Reading for Pleasure and Purpose.* London: Ofsted Publications.

Pressley, M (2000) What should comprehension be the instruction of?, in ML Kimel, PB Mosenthal, PD Pearson and R Barr (eds) *Handbook of Reading Research*, Vol. 3. Mahwah, NJ: Lawrence Erlbaum Associates.

Primary National Strategy (2006) *Developing Reading Comprehension.* London: Primary National Strategy.

Rooke, J (2013) *Transforming Writing Evaluation Report.* London: Literacy Trust. Available at: **www.literacytrust.org.uk/assets/0001/9256/Transforming_Writing_Final_Report.pdf** (accessed 17 January 2014).

Snow, CE, Griffin, P and Burns, S (2005) *Knowledge to Support the Teaching of Reading: Preparing Teachers for a Changing World.* San Francisco, CA: Jossey-Bass.

Yuill, N and Oakhill, J (1988) Effects of inference awareness training on poor reading comprehension. *Applied Cognitive Psychology*, 2(1): 33–45.

Yuill, NM and Oakhill, JV (1991) *Children's Problems in Text Comprehension: An Experimental Investigation.* Cambridge: Cambridge University Press.

4 Spelling

Kate Allott

Learning outcomes

Learning outcomes

By reading this chapter you will develop your understanding of:

- why children need to develop good spelling;
- what children need to learn about spelling;
- how to teach spelling effectively.

Teachers' Standards
3. Demonstrate good subject and curriculum knowledge:

- have a secure knowledge of the relevant subject(s) and curriculum areas, foster and maintain pupils' interest in the subject, and address misunderstandings;
- demonstrate a critical understanding of developments in the subject and curriculum areas, and promote the value of scholarship;
- demonstrate an understanding of, and take responsibility for, promoting high standards of literacy, articulacy and the correct use of standard English, whatever the teacher's specialist subject.

Introduction: why spelling matters

Does spelling matter in the age of the spell checker? In extreme cases, writers' attempts at spellings are so different from the intended word that the spell checker cannot help, and if writers do not read the suggested alternatives accurately, they may find that they have written something quite different from what they had intended – suntanned instead of sustained, for example. With young or struggling writers the reader may simply not be able to read their work – indeed, in the very early stages some children find it difficult or impossible to read back what they themselves have written. But if it is possible to read most misspelled words quite easily, does spelling really matter?

Research focus: children's views of spelling

The National Literacy Trust carries out an annual survey of children's attitudes to literacy (Clark, 2013). In 2012, more than 34,000 children were surveyed, and they were asked whether they agreed that if they could use a spell checker they did not need to learn to spell. About a quarter agreed; children receiving free school meals were more likely to agree, and those who agreed were more likely to be below their expected level in writing than those who disagreed with the statement.

However, children often worry about spellings, and write more slowly and with less confidence because of the effort they make with this aspect of writing. Again, it could be argued that if adults gave less emphasis to correct spelling children would be less inhibited by their worries about it. There is some truth in this, and certainly it is important that the right sort of attention is given to spelling – an emphasis on developing an interest in words and how they are spelled, rather than on rote learning and testing. However, some children are very keen to know that they have used the correct spelling, and cannot be fobbed off with praise such as 'good try' or 'I can read it'. In the end, spelling is a skill, and developing a skill to the point of automaticity, whether it is changing gear in a car or sight-reading music, leaves us free to attend to more important aspects of the activity. Young writers who can spell most of the words they write, and know that others that they are unsure of can be checked later, are able to focus on composition. The 2014 National Curriculum states that *writing down ideas fluently depends on effective transcription: that is, on spelling quickly and accurately* (DfE, 2013, p15).

Activity: investigating attitudes to spelling

Talk to three people – perhaps three people of very different ages, or different occupations, or three trainee teachers – about spelling. Do they think spelling is important? Do they consider themselves to be good at spelling? Do they remember being taught spelling at school? What strategies do they use when they are not sure how to spell a word?

Spelling also matters for primary teachers. Every day in the classroom they are faced with the need to write, whether on the board, in children's books, in notes and records. If they have difficulties with spelling, there are, of course, strategies that can be used to support them, but even so, it is worth working on improving their spelling as well (using those techniques they will be teaching to their pupils). Careful preparation of material to be presented to children is important, but for some, there will be moments when, for example, a child suggests a word in shared writing which the teacher cannot spell. If the teacher is aware of this, it is possible to model checking the spelling before writing it, which can be useful for children (though doing this too often would slow the pace of the teaching, and this is not the stage of the writing process at which spellings would normally be checked). However, there may also be times when teachers are simply not aware that they have misspelled words, unless this is drawn to their attention by another adult, or even by a child.

Case study: spelling and self-image

Laura, a postgraduate trainee, was concerned that her spelling was weak and that in the Year 5 class in which she had been placed for her first experience in school, the children might notice if she made mistakes. She explained this to her class teacher, who offered to check through teaching materials she had prepared and also her marking comments, so that Laura could alter spellings before the children saw them. When she was writing on the board, her teacher mentioned any errors unobtrusively at the first opportunity, so that misspelled words were not seen by the class for any length of time. Children did also point out errors, and Laura found this a difficult experience. At the end of her time in school she decided to work systematically on improving her spelling, acknowledging that she had not done this for some years, as she had relied on spell checkers during her degree course. Laura linked this experience to what she had been learning about fixed and growth mindsets – that some learners believe that ability is innate and fixed, while others think that they can improve through commitment and hard work (Dweck, 2008). She recognised that she had labelled herself as a poor speller, but now saw herself as someone who, with hard work, could over time improve her spelling.

What children need to learn about spelling

To become competent spellers, children need to learn:

- the basic alphabetic code – the way in which written symbols (graphemes) represent sounds, or phonemes;
- more complex aspects of the English spelling system;
- how to attempt the spelling of unknown words;
- how to learn spellings.

The alphabetic code

Early phonics teaching provides children with the skill of segmenting words – hearing all the phonemes separately and in sequence. This skill continues to underpin spelling at every stage, developing into the skill of breaking longer words into syllables and writing each in order, and reading back what has been written to check that it is indeed a plausible representation of the target word. Weak spellers in Key Stage 2 and beyond often fail to do these things, resulting in misspellings such as 'delcate' for 'delicate', where a phoneme has been omitted, and 'oragnise' for 'organise', where the phonemes are in the wrong order. 'Disscusion' for 'discussion' suggests the writer is aware that there is a double s somewhere in the word, but has not realised that the word ending as written is now similar to that of 'fusion' and 'exclusion', and would sound the same. The National Curriculum programme of study (DfE, 2013) emphasises the importance of making links to the phonic basis of the alphabetic code wherever appropriate.

Along with learning the phonic skills needed for spelling, children in the Early Years learn, in the first instance, at least one way of representing every phoneme they use. This includes some digraphs, such as *ll*, *ck* and *ai*, so that children are aware from very early on that they may need to use two or more letters to represent a phoneme. For many children (and their teachers and parents), this stage is very exciting, as quite quickly they are able to write anything they want to, and much of what they do write can be read by others. Even when children are finding pencil control and letter formation a challenge, they may enjoy composing words and messages using, for example, magnetic letters or keyboards. If they have not yet learned a way of representing a particular phoneme, they are likely to invent their own way of doing so – for example, using the upper case A to represent the long vowel /ai/. Look, for example, at Meg's shopping list, written at 5.1 years, after a term in Reception. At this stage she is reversing the

Figure 4.1 Meg's shopping list

letters b and d. She has not yet learned ways of representing long vowel phonemes, but has invented her own way of doing so.

Phonics teaching used to cover only single letter graphemes and a few digraphs, but children now learn all the common ways of representing each phoneme – that the phoneme /k/, for example, can be represented by *c, k, ck* and *ch*. Different ways of representing vowel phonemes in particular are detailed in the Year 1 section of Appendix 1: Spelling in the National Curriculum (DfE, 2013), and this continues into Year 2. Of course, not every possible grapheme–phoneme correspondence can be listed, as some are very unusual, but the Appendix includes ones that children are likely to encounter in their reading and writing. Learning about all the alternative options for representing each phoneme in many ways simply opens up a host of new possible misspellings, and Key Stage 1 writing is full of interesting applications of new knowledge such as 'waicke', 'borll', 'ferst' and 'fighnd'. However, children need to move from knowing that there are many possible ways to spell a word to knowing which is the correct one, and this knowledge of orthography (the spelling system) will not be complete by the end of Key Stage 2; indeed, many of us continue to develop this knowledge throughout our lives, as we learn new words.

The English spelling system

Learning the spellings of the many thousands of words children are likely to want to write may appear to be a daunting task, especially as the English spelling system is particularly complex. Crystal (2012) says of it, *We search for rules, and just when we think we have found some, we encounter a host of anomalies, variations and exceptions* (p3). There is some recognition of the complexity of the English spelling system in the National Curriculum: the guidance for Year 1 states that *it is important to recognise that phoneme-grapheme correspondences (which underpin spelling) are more variable than GPCs (which underpin reading)* (DfE, 2013, p21). But it is not necessary to learn each word as a separate item. There are many patterns by which words can be grouped, and learning groups with a common pattern is a simple and efficient approach, recommended by the National Curriculum. For example, it is difficult to know how to spell words where the final syllable is an unstressed vowel, which can be represented by, among other graphemes, *er, or* and *ar*:

farmer	doctor	vicar	colour
reader	motor	collar	flavour
baker	tailor	cellar	humour
butcher	sailor	hangar	

Grouping words by spelling pattern and teaching them together makes it easier for children to remember the spelling. One would not, of course, teach these four patterns together, as this would invite confusion; best practice would be to teach the most common pattern, –er, first, and the others at intervals later on.

In addition to these patterns, there are rules which govern aspects of the spelling system, such as the rules for making nouns plural, or for adding prefixes and suffixes to words. This is part of morphology, or the study of how words are built from root words and affixes (prefixes and suffixes), which also carry meaning. The National Curriculum builds this in from Year 1 onwards, as follows.

Year(s)	Spelling words with affixes	Examples
1	Adding –s and –es to words (plural of nouns and the third person singular of verbs)	cats, foxes, spends, catches
	Adding the endings –ing, –ed and –er to verbs where no change is needed to the root word	jumping, jumped, jumper
	Adding –er and –est to adjectives where no change is needed to the root word	quicker, quickest
	Adding the prefix –un	unfair, unlock
2	Adding –es to nouns and verbs ending in –y	babies, carries
	Adding –ed, –ing, –er and –est to a root word ending in –y with a consonant before it	copied, copier, happiest, copying
	Adding the endings –ing, –ed, –er, –est and –y to words ending in –e with a consonant before it	making, likes, biker, nicer, finest, shiny
	Adding –ing, –ed, –er, –est and –y to words of one syllable ending in a single consonant letter after a single vowel letter	patting, patted, fatter, fattest, runny
	The suffixes –ment, –ness, –ful, –less and –ly	enjoyment, sadness, careful, hopeless, badly
3 and 4	Adding suffixes beginning with vowel letters to words of more than one syllable	forgetting, beginner
		gardening, gardener
	More prefixes	disagree, mislead, incorrect, reappear, intercity, superman
	The suffix –ation	information, sensation
	The suffix –ly	happily, gently, basically
	The suffix –ous	poisonous, dangerous
5 and 6	Adding suffixes –cious, –tious, –ant,	vicious, cautious, expectant,
	–ance/–ancy, –ence/–ency, –able, –ible, –ably, –ibly	tolerance, frequency, adorable, sensible
	Adding suffixes beginning with vowel letters to words ending in –fer	preferring, preference

For each of the examples, consider whether you understand the rule and could explain it to the relevant age group. Use the National Curriculum spelling appendix to check your explanations.

Activity: investigating a suffix

Add the suffix *–ing* to the following list of words, and generate some rules about what happens. Decide on an appropriate order for introducing these rules to children. Investigations can be useful and interesting ways of introducing or revising spelling rules.

stand	play	target	run	focus	cry
sit	fight	wait	repel	shoot	begin
leap	pat	kick	moan	lie	parade
slide	see	hope	jump	bet	solve

(Possible answers can be found at the end of the chapter.)

There are often complaints that every rule has its exceptions, even those related to affixes, but sometimes this is more a consequence of a misunderstanding of the rule. For example, the well-known saying 'i before e except after c' works well, but only when the phoneme being represented is /ee/. Even when there are exceptions, rules which apply to the vast majority of words are still useful.

Research focus

A project carried out as part of the Teaching and Learning Research Programme (2006) focused on teaching children about morphemes in order to support their learning of spellings which cannot be predicted by how the word sounds, such as *magician* and *commotion*, where the ending of the words sounds the same. Children's (and teachers') awareness of morphemes was developed through a range of enjoyable activities, and both higher and lower attaining children's spelling improved as a result of the programme.

Activity: morphemes and spelling knowledge

Very few words cannot be altered by adding affixes to them, so when children learn to spell one word they are likely to be able to spell related words: once they have mastered the unusual spelling *guard*, from the 2014 National Curriculum word list for Years 3 and 4, they will also be able to spell *guarded, guarding, guards, unguarded, guardroom* and *guardian*. This approach is likely to have a significant impact on children's spelling.

For each of the following words, see how many new words you can make by adding affixes.

believe	build	centre	consider	describe
earth	fruit	height	learn	often
perhaps	recent	straight	strange	through

(Possible answers can be found at the end of the chapter.)

However, mature spellers do not on the whole rely entirely on remembering rules, and in many cases there simply is no rule – for example, to explain the different endings of *sailor* and *baker*. Good spellers have developed a visual approach to spelling, where they are able to remember the structure and appearance of words, and check their spelling by judging whether words 'look right'. Children need to develop this approach.

Spelling strategies for unknown words

Children need to learn strategies both for attempting unknown words and for learning spellings. When trying to write a word we are not sure of – perhaps a word we have heard used but not seen written down – there are several strategies which can be adopted. These include the following:

- Spelling the word the way it sounds – the phonic approach. This is what early writers do, and it should mean that even if the word is not correctly spelled it can be read successfully.

- Spelling using known spelling patterns – for example, in spelling the word *cognition* the writer might think of the *–tion* ending as in *nation* or the *–ssion* ending as in *mission*.

- Spelling by analogy with other known spellings – for example, the writer may well know the word *recognition* and use this knowledge when attempting *cognition*.

- Trying alternative spellings and judging which looks right – *cognition* or *cognission*. This self-testing technique is a mark of a good speller.

- Looking the word up in a dictionary.

Teaching spelling should include the teaching of all these strategies, so that children have access to a range of approaches and are able to make considered choices. Dictionary use needs to be taught and practised; this will include knowledge of the alphabet so that children can find words quickly. They need to know not only that *enormous* will come before *gigantic*, but also that *extraordinary* will come after *enormous*. Teaching the quartiles (E, M and S are roughly one quarter, a half and three-quarters of the way through the dictionary) can be helpful. For children with significant difficulties with spelling, a conventional dictionary may not be very helpful: looking up *watch* by finding *w* and then *o* will not work, or going to the *j* section for giant. The *ACE Spelling Dictionary* (Moseley, 1995) was devised to provide support for such children and can be a very useful resource in the Key Stage 2 classroom, although children do need to be trained in its use. A decision also needs to be made about when dictionaries are to be used: whether they will be available for children to consult as they write, or whether they are to be used for checking spellings during the editing stage of the writing process. Some children find it difficult to regain their train of thought when they have stopped to look up a word, so they will write less and may lose the flow of their thoughts; others dislike writing words they are conscious they have probably misspelled, and are able to check very quickly.

Case study: developing independence in spelling

Matt was concerned that the children in his Year 2 class were reluctant to try out spellings for themselves. Many of them regularly asked adults for spellings, and then copied them, and Matt felt that this was not leading to effective learning. He told the children that from now on they should have a go at spelling words, and then when they had finished their writing should identify three words they had not been sure of and check the spelling. They were not to ask for spellings, as Matt wanted to break their dependence on adults and also ensure that teaching time was given to other aspects of writing. At the same time he compiled a list of common misspellings and planned the teaching of these words into his regular spelling sessions. He also explicitly taught strategies for having a go at unknown words and for learning spellings.

Strategies for learning spellings

Strategies for learning spellings are hugely important. In the past, the system of setting spellings to be taken home and learned (with no indication for pupil or parent of how this was to be done) and then testing them in the weekly class spelling test, resulted in some children always scoring very low marks. (Others always did well, but this was not necessarily evidence of effective learning, as they may well have known all the spellings on the list already.) Children need to be taught how to learn spellings, and this teaching should only stop when they can explain what strategies are available to them and consciously choose an appropriate strategy for each word or group of words. The strategies children should know include the following:

- Paying careful attention to the structure of the word. How many syllables are there? Are there prefixes or suffixes? Children need to 'notice' word structure (which does not necessarily happen when reading), and should be encouraged to share their observations with others – for example, noting points of interest in their names (Charmaine starts with the same grapheme as Chloe and Charlie, and has five smaller words within it); finding palindromes such as *madam*, which reads the same backwards as forwards; looking for interesting patterns such as the repeated *ue* in *queue*. Peters (1985) described this strategy as 'looking with intent', and it is fundamental to becoming a good speller.

- Identifying the 'tricky' part of the word. Attention needs to be focused on the part or parts of the word likely to cause difficulties. For example, in people the unusual *eo* grapheme and the *le* ending are most likely to lead to errors. It is also reassuring for children to realise that they can spell most of the word successfully already.

- Learning about the words they are learning to spell: words such as *night* and *might* become less baffling and more interesting when one realises that the *gh* used to be pronounced, using the phoneme heard at the end of *loch* – and of course, it still is in some regional accents, as the representation of the Scottish accent in 'braw, bricht, moonlicht nicht' suggests. The 2014 National Curriculum refers to the role of etymology (the study of word origins) in learning spellings.

- Storing the word in the visual memory: simply looking at it is unlikely to do this, while an active approach such as the well-known 'Look, Say, Cover, Write, Check' method is usually very successful, since it uses both visual and kinaesthetic learning. When teaching this method, it is important to build in a short delay between looking and writing, as it is possible to look at a word, write it and then forget it immediately, much as we can remember a phone number just long enough to call it. It is also important to repeat the process for each word three or so times during the session, even if it was correctly spelled the first time, and then to repeat it on other days to ensure that it is not simply remembered in the short term. Cripps (1989) suggests that joined handwriting also supports the learning: the sequence of movements is also learned. Auditory learning can also be involved if the letter names are said as the letters are written.

Teaching words in groups with the same spelling pattern also helps with visual memory: *eight*, *eighth* and *weight* from the 2014 National Curriculum word list for Years 3 and 4 could be linked with *neigh* and *sleigh*, for example. Asking children to find more words to add to spelling pattern lists encourages that awareness of words and interest in them which will support spelling. It is possible to group words by pattern even when they sound different – for example, *heard* and *heart* from the Years 3 and 4 list could be grouped with *hear*, *beard* and *year*, with the 'ear' grapheme representing three different phonemes.

- Inventing and sharing mnemonics: for words which are particularly troublesome and which cannot be learned using any of the methods described above, it may be necessary to use a mnemonic – a memory aid such as:

- o friend: *Fri*day is the *end* of the week;
- o friend: I'll be your fri*end* to the *end*;
- o piece: 'a *pie*ce of pie'.

Mnemonics for words such as *because* (Big Elephants Can't Always Use Small Exits) may start to seem more difficult to remember than the spelling itself. Mnemonics are probably most effective in supporting learning when children have devised their own for words they have particular difficulty with.

Teaching spelling: practical considerations

Spelling is a skill, and as with most skills it is best learned in regular short sessions. Ten minutes several times a week is more likely to be effective than a longer session once a week, although on occasion a longer session may be needed for carrying out a spelling investigation. Spelling sessions are likely to consist of a focus on a particular pattern or a particularly problematic word, with discussion and explanation followed by a short practice using the Look, Say, Cover, Write, Check approach. Sessions could also focus on strategies rather than spellings, until these strategies become second nature. Spelling investigations are a particularly enjoyable approach, and are also useful in providing children with a way of discovering and rediscovering rules.

It is important to note that children should be using letter names by Year 1; this helps to avoid confusion as to whether phonemes or graphemes are being referred to – for example, when discussing digraphs: the /f/ phoneme at the beginning of *photo* is represented by the letters 'p' and 'h', not the phonemes /p/ and /h/.

Case study: hard and soft c

Greg, working in a Years 4 and 5 class, planned an investigation of 'hard c' and 'soft c'. Two groups were given text extracts; they wrote all the words in the extracts containing the letter c on cards, and sorted them according to the phoneme represented. Other groups were given word lists to sort, matched to their level of knowledge about spelling. The groups then generated their own rules about the grapheme–phoneme correspondences they had identified, and reported back to the whole class. Their work was placed on the classroom 'working wall', and Greg asked them to continue to look out for examples to add, particularly ones which did not seem to fit the rules they had worked out. Two days later a boy added 'succulent' and 'accident', and there was some interesting discussion of how they fitted with the previous findings.

Choosing spellings to learn

The 2014 National Curriculum outlines spellings to be learned, both through the patterns listed for the year groups and through the word lists for Key Stage 2. The word lists are described as 'a mixture both of words pupils frequently use in their writing and those which they often misspell' (DfE, 2013, p50). They contain many words which do not fit neatly into spelling pattern groups, and indeed many of them are often misspelled by adults. Of course, spellings to be learned should be words that pupils are likely to use in their writing but do not already know how to spell, but inevitably in whole-class teaching this cannot always be the case for all children. However, careful focus on the structure of particular words, and discussion of why they are spelled as they are, develops skills which can be transferred to other words. Crystal (2012) suggests that words to be learned should belong together in some way – for example through sharing a common root (*finite, infinite, definite, infinity*) or common patterns (*was, wash, watch, swan, swallow*). He also feels strongly that words should be taught in a meaningful context, particularly where they are likely to be confused. Homophones – words which sound the same but are spelled differently, such as *plain* and *plane* – are often taught together, almost inviting confusion even when it did not previously exist. For example, rather than teaching *there, their* and *they're* in the same session, *there* can be taught in the meaningful context of *here, where, everywhere, nowhere*, linking it to other words by both meaning (location) and spelling pattern. *They're* can be taught with *we're* and *you're*, in the context of contractions. *Their* is more difficult because the spelling pattern is shared with very few words (*heir, weir, weird*), two of which children are very unlikely to use in their writing, but since *weird* is often misspelled, linking it to *their* can be useful.

Marking children's work

Many schools' marking policies state that where children's writing contains many misspellings, only a small number should be identified, so that children are not discouraged. These should be either high-frequency words, where there is a danger that the child uses the word so often that the misspelling starts to look right, or words containing a useful spelling pattern which could support the child's spelling of other words. The National Curriculum's advice to teachers is that if children have been taught a spelling, any misspellings of that word should be corrected, but that other misspellings should be noted for future teaching – for example, *taic*.

Activity: marking children's work

In this piece of writing from a six-year-old child, decide which two or three spelling errors you would pick out and how you would ask the child to respond.

A fairy story

Once upon a time. There was a girl a little girl her name was haelther. She was an ordonery girl but one day on her nineteenth birthday she maread a prince and she became princess haelther. But there was a wiked queen around those days and verey jelus. One day she said to her self I will get my revenge and kill her. One day she set her horse man out to capsher and she wud no becouse he wud bring her hart back in this box.

(Possible answers can be found at the end of the chapter.)

Using spelling errors diagnostically

Children's spelling errors can tell us a great deal about their understanding of the spelling system and the strategies they use, and this information should be used to plan next steps in learning. Individual spelling logs can be developed, in which children note words they need to learn and practise them; these words can be used for testing by a spelling partner.

Activity: analysing spelling errors

Look at the following list of misspellings from a piece of writing by Rory, a Year 3 pupil. The writing was 169 words long; 123 of the words were correctly spelled, including year, came, play, they, some; three could not be read.

target word	Rory's attempt	target word	Rory's attempt	target word	Rory's attempt
what	wot	happened	hapend	you	yoy
could	coed	sorts	sots	stuff	stuf
friends	frends	celebrate	selabret selabrat	house	hows
out	awt	very	verry	gone	gon (x4)

target word	Rory's attempt	target word	Rory's attempt	target word	Rory's attempt
anything	enithing	takeaway	takawey takerway	anything	enithing
people	peopl	parties	patys	times	tams
chocolate	choclot	finally	fanley	finishes	finishis
every	efrey	world	wold	strongest	strongist
should	shud	huge	huej	muscle	musul
ever	efer	looked	loot	tired	trayerd
sadly	sabley	they're	there	their	there

What do Rory's errors tell you about his understanding of the English spelling system? What targets would you set for him?

(Possible answers can be found at the end of the chapter.)

Developing an interest in words

David Crystal writes the following about spelling:

> We have to stop viewing it in solely negative terms – as a daunting barrier, as a hostile mountain, as an apparently perpetual process of rote learning – and start thinking of it as a voyage of exploration. The story of the English writing system is so intriguing, and the histories behind individual words so fascinating, that anyone who dares to treat spelling as an adventure will find the journey rewarding.
>
> (2012, pp277–8)

The teacher who is interested in words is likely to pass this interest on to their pupils. Knowing about words and their origins does support spelling, but it also develops a sense of confidence and a curiosity which will stand children in good stead on their voyage of exploration of the English language.

Case study: new words and old

Jenny asked her Year 2 class to write descriptions of monsters. One boy, Alex, described his monster's teeth as 'knifey'. This reminded Jenny of a poem by Gerard Manley Hopkins which used the words 'towery' and 'branchy' to describe Oxford. Jenny quickly found an image of

⟶

the city to display on the interactive whiteboard, and at the end of the lesson she showed it to the children and explained that a famous poet had invented two new words to describe the place. She then told them that Alex had invented his own new word to describe teeth, and Alex shared it with them. He drew the teeth to show how he had imagined them. Jenny explained that some writers do invent new words, and that new words have to be made up for new inventions such as the computer or the Internet. The children were very interested in the idea that many words did not exist until quite recently. One child commented on the *k* at the beginning of the word *knifey* and Jenny told them that long ago people pronounced the *k* as well as the *n*. She wrote it up on the wall, and over the next few days children added *knight, knot, knee, know, knock*. A parent saw the list and thought there was a connection with the Vikings. He emailed a Norwegian friend, who confirmed that modern Norwegian uses the words *kniv* for knife, *kne* for knee, *knakke* for knock, *knute* for knot and *kan* for know, pronouncing the k in all the words; this was reported back to the class by his son, and the children practised saying the Norwegian words.

Curriculum link

The children learned that language changes over time: continuity and change are important historical concepts.

Children looked on a map to see where Norway was and where the Vikings came from. They could also have investigated place names, noting that places with Viking names (ending in *–thorpe*, *–field* or *–by*) were more likely to be in the north-east, where the Vikings first landed.

Learning outcomes review

You should now know:

- why children need to develop good spelling;
- what children need to learn about spelling;
- how to teach spelling effectively.

Self-assessment questions
1. Can you now summarise what children need to learn to become good spellers?
2. Can you explain how you would teach a spelling pattern?
3. Can you describe what you would be looking for when using children's writing to assess their spelling?

Possible answers to activities

Investigating a suffix

You might begin with single-syllable words ending with a consonant, and have the children add the *–ing* suffix and sort according to whether the final letter needs to be doubled (*stand, sit, leap, fight, pat, wait, kick, run, moan, jump, shoot, bet*). The children should discover that where the vowel is short and a single-letter grapheme follows it the letter will need to be doubled (*sitting, patting, running, betting*). If the vowel is long (*leap, fight, wait, moan, shoot*) the consonant is not doubled. If the vowel is followed by a digraph (*kick*) or adjacent consonants (*stand, jump*) only the *–ing* suffix is added. You might then move on to look at two-syllable words – *target, focus, repel, begin* – where the consonant doubles if the second syllable is stressed (*repelling, beginning*). Finally, you could consider words with split digraphs (*parade, slide, hope, solve*) which drop the 'e' before adding *–ing*, and words ending in vowel phonemes (*play, cry, see, lie*).

Morphemes and spelling knowledge

believe	believes, believing, believed, believer, believable, unbeliever, unbelieving
build	builds, building, builder, rebuild, rebuilding
centre	centres, centring, centred, decentre, central
consider	considers, considering, consider, consideration, reconsider
describe	describes, describing, described, indescribable
earth	earthed, earthly, earthy, earthquake, earthworm, earthenware
fruit	fruits, fruited, fruity, fruitful, fruitless, fruition
height	heights, heighten, heightened, heightening
learn	learns, learning, learned, unlearn, learner
often	oftentimes, oftener, oftenest
perhaps	
recent	recently
straight	straighten, unstraighten, straighter, straightest, straightaway, straightforward
strange	stranger, strangest, strangely, strangeness
through	throughout, throughput

Marking children's work

Eleven words are misspelled in this writing: *Heather, ordinary, married, wicked, very, jealous, capture, would, know, because, heart.*

(Continued)

(Continued)

Very is in the 100 most frequently used words and therefore is an important spelling to learn. Children often add *–ey* inappropriately at the ends of words (e.g. lonley) so it would be useful to address this as well.

Although *would* is not in the 100 most frequently used words, *could* (which the child also misspells) is, and *would* is near the top of the second hundred. It would therefore be useful to teach the spelling pattern *–ould*, also seen in *should, boulder, mould*.

Analysing spelling errors

Rory is usually able to produce a plausible phonic attempt at words he wants to write; almost everything he writes can be read without too much difficulty, and he is not afraid to attempt more difficult words such as *celebrate* and *chocolate*. Some of his errors show a limited awareness of conventional spellings – for example, he produces split digraphs in *came* and *some*, but not in *huej, selabrat, gon* or *tams*; his spelling of *peopl* and *there* suggests that a visual approach is being used at times. He shows little or no awareness of common suffixes such as *–ed, –es* and *–est*. He often has difficulties representing long-vowel phonemes – *awt, sots, patys, fanley, wold*.

Targets might include the following.

- Learn to spell words in the 100 most frequently used word list (DfES, 2007): of Rory's errors the following are included in the list: *you, what, out, looked, very, their, people, could, house, time*.
- Learn to spell words with the *–ed* suffix.
- Learn at least one way of representing the phonemes /ur/, /ar/, /or/.

Further reading

For a fascinating history of the English language, read:

Crystal, D (2005) *The Stories of English*. London: Penguin.

For interesting case study material, look at:

O'Sullivan, O and Thomas, A (2007) *Understanding Spelling*. London: Routledge.

For interesting and practical guidance on teaching spelling, try:

Waugh, D, Warner, C and Waugh, R (2013) *Teaching Grammar, Punctuation and Spelling in Primary Schools*. London: SAGE.

For a clear and helpful explanation of the place of spelling in the primary English curriculum, read:

Waugh, D and Jolliffe, W (2012) *English 5–11: A Guide for Teachers*. London: Routledge.

References

Clark, C (2013) *Children's and Young People's Writing in 2012: Findings from the National Literacy Trust's Annual Survey*. London: National Literacy Trust.

Cripps, C (1989) *Joining the ABC*. Wisbech: LDA.

Crystal, D (2012) *Spell It Out: The Singular Story of English Spelling*. London: Profile Books.

Department for Education (DfE) (2013) *The National Curriculum in England: Key Stages 1 and 2 Framework Document*. London: DfE.

Department for Education and Skills (DfES) (2007) *Letters and Sounds: Principles and Practice of High Quality Phonics*. London: DfES.

Dweck, C (2008) *Mindset: The New Psychology of Success*. New York: Ballantine Books.

Moseley, D (1995) *ACE Spelling Dictionary*. Wisbech: LDA.

Peters, M (1985) *Spelling Caught or Taught*. London: Routledge.

Teaching and Learning Research Programme (2006) *TLRP Commentary*. London: Institute of Education.

5 Grammar and Punctuation

David Waugh

Learning outcomes

By reading this chapter you will develop your understanding of:

- what children need to understand about grammar and punctuation;
- what you need to know as a primary teacher in order to teach the 2014 English National Curriculum;
- some of the challenges you face when you teach children grammar and punctuation;
- approaches to teaching grammar and punctuation.

Teachers' Standards
3. Demonstrate good subject and curriculum knowledge:

- have a secure knowledge of the relevant subject(s) and curriculum areas, foster and maintain pupils' interest in the subject, and address misunderstandings;
- demonstrate a critical understanding of developments in the subject and curriculum areas, and promote the value of scholarship;
- demonstrate an understanding of, and take responsibility for, promoting high standards of literacy, articulacy and the correct use of standard English, whatever the teacher's specialist subject.

Introduction

Many trainee teachers, when faced with grammar workshops, tests and exercises, complain that they were never taught about grammar when they were at school. Of course, they did learn a lot about grammar, but perhaps not in an overt way which involved learning technical terms such as *clause*, *phrase*, *preposition* and *pronoun*. This has become less of a problem recently, since the advent of the National Literacy Strategy in primary schools in 1998 meant that such terms became part of the curriculum. However, many did not develop a deeper understanding of grammatical terminology, perhaps because the teachers who taught them did not possess sufficient knowledge to provide this.

Some teachers who lack this knowledge complain that they do not need it: they are literate and can write accurately so, they argue, why do they need to be able to name and define the language they use? In this chapter you will look at some of the reasons why developing this knowledge is important both for pupils and teachers, and how you can teach effectively what the National Curriculum requires children to learn.

It is interesting to compare the current situation with that described by Hudson in 1992 as another new national curriculum was about to be launched:

> One of the most bizarre facts about British education, when compared with the systems found in most other European countries, is the almost complete absence of grammar (in a narrow sense) from the curriculum of most schools … . This is true as of 1990, but the new National Curriculum for English looks set to push us into line with the rest of Europe.
>
> (p3)

But has this change actually occurred?

How have things changed?

Since 1988, the National Curriculum has been revised three times, the National Literacy Strategy has been issued in two versions, and the National Strategies produced *Grammar for Writing* (DfEE, 2000), a resource for teachers packed with ideas for teaching key aspects of grammar. In 2013, all Year 6 children sat the Spelling Punctuation and Grammar (SPAG) test as the government sought to ensure that grammatical knowledge and understanding was being taught in primary schools. And yet, despite all these initiatives, some of which were statutory requirements, the government produced a new National Curriculum in 2013 in which grammatical terminology features more strongly than in previous versions.

The 2014 curriculum includes two statutory appendices – Grammar and Punctuation, and Spelling, and includes statements about what is expected at different stages, for example in Year 2:

> The terms for discussing language should be embedded for pupils in the course of discussing their writing with them. Their attention should be drawn to the technical terms they need to learn.
>
> (DfE, 2013, p31)

For Year 3–4, grammar should be taught explicitly and the document states the following:

> The grammar of our first language is learnt naturally and implicitly through interactions with other speakers and from reading. Explicit knowledge of grammar is, however, very important, as it gives us more conscious control and choice in our language. Building this knowledge is best achieved

through a focus on grammar within the teaching of reading, writing and speaking. Once pupils are familiar with a grammatical concept (for example 'modal verb'), they should be encouraged to apply and explore this concept in the grammar of their own speech and writing and to note where it is used by others.

(DfE, 2013, p66)

This emphasis on knowledge of terminology is summed up by the following:

Throughout the programmes of study, teachers should teach pupils the vocabulary they need to discuss their reading, writing and spoken language. It is important that pupils learn the correct grammatical terms in English and that these terms are integrated within teaching.

(DfE, 2013, p15)

The latest version of the National Curriculum lists the terms that children should learn to recognise and use, and these will be explored throughout this chapter.

Terminology: what do children and their teachers need to know and understand?

The grammatical terms that pupils should learn are set out below. The National Curriculum states that pupils *should learn to recognise and use the terminology through discussion and practice* (DfE, 2013, p66).

Year	Terminology for pupils
1	letter, capital letter
	word, singular, plural
	sentence
	punctuation, full stop, question mark, exclamation mark
2	noun, noun phrase
	statement, question, exclamation, command
	compound, adjective, verb
	suffix
	tense (past, present)
	apostrophe, comma

Year	Terminology for pupils
3	adverb, preposition conjunction
	word family, prefix
	clause, subordinate clause
	direct speech
	consonant, consonant letter, vowel, vowel letter
	inverted commas (or 'speech marks')
4	determiner
	pronoun, possessive pronoun
	adverbial
5	modal verb, relative pronoun
	relative clause
	parenthesis, bracket, dash, cohesion, ambiguity
6	subject, object
	active, passive
	synonym, antonym
	ellipsis, hyphen, colon, semi-colon, bullet points

The final version of the National Curriculum has a much-improved (compared with the draft version) glossary which explains the terms above. How confident do you feel about your own knowledge of the terms and how well do you feel you could teach children about them?

Think about your own understanding of some of the terms in the table. Which ones are you unsure about? Developing your own understanding will help you to understand what children need if they are to develop their understanding. As you explore a topic, you begin to realise what you need to know and understand before you can fully understand the topic. Take, for example, the subordinate clause. What do you need to know before you can understand what a subordinate clause is and the role it plays? You need to know the following:

- the meaning of subordinate;
- the meaning of clause;
- what a main clause is;
- what a sentence is.

To gain this understanding, we make use of real examples. We might start with a simple sentence – for example:

Alex took the dog for a walk.

We might ask ourselves what more we would like to know:

- Who is Alex?
- What kind of dog?
- Where did they go?
- What was the weather like?

Now we can look at ways in which some of this information might be incorporated into the original sentence.

> *Alex, who had just got home from school, took the dog for a walk.*
>
> *Alex took the dog, a terrier which barked at everyone he met, for a walk.*
>
> *Alex took the dog for a walk in the woods near to her home.*
>
> *One windy day as the rain began to fall, Alex took the dog for a walk.*

In each of the sentences above, Alex took the dog for a walk is the main clause without which the additions would not make sense or be complete sentences. So the additions are less important but provide extra information – they are subordinate. All but one includes a verb, and clauses must have verbs – without them they are phrases. Can you spot which subordinate is a phrase rather than a clause?

> *Alex took the dog for a walk in the woods near to her home.*

In the sentence above *in the woods near to her home* does not include a verb, so it is a phrase rather than a clause.

The example above illustrates the importance of considering what the prerequisites for learning something new might be. For useful video clips which discuss this further try: **www.pearsonschoolsandfecolleges.co.uk/Primary/GlobalPages/ NewEnglishCurriculum/Debra-Myhill-Insights.aspx**

Why teach grammar?

The answer to this question for teachers in English schools might include the pragmatic:

- because it's a requirement of the National Curriculum;
- because Year 6 have to take the SPAG test and as a school we'll be judged on the children's performance.

However, one would hope that most teachers would consider the rationale for teaching grammar at a more intellectual level and would consider not only why but how they should teach grammar. It may be that after they have explored some of the possible pedagogical strategies for teaching grammar they will conclude that they not only have the knowledge and understanding to deliver the curriculum, but that they can also do this in a way that will engage and benefit their pupils. This is crucial and it may be that in the past teachers gave too little attention to making grammatical knowledge appear relevant, resulting in generations of people growing up without this knowledge and without any desire to acquire it. In the section below, Myhill (2012) reflects upon traditional approaches to grammar and their limitations.

Research focus: descriptive and prescriptive approaches to grammar

Most public and political discourses around grammar adopt a prescriptive view of grammar – that grammar sets out a set of rules which competent speakers and writers must obey. It is a deficit view of grammar, preoccupied with error, remediation, correctness and accuracy. It is this view that underpinned traditional grammar in schools – drills, exercises and rules.

In contrast to this is the descriptive view of contemporary linguistics, which sees grammar as description of how language is actually used, and the ways in which it varies according to context. As an academic discipline, linguistics is intellectually robust and rooted in rigorous investigations of language. Yet such descriptive views of grammar are often positioned as liberalism or cultural relativism.

Looking back

It is odd that we should ignore the intellectual and academic contribution of disciplinary linguistics in favour of old-fashioned and discredited linguistic ideas. In no other area of the curriculum would there be advocacy of old knowledge when new knowledge has superseded it.

It is also worth revisiting why grammar was dropped from the curriculum in English-speaking countries around the world. Successive studies showed that there was no correlation between learning grammar and developing greater proficiency as a language user: indeed, some studies suggested there was a harmful effect. Traditional grammar, therefore, lacked intellectual integrity and served no obvious educative purpose.

Myhill, D. (2012) 'The role for grammar in the curriculum' in *Meeting High Expectations: Looking for the heart of English*. p21. Available at: www.heartofenglish.com/sites/default/files/High_Expectations_LHE_web.pdf (accessed 15 December 2013).

What are the challenges for teachers?

All of this presents challenges for teachers, some of whom, despite the increased emphasis on grammatical knowledge in curricula since 1988, still lack the subject knowledge to teach children about grammar confidently, either using a traditional prescriptive or a descriptive approach. Further challenges lie in making grammar more interesting than it was when some teachers were in school, and convincing children and parents of the need for overt teaching of grammar.

Case study: developing teachers' knowledge of terminology

Sue, who was responsible for a group of eight School Direct trainees, discovered from their initial subject knowledge audit that all rated their knowledge and understanding of grammar no better than satisfactory and, in five cases, weak. In her discussions with the group, Sue discovered that most were confident readers and writers, but that it was knowledge of grammatical terminology rather than an ability to write accurately which required attention. Some recalled being taught terminology at school, but they had found this uninspiring and difficult to grasp.

Sue decided that she would try a creative approach to developing the trainees' knowledge of terminology and would link it to work on learning poems by heart: something children are required to do as part of the 2014 National Curriculum. She chose one of her favourite poems, 'Jim' by Hilaire Belloc, for an activity which would reinforce knowledge of word classes. She provided each trainee with basic definitions of key word classes taken from the glossary of Waugh *et al.* (2016, Appendix 1).

Adjective

Adjectives describe people and things – for example, a *red* rose; *three* dogs; a *heavy* weight. They *modify* nouns.

Adjectives can also follow the verb 'to be' – for example, York is *beautiful*; David is *happy*.

These are adjectival phrases and *complement* the verb. They provide more information about nouns and pronouns.

Adverb

Adverbs are used to modify a verb, an adjective or another adverb.

She ran *quickly* – modifies a verb.

York is *incredibly* beautiful – modifies an adjective.

He drove *extremely* slowly – modifies another adverb.

Fortunately, Rovers scored a last-minute goal – modifies a whole sentence.

Conjunctions/connectives

These are words used to join words, phrases or clauses – for example, *and, but* and *or*. There are two kinds of conjunction:

→

Coordinating conjunctions (and, but, or and *so)* link statements of equal status: *I ate the pizza and I drank the water.*

Subordinating conjunctions (when, while, before, after, since, until, if, because, although, that) link subordinate (less important) clauses to main clauses: *Before I went out*, I combed my hair; I enjoyed the film, *although it was rather violent in places.*

Determiner

These are words used with nouns to help define them – for example, *this* computer, *a* pencil, *the* book. The determiner limits, or determines, the reference of the noun in some way. Determiners include:

- articles (*a/an, the*);
- demonstratives (*this/that, these/those*);
- possessives (*my/your/his/her/its/our/their*);
- quantifiers (*some, any, no, many, few, all, either, each*);
- numbers (*one, two,* and so on);
- some question words (*which, what, whose*).

Words that are used as determiners are followed by a noun (though not necessarily immediately):

Which black pen is mine?

This book is yours.

Noun

Words used to identify people, places, things and ideas. The suffix 's' is often added to nouns to indicate a plural (more than one).

Collective nouns

These are nouns that refer to a group of things or people – for example, *collection, family.* Collective nouns may have either singular or plural agreement with a verb, depending on the intended meaning – for example, *his family is large* but we say *his family are all elderly* because we are eliding the members of his family.

Proper nouns

These nouns refer to the name of people, places or things that are unique and are normally written with an initial capital letter. Brand names of products and companies are proper nouns.

→

Noun phrases

These are groups of words doing the work of a single noun – for example, *the chairman of the board of governors*.

Preposition

Prepositions are usually attached to a noun or noun phrase, showing the position or relationship of one thing to another and include words such as *at*, *over*, *by* and *with*.

When a prepositional phrase is formed, it usually does the work of an adverb or adjective.

Pronoun

A word used in place of a noun, a noun phrase or several nouns – for example:

- personal pronouns: *I/me, you, he/him, she/her, we/us, they/them, it;*

- possessive pronouns: *mine, yours, his, hers, ours, theirs, its;*

- reflexive pronouns: *myself, herself, themselves;*

- indefinite pronouns: *someone, anything, nobody, everything;*

- interrogative pronouns (used in questions): *who/whom, whose, which, what;*

- relative pronouns: *who/whom, whose, which, that.*

Verb

A 'doing' or 'being' word that expresses an action or a state.

Verbs change their form, or tense, according to when the action takes place. So verbs may be in the past, present or future tense.

Modal verbs are ones such as *can, may, might, will,* which are used to express different degrees of certainty.

Sue asked the trainees to work in pairs and to look at two word classes each and prepare a short explanation, together with a poster, to explain each word class to the rest of the group. People were encouraged to ask questions and challenge definitions, as well as to find examples of word classes. Sue found that some trainees were surprised by some aspects of word classes; in particular the following:

- Some had not realised that determiners could be words other than *a, an* and *the.*

- Some did not realise that adverbs could modify adjectives and other adverbs, as well as verbs.

- Some had not heard of noun phrases or collective nouns.

- Some did not realise that *am, are* and *is* are verbs and part of the verb *to be.*

- No one had heard of modal verbs, although everyone understood their function.

Sue discussed these issues with the group and provided examples and discussed how they might teach the terms to children, showing them lists of terms for each year group similar to those found in this chapter. She then explained that they were going to learn part of a poem and that she was going to show it to them in rhyming couplets with some words missing. Their task was to consider both which word class was needed to complete the lines and to suggest possible words. She explained that the poem was one of Belloc's *Cautionary Tales* and involved a boy being eaten by a lion as a result of refusing to hold hands with his nanny. They talked about when the poem might be set and why Belloc might have written it. Sue explained that they might be surprised by some aspects of the poem's presentation and asked them to comment when they found anything unusual. Sue then showed them the opening lines:

There was a Boy whose name was Jim; His Friends were very good to ___.

Sue asked for suggestions for the missing word and everyone agreed it should be *him*, both because it rhymed and because putting *Jim* again would be repetitive. She asked them what word class *him* belonged to and people quickly decided him was a pronoun standing in for the proper noun *Jim*. She showed them the next couplet:

They gave him Tea, and Cakes, and Jam, And slices of _____ Ham,

People agreed that an adjective was needed to describe ham and made various suggestions including *boiled*, *roasted*, *delicious* and, from a vegetarian, *revolting*. Trainees commented that in the poem common nouns were given capital letters, which is not usual except at the beginnings of sentences, and there was speculation as to why this might be. One person, who had studied German, pointed out that all nouns in German have capital letters and wondered if Belloc might have been German. However, a quick search on the Internet showed that he was born in France and grew up in England. Further searches failed to explain the capital letters, but did reinforce trainees' understanding of their use for proper nouns. Sue showed the trainees the next three couplets together and asked them to complete them.

And Chocolate with pink inside And little _____ to ride,

And _____ him Stories through and through,

And even took him to the ___

But there it ____ the dreadful Fate

Befell him, which I now _____.

The trainees were asked to focus closely on the type of word which would be required to fill each gap before considering which would be the best word of that type to use. Sue found that they gradually increased in confidence in their use of terminology and supported each other's learning, as well as referring to and discussing the definitions provided.

Activity: 'Jim'

Look at the opening lines of 'Jim' above and decide what type of word is needed to fill each space and then choose appropriate words to put there. (Belloc's version can be found at the end of the chapter).

A cautionary note

Using poems and extracts from stories in the way described above can be very effective, but it is important to remember that poems and stories were written to entertain readers. Take care not to convey the impression to children that they are simply devices for teaching grammar. Read the whole poem to them if you discuss extracts, and discuss the content rather than simply the word classes.

Developing our own subject knowledge

Knowing grammatical terms is one thing, recognising the more subtle nuances another. For many teachers and student teachers who have not previously developed a knowledge and understanding of terminology, an initial feeling that 'this isn't all that difficult after all' can be dampened when they discover such concepts as word class mobility. Look at the sentences below and decide which word class (often called *part of speech*) each belongs to.

A *red* car was badly parked outside the house.

The *snow* covered the garden.

Tom *kicked* the ball through the window.

It began to snow *heavily*.

If you have a basic knowledge of grammatical terminology, you probably decided that *red* is an adjective in the first sentence, *snow* is a common noun in the second, and *kicked* is a verb (in the past tense) in the third. In the fourth sentence, *heavily* is an adverb, but which verb does it describe? In fact, it describes the verb *to snow*, so snow, which was a noun in the first sentence, can also be a verb. This is an example of word class mobility, a source of confusion for people learning grammatical terminology and, perhaps, a justification for learning about grammar in a descriptive rather than a prescriptive way. Because many words can perform different roles depending upon how they are used in sentences, it is important that we look at words in context of sentences rather than in isolation.

Activity: word class mobility

Each of the words below can belong to more than one word class, depending upon how they are used in sentences. Try using each of the words in sentences to see what parts of speech each can belong to:

chair

book

table

green

round

(Possible answers can be found at the end of the chapter.)

We can see, then, that developing an understanding of grammatical terminology presents some challenges and may not be as simple as it appears at first sight. As we have seen earlier from Myhill, there is much disagreement about both how this knowledge and understanding can best be acquired.

Research focus: reviewing effective teaching of grammar

Andrews *et al.* (2004) undertook two in-depth reviews: one on the teaching of formal grammar (syntax) and one on the teaching of sentence combining. Andrews *et al.* concluded *that the teaching of formal grammar (and its derivatives) is ineffective; and the teaching of sentence combining is one (of probably a number of) method(s) that is effective* (p2). The team maintained that

further research needs to move beyond studies of formal grammar and its effects on compositional skills; move beyond the USA into different contexts, taking into account the textual and contextual factors in learning to write; undertake some large-scale and longitudinal experimental studies to find out what works; improve the quality and reporting of such studies in the field and look at other ways of researching the effects, impact and nature of grammar(s) in learning to write.

(Andrews *et al.*, 2004, pp2–3)

The key to teaching grammar successfully, then, seems to be to set the teaching within meaningful contexts. The EPPI study (2004) found:

The results of our two in-depth reviews are that traditional grammar teaching, based on word classes and the teaching of syntax (using a meta-language to describe and classify parts of speech), is largely ineffective and that sentence combining is largely effective.

(pp49–50)

So spending time looking at lists of words and deciding which word class they might belong to may, at one extreme, be a poor use of time, but exploring ways in which sentences can be constructed and considering the kinds of words which might be used to enhance them may be much more productive. And if children can see that when discussing their writing a knowledge of terminology is helpful, they will be more likely to remember the terms and use them appropriately. For instance, take the example of expanded noun phrases, which the 2014 National Curriculum states that children should learn to use in Year 2. Your first response to the phrase *expanded noun phrase* might be to wonder what it means and then how you might teach it. In fact, there is nothing complicated about expanded noun phrases: we just need to think about the prerequisite knowledge we need before we can understand them. Clearly, we need to know what a noun is and what a phrase is and both are best understood by looking at the text.

The car stood in a field.

The rusty old car stood in a field.

In the second sentence the noun *car* has adjectives added to give more information. The *rusty old car* is a noun phrase and now that we know that we can think about changing the shape of the sentence, perhaps to vary our writing.

Rusty and old, the car stood in the field.

After looking at examples of expanded noun phrases we can see that another prerequisite is an understanding of adjectives and the roles they play in making writing more interesting.

At Year 2, children are expected to learn to use expanded noun phrases *to describe and specify, e.g.* the blue butterfly (DfE, 2013, p31). By Years 5–6 they should be *using expanded noun phrases to convey complicated information concisely* (p49).

Myhill (2013) argues that children will acquire this understanding best if the teaching of grammar is embedded in the teaching of writing. In the next section, examples of three children's writing are presented to enable you to reflect on their individual needs and to consider how you might model some of the grammatical knowledge and understanding which some of them lack.

Children's writing and what it can reveal about their knowledge of language

Consider three different Year 3 children with different strengths in language usage. In each case the words are typed exactly as the child wrote them.

Jade

Jade speaks and writes accurately but slowly. It takes her a long time to construct sentences but those she completes tend to be accurate. For example, in her school diary one day she wrote just two sentences.

On Sunday we went to the park. We fed the ducks.

Jade's writing was spelled and punctuated correctly.

Harry

Harry speaks and writes quickly and fluently, but although what he says and writes usually makes sense, he tends to make some grammatical errors, including missing words out. His diary entry read:

We wented to the seaside on sunday and me and my sisster played on sand with buckits and spayds and we builded sandcassuls and put flags in them. After that we goed to amyousments and road on the dodgums and the roundbout.

Harry's work is presented with his original spellings.

Ceri

Ceri's writing and speech tends to be accurate and she works at a good pace. However, her language tends to be quite restricted and not very interesting for readers and listeners. Her diary entry read:

On Saturday I went to Derby with my mum and dad. We bought a new pair of shoes for me and a new shirt for my dad. We went to a café for a sandwich and a drink later. It was good. I had apple juice and an egg sandwich. Then we went to some more shops and we got the bus and we went home again. I had a good time.

Activity: children's writing

In the 2014 National Curriculum children in Year 3 learn how to use adverbs, prepositions, conjunctions, clauses, subordinate clauses and direct speech. In Year 2 they will have learned about noun phrases, adjectives and past and present tense. How could you help develop each child's use of language by revisiting concepts from Year 2 and using those for Year 3? (See below for discussion.)

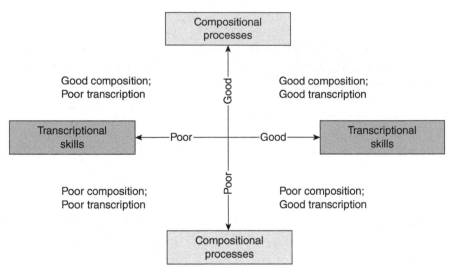

Figure 5.1 A simple view of writing

Source: Bevilacqua and Fenton (2009) Powerpoint presentation.

You may be familiar with the simple view of reading (SVOR) (Gough and Tunmer, 1986; Rose, 2006) which enables us to assess children's word recognition skills and their comprehension skills (see Chapter 6). A similar model has been devised for writing skills, which enables us to gauge children's compositional skills and their transcriptional skills (Berninger *et al.*, 2002). Some children will be good at both, but others may produce accurate writing (good transcription) which may be unimaginative or not very engaging for readers (weaker compositional skills). Others may compose interesting writing which lacks accuracy of spelling, grammar and punctuation (good composition, weaker transcription), while yet others may be weak in both areas. By viewing children's writing in this way we can identify targets for them and support them as they develop their writing.

Let us look at each child's writing and needs in turn. Jade might be said to have good transcriptional skills in that her work is accurate and well presented. However, her compositional skills are weaker and she had limited ideas about what to write or how to make her writing interesting for a reader. She might be asked to look at her writing again and consider how she could describe the park, what the ducks might have looked like, how they might have behaved, where they were, etc. This would present an opportunity to talk about adjectives, adverbs and prepositions, and for the teacher to model using them in a shared writing activity with children contributing ideas and vocabulary and the teacher acting as a scribe.

Harry's compositional skills are quite good since he is happy to convey his ideas in some detail, but he has transcriptional problems in that his spelling is often inaccurate and he has some errors in irregular past tense verb forms (*wented*, *goed* and *builded*). Harry has been adventurous in his use of vocabulary and it would be a shame to discourage him from using words such as *amusements*, *dodgems* and *sandcastles* because he could not spell them accurately. In fact, some of his attempts at spelling are phonically plausible and once he has written a more challenging word incorrectly, the teacher has an opportunity to show him how to spell it correctly.

Ceri's writing is very accurate, but rather uninspiring. She has very good transcriptional skills but could develop her compositional skills by considering using a wider range of verbs, adverbs and adjectives. She might also be shown how to vary sentence structure, perhaps fronting an occasional adverbial and exploring ways in which published writers present their work. It is important not to discourage Ceri, but she is clearly ready to develop her already accurate work into something which will be more engaging for her readers.

A key question to ask when devising writing activities for children is: what grammar is needed for this kind of writing – for example, past tense, use of adjectives, multi-clause sentences, fronted adverbials, expanded noun phrases? If we do this, we will be able to share examples with children before they write, model the writing through shared writing, and plan guided writing for groups which draws attention to key elements of grammar. Our assessment of writing and the checklists we provide for children will focus on the elements identified and children will be able to evaluate their own and others' writing in light of certain criteria. The two case studies below provide examples of teachers using this approach to teach two elements of the 2014 National Curriculum which have challenged some teachers and trainees.

Case study: active and passive voice

Glen was asked to teach his Year 6 class about the active and passive voice. He read about the terms and ensured that he understood what they meant. He then considered how he might introduce them to his class. He decided that he would begin with a short dramatic activity and chose two children to come out to the front of the class. He explained that he was going to ask Alesha to do something or give something to Mark but that this could not involve any physical contact (he had visions of punches and kicks). Alesha handed Mark a pencil. Glen then asked Alesha to say what she had done in a complete sentence: *I gave Mark a pencil.*

Glen then asked Mark to say what had happened but to begin his sentence with *A pencil* – *A pencil was given to me by Alesha.*

Glen continued the activity with other actions and other children. This time he asked the children who were watching to suggest a sentence from the person performing the action's point of view and another from the receiver's point of view. Once the children had grasped

$\longrightarrow$

the concept, Glen explained that one type of sentence was called active and the other passive and asked the children to discuss which was which. When it was clear that they understood, Glen asked children to find examples in a piece of text he had prepared and then to look for examples of each in a range of texts in the classroom.

In a subsequent lesson, Glen asked children to include at least three examples of both active and passive sentences.

Activity

Bearing in mind the earlier discussion about identifying prerequisite knowledge and understanding, what do you consider it important that teachers and children know and understand before teaching and learning about the passive?

Curriculum link

The National Curriculum states that children *should learn to recognise and use the terminology through discussion and practice* (DfE, 2013, p66). Glen's lesson began in a very practical way and helped children to develop their understanding through physical activity and discussion.

Case study: fronted adverbials

Anna, a final year BA trainee teacher, was asked to work with her Year 4 class to encourage their use and understanding of fronted adverbials. The term wasn't one Anna had previously encountered and she felt anxious about teaching it and sought advice from her tutor.

The tutor explained that there was nothing very complex about fronted adverbials and that Anna almost certainly used them in her own writing, and certainly encountered them in her reading. He gave her a few simple sentences to consider.

The door opened suddenly.

The Tardis departed rapidly and in a cloud of dust.

Louis ran in one direction hastily and nervously.

He asked Anna to consider how each action was performed, looking at the verbs (*opened*, *departed* and *ran*), and invited her to change the order of the sentences so that each conveyed the same information but with a different structure. Anna came up with the following.

→

Suddenly, the door opened.

Rapidly and in a cloud of dust, the Tardis departed.

Hastily and nervously, Louis ran in one direction.

The tutor then asked Anna to suggest what a fronted adverbial might be, and she stated that it simply meant moving the adverb or adverbial phrase to the front of a sentence. Notice that a comma follows the fronted adverbial.

Anna went away to look for examples from texts that were well known to her class and considered how she might teach them to use fronted adverbials in their writing.

She planned a shared writing session in which she would first explore a piece of text which included fronted adverbials and then write a story opening with the children. Her tutor suggested that she should not try to produce writing in which too many sentences had fronted adverbials, but should discuss with the children the value of changing sentence structure occasionally. He also suggested that the creation of a poem in which every line had a fronted adverbial might help show children how this sentence structure worked in a genre in which repetition of style is often a strong feature.

Curriculum link

Fronting is a strategy writers use to vary the structure of their sentences. It is mentioned in the National Curriculum statutory guidance for Year 3–4, but might be discussed through examples with younger children, especially during shared reading and writing where they might be shown ways in which they could write. A classic example of fronting is the opening for many traditional tales. For example, we would be surprised to read:

There were three bears once upon a time.

and would expect the adverbial phrase to appear at the front of the sentence:

Once upon a time, there were three bears.

Ultimately, in English primary schools, children's grammatical knowledge and understanding will be assessed through national tests in Year 2 and Year 6.

The Spelling, Punctuation and Grammar (SPAG) Test

The test includes grammar, punctuation and vocabulary questions. Allott (2014) analysed the 2013 test and found the following.

The grammar questions include:

- adding missing elements to complete a sentence, such as a preposition, pronoun, adverb or adverbial, or the correct tense of a verb;
- identifying word classes, connectives, non-standard forms, imperative verbs, subordinate clauses;
- identifying type of sentence (e.g. statement or command);
- subject–verb agreement (the focus of more than one question).

The punctuation questions include:

- adding sentence punctuation, including commas to mark subordinate clauses;
- identifying correct punctuation of direct speech;
- identifying correct use of apostrophes;
- use of brackets;
- contracting verbs.

The vocabulary questions include:

- identifying homonyms and antonyms;
- choosing correct word meanings.

Typical questions

In the 2013 SPAG Test, children were asked to choose which of the following prepositions, *with*, *beside*, *near* and *from*, would be best to complete the following sentence:

> *The postcard was _____ my uncle.*

It is assumed that the correct answer is 'from' and this might be felt to be the best choice. However, all the other prepositions would fit and the sentence would still be grammatically accurate and would make sense.

> *The postcard was with my uncle.*
>
> *The postcard was near my uncle.*
>
> *The postcard was beside my uncle.*

Many other questions use grammatical terminology, but some can be answered without children knowing the terminology where they are given choices from selections of words to fill in gaps in sentences. In fact, just under half the questions can be answered without knowing grammatical terminology if children choose words which fit into sentences and sound right.

The point here is not that children should not learn correct terminology and be able to use it accurately, but that if they are exposed to a wide range of texts and discuss language, they will be well equipped to answer some questions, even if they do not always recall the definitions of all of the terms.

Activity

The questions below are similar to those found in the SPAG test. In the first two, terminology is used to indicate the appropriate word class needed to complete the sentences. In the second two, you are simply asked to choose the appropriate word.

Choose the correct form of the verb to complete the following sentence:

> *The dog (barks/bark) at the cat.*

Complete the following sentence with an adverb that makes sense:

> *John ran _____ to escape from the savage dog.*

Choose the correct word to complete the following sentence:

> *A tall ship (sail/sailed) into the harbour.*

Complete the following sentence with a word that makes sense:

> *The snow fell (heavy/heavily) and the wind howled.*

Consider whether a knowledge of the terms 'verb' and 'adverb' were helpful in enabling you to complete the first two sentences. When you completed the second two, were you able to do so easily without knowing that the word 'choice' needed was a verb in the first and an adverb in the second?

Punctuation

Although there are many rules and conventions for grammar, we can be flexible in the way we convey information. For example, look at the following sentences.

> *Saima skipped happily along the road to the shop.*
>
> *Happily, Saima skipped along the road to the shop.*

As you've probably recognised, if you have read the rest of the chapter, the adverbial 'happily' has been 'fronted' in the second sentence and a comma is now used between it and the rest of the sentence. Punctuation has two main aspects: rules and conventions. Rules include the following:

- All sentences begin with capital letters.

- Sentences must end with full stops, question marks or exclamation marks.

- Apostrophes are used to show elision (*don't, wouldn't*, etc.) and to show possession (*Hanif's, Manuel's* etc.).

Some uses of punctuation may follow conventions, but writers may choose to use punctuation marks in different ways. For example, some people use far more exclamation marks than others, while others include more commas in their writing. Some people separate items in lists with commas regardless of the length of the items, while others use semi-colons. However, if we do not use punctuation carefully, we can inadvertently convey an unintended meaning to our readers. Look at the two sentences below, for example:

> *I'm sure the oak floor will look great. Like you, I was very surprised no one thought of this before.*

> *I'm sure the oak floor will look great like you. I was very surprised no one thought of this before.*

The table below shows when concepts should be introduced first, not necessarily when they should be completely understood.

Year	Punctuation concept
1	Separation of words with spaces
	Introduction to capital letters, full stops, question marks and exclamation marks to demarcate sentences
	Capital letters for names and for the personal pronoun I
2	Use of capital letters, full stops, question marks and exclamation marks to demarcate sentences
	Commas to separate items in a list
	Apostrophes to mark where letters are missing in spelling
3	Introduction to inverted commas to punctuate direct speech
4	Use of inverted commas and other punctuation to indicate direct speech – e.g. a comma after the reporting clause; end punctuation within inverted commas – e.g. *The conductor shouted, 'Sit down!'*
	Apostrophes to mark singular and plural possession – e.g. *the girl's name, the girls' names*
	Use of commas after fronted adverbials

Year	Punctuation concept
5	Brackets, dashes or commas to indicate parenthesis
	Use of commas to clarify meaning or avoid ambiguity
6	Use of the semi-colon, colon and dash to mark the boundary between independent clauses – e.g, *It's raining; I'm fed up*
	Use of the colon to introduce a list
	Punctuation of bullet points to list information
	How hyphens can be used to avoid ambiguity – e.g. *man eating shark* versus *man-eating shark*, or *recover* versus *re-cover*)

(DfE, 2013, pp67–9)

As you looked through the list above, you may have felt much more confident about some items than others. Teachers tend to be less sure about how to teach possessive apostrophes, parenthesis and ambiguity than how to teach full stops, commas and direct speech, so we have focused on these aspects below. For more detailed explanations of other terms, see Waugh *et al.* (2016) and the National Curriculum glossary (DfE, 2013).

Possessive apostrophes

Possessive apostrophes are probably the most widely misused of all punctuation marks and arouse strong feelings. See below for a simple explanation.

For singular nouns, we show possession by adding *'s* – *Bob's truck, Sue's class.*

For plurals, the apostrophe follows the plural – e.g. *the boys' toilets, the children's books.* In *boys* the plural of boy is formed by adding an 's' so the apostrophe follows the 's'. *Children* is the plural of *child* so the apostrophe goes after *children* – the 's' is added to make it easier to say.

Pronouns do not have apostrophes to show possession, with the exception of one's and pronouns which end with *one's* – *anyone's, someone's, no one's.* So it is never correct to write *your's, her's* or *their's,* and *it's* only has an apostrophe when it is short for *it is* and not in sentences such as *The cat licked its paws.*

Parenthesis

In order to separate a word or phrase from the rest of the sentence, we use devices such as brackets or dashes, known as parentheses (the plural of parenthesis).

> *She strode into the room (the butler had been unable to stop her) and faced Lady Manson.*

Rounded or squared brackets – ( ) or [ ] – are often also called parentheses.

Ambiguity

Ambiguity occurs in sentences when it is unclear who is performing an action or what the action is – for example:

> *Dogs must be carried on the Underground.*

Does this mean that you must pick your dog up if you take a Tube train, or is it compulsory to carry a dog?

> *Please sign up for an appointment on Friday.*

Does this mean that you need to wait until Friday to sign up, or that the meeting is on Friday?

To avoid ambiguity, it is important to re-read what you write to ensure that it can't be misconstrued.

Case study: punctuation

Liam planned to teach his Year 5 class about the use of punctuation to avoid ambiguity. He was unsure about the meaning of the word *ambiguity* and so looked in dictionaries to find that it means *having more than one meaning, not clear*. He discovered that the *ambi-* prefix means on both sides. He discovered that the word *ambidextrous*, which means able to use both hands equally well, had the same prefix and even noted that the sign to *Huttons Ambo*, which he passed every day on his way to school, referred to two villages – *High Hutton* and *Low Hutton*.

He then set about finding examples of ambiguity which could be avoided with careful use of commas. He found some examples, including the following.

A sign:

> *Slow children at play.*

> which could have read:

> *Slow, children at play.*

A letter:

> *Most of the time, travellers worry about their luggage.*

> which could have read:

> *Most of the time-travellers worry about their luggage.*

→

A round robin Christmas letter:

Sam loves cooking her family and her dog.

which should have read:

Sam loves cooking, her family, and her dog.

A piece of dialogue from a child's story:

Shall we eat Grandma?

which should have read:

Shall we eat, Grandma?

An advertisement for a job:

You will be required to work twenty four-hour shifts.

which could have read:

You will be required to work twenty-four hour shifts.

And which probably should have read:

You will be required to work twenty-four-hour shifts.

And from several websites:

King Charles 1 prayed half an hour after he was beheaded.

which should have read:

King Charles 1 prayed. Half an hour after, he was beheaded.

What is this thing called, love?

which could have read:

What is this thing called love?

Liam showed the examples one by one using the interactive whiteboard and asked children to tell each other and then the class what they thought each meant. He asked them to suggest ways in which the punctuation could be changed so that the meaning was unambiguous. This led to discussions about commas, full stops, question marks and hyphens. Some children pointed out that signs don't usually have punctuation, so it is especially important that the information they provide is unambiguous.

Liam's class went on to work in small groups to look at further examples of texts whose meanings could be altered by changing punctuation. He encouraged them to look at their own writing to check that punctuation made the meaning clear.

As you have seen in the case studies, when grammar and punctuation are taught as part of reading and writing, children are able to learn effectively and with enjoyment. Teaching grammar and punctuation does not have to be dull and boring to teach and to learn, and there is a wealth of material available to ensure that it need not be.

Myhill (2013) sums up her top tips for teaching grammar and punctuation as follows:

- Embedding grammar in the teaching of writing has a real impact on attainment in writing.

- Think about what elements of grammar would help children become more effective writers of each text type.

- Narrow the focus of your teaching of grammar or punctuation to just three or four points for a piece of writing.

- Good grammar, punctuation and spelling skills give children conscious control over the language they use.

Learning outcomes review

You should now know:

- what children need to understand about grammar and punctuation;
- what we need to know as primary teachers;
- some of the challenges we face when we teach children grammar and punctuation;
- approaches to teaching grammar and punctuation.

Self-assessment questions
1. Can you now confidently define the following word classes: noun, verb, adjective, adverb, pronoun, determiner, preposition?
2. Do you understand the following: noun phrases, fronted adverbials, parenthesis, ambiguity, possessive apostrophes?

Answers to activities

Jim: Who ran away from his Nurse and was eaten by a Lion

The opening lines are:

There was a Boy whose name was Jim;

His Friends were very good to him.

They gave him Tea, and Cakes, and Jam,

And slices of delicious Ham,

And Chocolate with pink inside

And little Tricycles to ride,

And read him Stories through and through,

And even took him to the Zoo—

But there it was the dreadful Fate

Befell him, which I now relate.

You can find the complete poem at: **www.poemhunter.com/poem/jim/**

For a collection of Belloc's cautionary tales see:

Belloc, H (2008) *Cautionary Tales for Children* (first published in 1907). Radford, VA: Wilder Publications.

Word class mobility

Each of the words below can belong to more than one word class, depending upon how they are used in sentences. The following are some suggestions:

chair – a small chair (noun), to chair a meeting (verb)

book – a new book (noun), book a ticket (verb)

table – a round table (noun), table a question (verb)

green – a green car (adjective), eat your greens (noun), the leaves began to green (verb)

round – round up the sheep (verb), a round table (adjective), it's your round (noun), she ran round the corner (preposition), he went round to the pub (adverb)

Further reading

Myhill, D, Jones, SM, Lines, H and Watson, A (2012) *Grammar for Writing? The Impact of Contextualised Grammar Teaching on Pupils' Writing and Pupils' Metalinguistic Understanding.* Economic and Social Research Council Impact Report, RES-062-23-0775. Swindon: ESRC.

For short video clips about the National Curriculum requirements, see:

Myhill, D (2013) *Insights into the New Grammar Curriculum with Debra Myhill* (video series). Available at: **www.pearsonschoolsandfecolleges.co.uk/Primary/GlobalPages/ NewEnglishCurriculum/Debra-Myhill-Insights.aspx** (accessed 18 December 2013).

For an entertaining and interesting look at punctuation, with lots of examples, Lynn Truss's book is ideal:

Truss, L (2003) *Eats, Shoots & Leaves: The Zero Tolerance Approach to Punctuation.* London: Profile Books.

References

Allott, K (2014) 'The SPAG test' in D Waugh, K Allott, E Bulmer, E English and R Waugh, *TeachLearn Primary SPAG*. Available at: **www.cc-apps.co.uk** (accessed 13 June 2014).

Andrews, R, Torgerson, C, Beverton, S, Freeman, A, Locke, T, Low, G, Robinson, A and Zhu, D (2004) *The Effect of Grammar Teaching (Sentence Combining) in English on 5 to 16 year olds' Accuracy and Quality in Written Composition: Review Summary*. York: University of York.

Berninger, VW, Vaughn, K, Abbot, RD, Begay, K, Coleman, K, Curtin, G, Hawkins, JM and Graham, S (2002) Teaching spelling and composition alone and together: implications for the 'simple view of writing'. *Journal of Educational Psychology*, 94: 291–304.

Bevilacqua, P and Fenton, S (2009) *Communication, Language and Literacy Development: Letters and Sounds: Working on Phase 5*. Powerpoint presentation for National Strategies, 20 October (no longer available).

DfE (2013) *The National Curriculum in England: Key Stages 1 and 2 Framework Document.* London: DfE.

Department for Education and Employment (DfEE) (2000) *Grammar for Writing: National Literacy Strategy.* London: DfEE. Available at: **http://webarchive.nationalarchives.gov. uk/20100612050234/nationalstrategies.standards.dcsf.gov.uk/node/153924** (accessed 13 June 2014).

EPPI-Centre English Review Group (2004) The effect of grammar teaching (sentence combining) in English on 5 to 16 year olds' accuracy and quality in written composition. London: Institute of Education, University of London.

Gough, PB and Tunmer, WE (1986) Decoding, reading, and reading disability. *Remedial and Special Education*, 7: 6–10.

Hudson, R (1992) *Teaching Grammar: A Guide for the National Curriculum.* Oxford: Blackwell.

Myhill, D (2012) The role for grammar in the curriculum, in *Meeting High Expectations: Looking for the heart of English*, pp21–2. Available at: **www.heartofenglish.com/sites/default/files/ High_Expectations_LHE_web.pdf** (accessed 15 December 2013).

Myhill, D (2013) *Debbie Myhill's video summaries.* Available at: **www.pearsonschoolsandfecolleges.co.uk/AssetsLibrary/SECTORS/PRIMARYASSETSNEW/Literacy/GrammarandSpellingBug/Debra_Myhill_Video_Summaries.pdf** (accessed 17 December 2013).

Rose, J (2006) *Independent Review of the Teaching of Early Reading.* Nottingham: DfES.

Waugh, D, Warner, C and Waugh, R (2016) *Teaching Grammar, Punctuation and Spelling in Primary Schools* (2nd edn). London: SAGE.

6 Reading

Ruth Harrison-Palmer

Learning outcomes

By reading this chapter you will develop your understanding of:

- the importance of developing a love of literature and reading for pleasure;
- the two dimensions involved in the reading process: word reading and comprehension (listening and reading);
- how to teach systematic synthetic phonics and comprehension effectively.

Teachers' Standards
3. Demonstrate good subject and curriculum knowledge:

- have a secure knowledge of the relevant subject(s) and curriculum areas, foster and maintain pupils' interest in the subject, and address misunderstandings;
- demonstrate a critical understanding of developments in the subject and curriculum areas, and promote the value of scholarship;
- demonstrate an understanding of, and take responsibility for, promoting high standards of literacy, articulacy and the correct use of standard English, whatever the teacher's specialist subject;
- if teaching early reading, demonstrate a clear understanding of systematic synthetic phonics.

Introduction: a balanced approach to teaching reading

The National Curriculum aims to provide a balance between reading for pleasure and reading instruction or, in the words of Teresa Cremin, *the will* and *the skill* (2008, p3). Both are necessary, but neither is sufficient alone. Just as it would be ineffective to teach the skills associated with reading to a class of pupils who show little interest and motivation, it would be unproductive to generate enthusiasm for and a love of literature without providing the skills to enable pupils to access this independently.

Reading for pleasure is fundamental to reading in the National Curriculum. Indeed, it states that pupils should *develop their love of literature through widespread reading for enjoyment* (DfE, 2013, p13). Alongside this, the skills associated with the teaching of reading focus on the two dimensions of 'word reading' and 'comprehension' at both Key Stages 1 and 2. These two dimensions require different approaches to teaching and a different body of knowledge.

> Skilled word reading involves both the speedy working out of the pronunciation of unfamiliar printed words (decoding) and the speedy recognition of familiar printed words. Underpinning both is the understanding that the letters on the page represent the sounds in spoken words. This is why phonics should be emphasised in the early teaching of reading to beginners (i.e. unskilled readers) when they start school.
>
> Good comprehension draws from linguistic knowledge (in particular of vocabulary and grammar) and on knowledge of the world. Comprehension skills develop through pupils' experience of high-quality discussion with the teacher, as well as from reading and discussing a range of stories, poems and non-fiction.
>
> (DfE, 2013, p14)

National data (DfE, 2016), based on revised Key Stage 2 assessments for reading, shows a drop in pupils achieving the required standard of level 4 in reading of 66 per cent compared with 89 per cent in 2015. At the time of writing, results for Key Stage 1 are not available for 2016, and in 2015 only 69 per cent of Year 1 pupils met the expected standard of phonic decoding in the Year 1 screening check and 11 per cent failed to achieve level 2 at the end of Year 2. Within this context, the curriculum emphasises the importance of supporting *struggling readers: through a rigorous and systematic phonics programme so that they catch up rapidly with their peers.* However, they should follow the Programme of Study for their year group in *terms of listening to new books, hearing and learning new vocabulary and grammatical structures, and discussing these* (DfE, 2013, p33).

The curriculum stresses the importance of spoken language in the development of reading. While this chapter does not include a specific section on this, there is an emphasis on vocabulary and oral language development. To find out more about the relationship between speaking and listening and reading, see Chapter 2, and to explore the importance of vocabulary in reading comprehension, see Chapter 3.

The importance of reading

Reading changes lives. The OECD report *Reading for Change* (2002) stresses the essential links between ability in reading and opportunities in later life such as *employment opportunities, work satisfaction, income, longevity and health* (p102). The curriculum eloquently states that *Reading … feeds pupils' imagination and opens up a treasure-house of wonder and joy for curious young minds* (DfE, 2013, p14). Furthermore, through becoming confident and competent readers, *pupils have a chance to develop culturally, emotionally, intellectually, socially and spiritually* (DfE, 2013, p13).

Activity: why do you read?

First consider your response to this question by noting down five reasons why you might read – e.g. reading a recipe to learn how to cook something. Now try asking some beginner or struggling readers the same question. How does their response differ from yours? What might the reasons be for this? How might you address this?

'If you enjoyed that book, you will love this one'

Just because children are able to read, it does not mean that they will choose to do so. The introduction to the National Curriculum states that *Schools should do everything to promote wider reading. They should provide library facilities and set ambitious expectations for reading at home* (DfE, 2013, p11). The curriculum emphasises the importance of reading books to pupils and discussing books with them. All teachers of reading need to be reading teachers (Cremin *et al.*, 2009). If you are to create a rich reading environment in which 'book talk' flourishes, you need to have read a wealth of children's literature yourself, from classics such as *Swallows and Amazons* by Arthur Ransome or *Treasure Island* by Robert Louis Stevenson to the latest publications by up-coming authors. There is a wealth of websites, such as the ones below, dedicated to keeping teachers and parents up-to-date with high quality children's books and ideas for using them:

www.booktrust.org.uk/books/

wordsforlife.literacytrust.org.uk/

www.lovereading4kids.co.uk/

booksforkeeps.co.uk/

www.readingrevolution.co.uk/

http://readinggroups.org/chatterbooks/

Making time to read children's literature may appear to be a luxury, but if you are to develop a love of reading and reading for pleasure it is essential. A number of schools use approaches such as ERIC (Everyone Read in Class) or DEAR (Drop Everything and Read), which aim to engender a culture in which reading is both a valuable and a normal activity that both adults and pupils do for pleasure. This provides an opportunity for busy teachers to catch up with the latest children's book too. Being able to use your knowledge of children's literature to discuss a book with a child, and sharing your different reactions and interpretations of it, can be a powerful learning opportunity. Equally, being able to recommend a book to children based on their interests and books that they have enjoyed previously helps to broaden the breadth and depth of their reading, while maintaining motivation. Discussing books that pupils have read and have had read to them is a central aspect to developing pleasure in reading in the curriculum, which states: *Throughout the programmes of study, teachers should teach pupils the vocabulary they need to discuss their reading, writing and spoken language* (DfE, 2013, p15) and that *Pupils should develop a capacity to explain their understanding of books and other reading* (DfE, 2013, p14).

Please read us a book!

The National Curriculum emphasises reading aloud to pupils up to and including Year 6 to introduce them to a wide range of high quality books and authors. In a packed curriculum 'story time' is often squeezed out, particularly in Key Stage 2. Unfortunately, research suggests that it is these pupils who are less likely to have stories read to them at home. Bowker (2012) indicates that 95 per cent of 3–4-year-olds have books read to them, with over a third of parents (42 per cent) reading to them every day. Only 33 per cent of 8–10-year-olds are read to several times a week. As well as developing reading for pleasure, reading to pupils has many benefits such as developing vocabulary and sophisticated language structures, modelling expressive reading, and demonstrating the connections between speech and print. Cliff-Hodges (2011) claims that listening to someone reading aloud facilitates a deep *reciprocal social companionship from which there is something to be gained by both participants* (p20).

Using 'book talk' and reading to pupils to develop pleasure and motivation in reading throughout the Programmes of Study

The table below (DfE, 2013) shows progression in terms of discussing books, reading aloud and reading for pleasure.

Year	Programme of Study	Notes and Guidance (Non-statutory)
1	• Listening to and discussing a wide range of poems, stories and non-fiction at a level beyond that at which they can read independently. • Participate in discussion about what is read to them, taking turns and listening to what others say. • Explain clearly their understanding of what is read to them.	• Pupils should have extensive experience of listening to, sharing and discussing a wide range of high-quality books with the teacher, other adults and each other to engender a love of reading at the same time as they are reading independently. • Pupils' vocabulary should be developed when they listen to books read aloud and when they discuss what they have heard. • By listening frequently to stories, poems and non-fiction that they cannot yet read for themselves, pupils begin to understand how written language can be structured in order, for example, to build surprise in narratives or to present facts in non-fiction.
2	• Participate in discussion about books, poems and other works that are read to them and those that they can read for themselves, taking turns and listening to what others say. • Explain and discuss their understanding of books, poems and other material, both those that they listen to and those that they read for themselves.	• 'Thinking aloud' when reading to pupils may help them to understand what skilled readers do.
3 and 4	• Participate in discussion about both books that are read to them and those they can read for themselves, taking turns and listening to what others say.	• Pupils should also have opportunities to exercise choice in selecting books and be taught how to do so, with teachers making use of any library services and expertise to support this.
5 and 6	• Participate in discussions about books that are read to them and those they can read for themselves, building on their own and others' ideas and challenging views courteously. • Explain and discuss their understanding of what they have read, including through formal presentations and debates, maintaining a focus on the topic and using notes where necessary. • Provide reasoned justifications for their views.	• Pupils should have guidance about and feedback on the quality of their explanations and contributions to discussions. • Even though pupils can now read independently, reading aloud to them should include whole books so that they meet books and authors that they might not choose to read themselves.

Research focus: reading teachers as teachers of reading

Research carried out by Cremin *et al.* (2008), which surveyed 1,200 primary teachers nationally, revealed that teachers' knowledge of children's books was worryingly narrow. Teachers tended to rely on favourites from their childhood. The findings suggest that these teachers were not knowledgeable enough about children's books to enable them to nurture reading development and to be able to recommend a wide range of books to pupils with diverse needs and interests. This project was followed up with 'Teachers as Readers: building communities of readers' (Cremin *et al.*, 2009), the aim of which was to support teachers to improve their knowledge of and use of literature and enable them to increase pupils' motivation and enthusiasm for reading. The project concluded that while it

> made a positive impact upon children's attainment, achievement and dispositions, and identified a coherent strategy to develop children's reading for pleasure by enhancing teachers' subject knowledge and pedagogic practice, it also revealed that reading for pleasure urgently requires a higher profile in primary education. It is clear that teachers need considerable support in order to find the time and space to widen their reading repertoires and develop an appropriately personalised reading curriculum which is both responsive and inclusive.

> (p26)

Case study: a whole-school approach to developing reading for pleasure

A small village school had developing reading for pleasure as a means of raising attainment in reading as a focus for the school development plan. This was developed in a number of ways. First, staff implemented whole-school reading on Friday mornings. This entailed all pupils, teachers, parents and members of the community spending half an hour together in various 'reading spaces' set up around the school to read, share books and discuss their reading. The school particularly encouraged male members of the community to be involved in order to be positive reading role models for the boys in the school. This is what some of the pupils had to say about the initiative.

'I like talking to other people about what I am reading.'

'It's sociable.'

'You get to share good books.'

→

In addition, a whole-school approach was taken to 'Drop Everything and Read' (DEAR). This happened at least three times a week. When the school bell rang, all pupils and teachers picked up the book of choice and read. Some of the responses from pupils are below.

'It's exciting and you don't need to do any work.'

'I like it because I've got a good book at the moment.'

'I think we should do it more often, like every day.'

Pupils, teachers, parents and members of the community were also encouraged to take photos of themselves reading in different places such as on a train, in the garden and even up a mountain. These were added to a display called 'Where have you been reading lately?'

In a short time there was a notable difference in the pupils, both academically and in attitude. The pupils' confidence and willingness to read, and the positive attitude they had developed translated into the classroom. Pupils were more enthusiastic about guided reading, and their comprehension of what they were reading had improved too.

Curriculum link

The pupils above were developing 'the habit of reading widely and often' for pleasure (DfE, 2013, p13). They developed a positive attitude to reading through being given frequent opportunities to read books of their choice for enjoyment. Reading was viewed as something that many people do for pleasure 'in real life' not just an activity for the teacher. They were also provided with many purposeful opportunities to discuss their reading, with peers, teachers, parents and members of the community, to further develop their vocabulary and comprehension.

Activity: what can you/do you do to create a classroom environment in which reading for enjoyment can thrive?

How do you/might you:

- make your own enthusiasm for reading explicit?
- demonstrate reading behaviours to pupils – e.g. how do you select a text to read for pleasure?
- provide frequent opportunities for pupils to read for pleasure?
- keep abreast of high-quality children's books?
- find opportunities to read aloud to pupils for pleasure rather than as a tool for teaching?

Now look at the end of the chapter for some possible suggestions.

The Simple View of Reading

The two dimensions involved in the reading process: word reading and comprehension (listening and reading)

The two dimensions of word reading and comprehension, which are central to the process of reading in the National Curriculum, are illustrated in the 'Simple View of Reading' below. This model was first introduced by Gough and Tunmer in 1986. Following Rose's (2006) *Review into the Teaching of Early Reading*, it became a recommended national model for the process of learning to read.

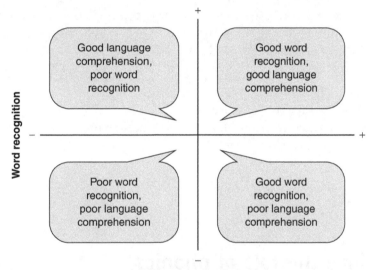

Figure 6.1 A simple view of reading

Source: **https://portfolio.pebblepad.co.uk/cumbria/viewasset.aspx?oid=506154&type=webfolio&pageoid=506166#** (accessed 17 April 2014).

This model makes it clear that effective reading comprehension is dependent on both word recognition skills and language comprehension skills. Rose (2006) exemplifies this as follows

> A useful illustration of the necessity for reading of both components and the insufficiency for reading of each component on its own is the story of Milton in his blindness. Wishing to read ancient Greek texts, but unable to do so because he could no longer see the words, Milton encouraged his daughters to learn to pronounce each alphabetic symbol of the ancient Greek alphabet. His daughters then used these phonic skills to read aloud the texts to their

father. Their father could understand what they uncomprehendingly read aloud to him. The daughters possessed word recognition skills, which did not enable them to understand the text; Milton, despite his ability to understand the Greek language, was no longer able to use his word recognition skills and so was no longer able to understand Greek text without harnessing his daughters' skills.

(p76)

Activity: check your subject knowledge

Before you read on, check your subject knowledge, in relation to word reading, by providing definitions for the following terms from the (non-statutory) glossary in the National Curriculum:

- grapheme;
- phoneme;
- grapheme–phoneme correspondences;
- digraph (including split digraph and consonant digraph);
- trigraph;
- schwa.

Now check your answers at the end of this chapter.

Word reading: the role of phonics

I wish commentators would make it clear that phonics is a body of knowledge we all need. No maths teacher would dream of expecting children to remember numbers as strings of digits – they teach the concept of place value. In the same way, children need to understand that letters represent sounds.

(Letter from Mary Kelly in the *Times Educational Supplement*, 10 June 2011)

The curriculum recognises phonics as a body of knowledge as it repeatedly states the phonic knowledge that needs to be taught to specific year groups. This knowledge pertains to grapheme–phoneme correspondences (GPCs), which should be taught in a systematic way. In addition, pupils need to develop the skill of blending phonemes all through a word in order to decode it.

Most schools use a phonics programme – for example, Letters and Sounds (DfES, 2007) – to teach the GPCs in an incremental, systematic way along with the skill of blending. By the time pupils reach Year 3, there should no longer be a need to explicitly focus on phonics for word reading (although this will continue to be a focus for teaching spelling), but if some pupils are not yet secure, this work needs to continue throughout Key Stage 2 until they catch up with their peers. A range of systematic phonics programmes is available. To support schools with choosing an effective programme, 'core criteria' were developed and can be accessed at **www.gov. uk/choose-a-phonics-programme**.

Teaching phonics effectively

The effective teaching of phonics, as defined by Rose (2006), should include a *vigorous programme of phonic work to be securely embedded within a broad and language-rich curriculum* (p16). The framework from one programme should be used consistently rather than using a 'pick-and-mix' approach from a variety of programmes, as this does not allow for a systematic approach to progression in which GPCs are taught in a clearly defined sequence. This sequence typically moves from the simple (one grapheme for each of the 44 phonemes) to the complex (multiple graphemes for a single phoneme).

Phonics should be taught through 'relatively short discrete daily sessions' (Rose, 2006, p16). These lessons should be sensory, including visual, auditory and kinaesthetic activities such as using pictures to support learning GPCs – for example, a snake for the phoneme /s/, songs to support learning a particular GPC, or physically moving to the grapheme that represents the phoneme in a given word. However, it is important to note that the focus should remain on the appropriate phonemes and skills rather than the activities. Assessment should be used to clearly identify next steps for both individuals and groups. Rose (2006) suggests that the most effective assessment was simple, rigorous and purposeful, [and] assessed:

- recognition of letters (and groups of letters, such as digraphs)
- the ability to sound out phonemes
- the ability to hear and blend phonemes
- the reading of phonically regular words
- the reading of some irregular words.

(p22)

A possible teaching sequence for an effective phonics lesson

Rose (2006) emphasises the importance of consistently using one programme to teach phonics, rather than a 'pick-and-mix' approach, to ensure that GPCs are taught in a clearly defined, incremental sequence. Like the National Curriculum, Rose stresses the importance of teaching phonics within a *broad and rich language curriculum* (p70). While a approach to teaching phonics is recommended to capture pupils' *interest, sustain motivation, and reinforce learning in imaginative and exciting ways* (p70), this should not detract from the learning objective for the lesson. An effective phonics lesson should include frequent opportunities for teachers to model and teach segmenting and blending and for pupils to practise these skills. Below is a possible teaching sequence for an effective phonics lesson which has been adapted from *Letters and Sounds* (DfES, 2007, p49).

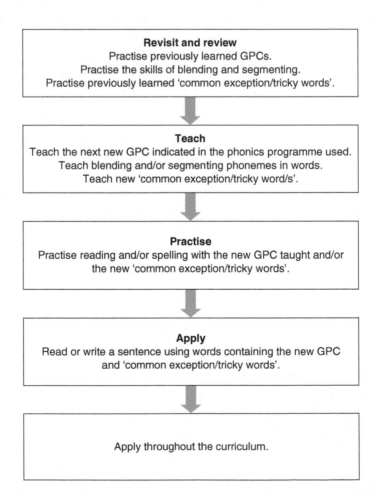

Revisit and review
Practise previously learned GPCs.
Practise the skills of blending and segmenting.
Practise previously learned 'common exception/tricky words'.

Teach
Teach the next new GPC indicated in the phonics programme used.
Teach blending and/or segmenting phonemes in words.
Teach new 'common exception/tricky word/s'.

Practise
Practise reading and/or spelling with the new GPC taught and/or the new 'common exception/tricky words'.

Apply
Read or write a sentence using words containing the new GPC and 'common exception/tricky words'.

Apply throughout the curriculum.

Right from the start of the programme, provide frequent opportunities for pupils to apply their phonic knowledge in reading and writing activities throughout the week. It is, after all, what it is for.

Curriculum links: word reading in the National Curriculum: progression and expectations

The curriculum states that in Year 1 pupils' word recognition skills should build on what they have learned in the EYFS to ensure that they *can sound out and blend unfamiliar words quickly* (DfE, 2013, p18). As well as learning new GPCs, they should consolidate ones taught earlier. The link between letters and sounds should be central to pupils' reading of all words. This includes words in which there are unusual GPCs such as 'said', in which the /e/ phoneme is represented by the grapheme 'ai'. These are often called 'tricky words', but are referred to as 'common exception words' in the National Curriculum. By using decodable texts that correspond to pupils' developing knowledge of GPCs, they can experience success in word reading through sounding out and blending to read unfamiliar words after learning only a few GPCs. There is an expectation that *Pupils should be helped to read words without overt sounding and blending after a few encounters. Those who are slow to develop this skill should have extra practice* (DfE, 2013, p18).

Pupils moving into Year 2 should have developed their knowledge of all the common graphemes for the 44 phonemes in the English language. For example, they should know that the /igh/ phoneme is commonly represented by the graphemes 'i', 'i-e', 'igh' and 'y'. There is an emphasis on fluent and speedy word reading with an expectation that pupils *should also be able to read many common words containing GPCs taught so far {for example, shout, hand, stop, or dream}, without needing to blend the sounds out loud first* (DfE, 2013, p25), and be secure in reading many *common exception words*. It is important to note that if pupils have not yet developed the phonic knowledge and skills needed for the Year 2 Programme of Study, they should continue working with the Year 1 Programme of Study, but follow the Year 2 Programme for developing comprehension.

In Years 3 and 4, there is an expectation that most pupils will have *increasingly secure* (DfE, 2013, p33) decoding skills and thus will not need explicit teaching of word reading skills. This allows for an increased focus on reading for meaning rather than decoding. For those pupils who are having difficulties with decoding, the curriculum states that they should *be taught to do this urgently through a rigorous and systematic phonics programme so that they catch up rapidly with their peers* (DfE, 2013, p33) but follow the Years 3 and 4 Programme of Study for comprehension.

By Years 5 and 6, pupils should be able to apply their word reading skills to *effortlessly* read most words and work out unfamiliar words *with increasing automaticity* (DfE, 2013, p41). As

(Continued)

(Continued)

with Years 3 and 4, those pupils with poor decoding skills should be *taught through a rigorous and systematic phonics programme so that they catch up rapidly with their peers in terms of their decoding* (DfE, 2013, p41) but follow the Years 5 and 6 Programme of Study for comprehension.

It is important to note that *The single year blocks at key stage 1 reflect the rapid pace of development in word reading during these two years* (DfE, 2013, p15). As schools are only required to have taught the Programme of Study by the end of the Key Stage, they may introduce content earlier or later, or make use of content in an earlier or later Key Stage.

Research focus: why systematic phonics?

Evidence from both UK (Johnston and Watson, 2007; MacKay, 2007) and international research (Department of Education, Science and Training, Australia, 2005; National Reading Panel (NRP), US, 2000) demonstrates that the most effective way to teach pupils word reading is through systematic phonics. The NRP report (2000) concluded that:

> systematic phonics instruction proved to be universally effective, it should be implemented as part of literacy programs to teach beginning reading, as well as to prevent and remediate reading difficulties.

> (p89)

Likewise, the Australian findings (2005) convincingly established that:

> systematic phonics teaching within a stimulating and rich literacy environment is essential to the effective teaching of reading during children's first three years of schooling, and thereafter where necessary.

> (pp37–8)

Rose (2006) describes the particular challenges relating to the English language and learning to read and the importance of a systematic approach:

> it is generally accepted that is harder to learn to read and write in English because the relationship between sounds and letters is more complex than in many other alphabetic languages. It is therefore crucial to teach phonic work systematically, regularly and explicitly, because children are highly unlikely to work out this relationship for themselves. It cannot be left to chance, or for children to ferret out, on their own, how the alphabetic code works.

> (pp19–20)

→

English has a more complex orthographic system (relationship between phonemes and graphemes) than some other languages such as Italian. This is because most phonemes can be represented by more than one grapheme. Some phonemes can be represented by many different graphemes.

Reading difficulties and dyslexia

Some children find word reading – decoding text – extremely difficult, and take much longer than most children to develop the skills involved. Even with well-planned interventions their progress may be very slow. The term 'dyslexia' is used to describe these difficulties. The Rose Report (2006) on dyslexia included the following points in its definition of the term.

- Dyslexia is a learning difficulty that primarily affects the skills involved in accurate and fluent word reading and spelling.
- Characteristic features of dyslexia are difficulties in phonological awareness, verbal memory and verbal processing speed.
- Dyslexia occurs across the range of intellectual abilities.
- It is best thought of as a continuum, not a distinct category, and there are no clear cut-off points.

(p9)

Estimates of how common it is vary considerably, according to the definition used and the cut-off points. Evidence that there is a genetic component come from twin studies (e.g. Gayan and Olson, 2001) but the environment also matters. While the Rose Report advocates early identification, it suggests that screening is not reliable and that the best approach is to observe and assess young children engaged in pre-reading and early reading activities, and note those who in comparison with their peers seem to find such activities difficult. Teachers might note, for example, children in the early years who have significant difficulty rhyming and hearing sounds in words, who are slow to learn grapheme–phoneme correspondences and have poor word attack skills. Later on in primary school, children may have difficulty reading new words, read slowly and inaccurately, and produce bizarre spellings. Whatever the difficulty observed, the crucial point is that subsequent teaching addresses that learning need directly and effectively.

The Rose Report emphasised the importance of high-quality teaching of reading and the 'waves' model of intervention, where the first wave of effective teaching includes additional in-class support for individuals who are struggling. This could include modelling blending and segmenting briefly at every opportunity through the day, or showing the child a grapheme card and reminding her what phoneme it represents several times in the day.

Quality first teaching is supported by a second wave of time-limited group or individual intervention programmes, aimed at helping children who are falling behind to catch up and keep up, and then a third wave of intensive long-term intervention for children who are still failing to make good progress. Intervention programmes which teach phonological skills systematically and thoroughly have been shown to be effective (Singleton, 2009). In other words, children are taught to recognise and manipulate sounds in words. They also need to be taught to sound out and blend words to read, including multi-syllable words, and to segment words to spell them. Programmes also need to include sufficient reading practice to allow children to develop speed and fluency in their reading. The teaching needs to be 'little and often' – if possible, daily – and it is essential that interventions are carried out by well-trained staff, whether these are teachers or teaching assistants, and that children's progress during the intervention is carefully monitored. Early intervention will help avoid children developing perceptions of themselves as poor readers. For children at the extreme end of the continuum, even intensive teaching may only result in slow progress, so it is important that support also involves building self-efficacy and confidence.

For trainee teachers, it is important that they ensure they have a secure grasp of phonics, understanding both the alphabetic code and also the skills children need, and knowing how to teach these effectively. They must make sure that their teaching gives children sufficient experience to develop phonological awareness. For example, in nursery the priority should not be teaching grapheme–phoneme correspondences, but developing an awareness of sounds within words, and an ability to manipulate them, through a rich diet of rhymes and word-play.

Reading 'floats on a sea of talk'
(Britton, 1970, p164)

Rose (2006) states that *As reading comprehension has now been shown to depend crucially on language comprehension, teachers also need to have good knowledge and understanding of oral language development, and of ways to foster language comprehension* (p40).

The National Reading Panel Report (2000) identified three key strands to developing comprehension. Note how they are all based on oral language development and language comprehension.

Learning about words

Throughout the Programmes of Study in the curriculum, pupils should *acquire a wide vocabulary, an understanding of grammar and knowledge of linguistic conventions for reading, writing and spoken language* (DfE, 2013, p13). Furthermore, *teachers should teach pupils the vocabulary they need to discuss their reading* (DfE, 2013, p15). Below are some useful examples of how you might approach this from the DCSF publication *Teaching Effective Vocabulary* (2008).

- Encouraging 'word of the day'. Both teachers and pupils decide on a new word each day with a view to using it in context as many times as possible.

- Pre-teaching vocabulary before meeting it in a text – for example, key words such as technical terms or words in unfamiliar contexts.

- Providing clear objectives for developing vocabulary – for example, giving pupils four words and asking them to use them during the lesson.

- Developing STOP REWIND activities. Pupils are given a catch phrase such as 'rewind' that they use when they are listening to the teacher reading and do not understand the meaning of a word or phrase. The teacher stops reading and a discussion of the word or phrase takes place to explore meaning.

- Showing a short film (e.g. BFI story shorts) without sound and asking pupils to discuss the dialogue that they would expect to hear.

For more ideas for teaching vocabulary, see Chapter 3.

Interacting with the text and explicitly teaching reading comprehension strategies

Comprehension is an active process between the reader and the text. Throughout Key Stage 1, the curriculum expects pupils to make use of higher order reading skills such as inference and prediction. By Key Stage 2, teaching should focus on reading comprehension, rather than word reading skills. Pupils should continue to develop their vocabulary to support their reading. Pupils should demonstrate their understanding by *drawing inferences such as inferring characters' feelings, thoughts and motives from their actions and justifying inferences with evidence* (DfE, 2013, p44). Asking pupils questions about the text is one way of developing interaction. In order to develop higher order reading skills, different types of questions should be used. Pupils should also be encouraged to generate their own questions.

Deductive or inferential questions require pupils to be detectives and work out the answers by 'reading between the lines' and going beyond the information given in the text. An example of a deductive question from the text, 'Jason was lounging on the beach. He applied another layer of sun cream' might be 'What was the weather like?' The reader has to work out the answer from the clues in the text.

By Years 5 and 6 pupils are expected to *discuss and evaluate how authors use language, including figurative language, considering the impact on the reader* (DfE, 2013, p45). Evaluative questions require pupils to make judgements about what they have read. An example of some evaluative questions in relation to a piece of suspense text might be 'Do you think the author creates a feeling of suspense effectively? How does he do it? Could he have done this better? How?'

The 2014 curriculum recognises that:

> The knowledge and skills that pupils need in order to comprehend are very similar at different ages. This is why the programmes of study for comprehension in years 3 and 4 and years 5 and 6 are similar: the complexity of the writing increases the level of challenge.

(DfE, 2013, p35)

There are many effective strategies for teaching comprehension through interacting with texts, such as the examples below taken from *Understanding Reading Comprehension: 2* (DfES, 2005a) and *Understanding Reading Comprehension: 3* (DfES, 2005b).

- **The author's chair** A pupil takes on the role of the author. Other pupils ask the author questions about the book. The 'author' provides answers.

- **Criteria rating** Discuss a particular scene from a story at a critical point and rate it in relation to mostly likely to happen/least likely to happen, mostly likely to be true/least likely to be true.

- **Hot-seating** The teacher or a pupil takes on the role of a character from the story. Pupils create questions for the 'character' who answers in role. Pupils should be encouraged to progress further than factual questions to investigate – for example, motives or consequences.

- **Visualisation** The teacher reads aloud from a fiction or non-fiction text and describes the pictures that they had in their head while they were reading. Ask pupils to think of the picture that they had in their heads. Then read another passage; pupils work in pairs describing their image to one another.

Activity: do you understand this?

Read the passage below and explain to someone else what it means (Waugh, 2013).

> A new gadolinium isotope decaying by electron capture with a 29-hour half-life was found. Its mass number was determined to be 147 by examination of its excitation function for production by alpha particle bombardment of Sm21*7Oz. The electron-capture isotope Gd 14e was also studied, and its half-life was redetermined to be 9.3+0.3 days.

(Shirley *et al.*, 1957)

You were probably able to apply your word reading skills to actually read the text, but were you able to understand it? It is likely that you were unsure of how to pronounce many of the words because they are not part of your vocabulary. This reminds us that comprehension needs to be explicitly taught if pupils are able to read for meaning, and vocabulary development is an integral part of this.

The teaching of word reading through systematic phonics has been a focus for government policy for a number of years. This has been formalised by making it a statutory requirement in the curriculum. There is an increased focus on the role of oral language development in the development of comprehension. Comprehension is viewed as a dynamic, active process, which should be taught to beginning readers alongside word reading from the start. Perhaps the biggest impact of the 2014 National Curriculum in terms of reading achievement will be seen due to phonics continuing to be taught in Key Stage 2 to pupils with poor word reading skills, and the permeating emphasis on reading for pleasure throughout the Programmes of Study. If, as the OECD (2002) report suggests, the 'will' influences the 'skill', an emphasis on reading for pleasure should have a direct impact on achievement in reading.

Learning outcomes review

You should now know:

- what pupils need to understand about word reading and comprehension;
- what we need to know and do as primary teachers to foster reading for pleasure;
- some approaches to teaching comprehension;
- how phonics underpins the teaching of word reading.

Self-assessment questions

1. Why is it important to develop reading for pleasure, from the very start, alongside teaching word reading and comprehension?
2. Why is providing opportunities for children to discuss their reading, focusing on language development, important?
3. Why is phonics needed to develop pupils' word reading?
4. If pupils in Key Stage 2 are struggling with word reading, what should you do?

Answers to activities

What can you/do you do to create a classroom environment in which reading for enjoyment can thrive?

How do you/might you:	Some suggestions
make your own enthusiasm for reading explicit?	• Talk to pupils about what you are reading. • Come into the classroom reading a book and explain that the pupils will need to wait for a moment as you have got to a really exciting part. Try to be as animated as possible as you read it. • Share your excitement about new titles and authors and where you found out about them.
demonstrate reading behaviours to pupils – e.g. how you select a text to read for pleasure?	• Model some of the behaviours suggested in Daniel Pennac's 'The Rights of the Reader', www.broad-street.com/images/uploaded/Ten%20rights%20of%20readers%20poster.pdf (accessed 29 April 2014). • Look at websites with pupils, such as the ones suggested earlier in this chapter, to find out about books you might like to read. • Visit the local library.
provide frequent opportunities for pupils to read for pleasure?	• Try the 'Everyone Read in Class' or 'Drop Everything and Read' approach discussed earlier in the chapter. • Set up a book club during lunchtime or after school. • Allow pupils to take books to read outside at playtime.
keep abreast with high-quality children's books?	• Talk to pupils about what they are reading. • Use the websites suggested earlier in the chapter. • Talk to other teachers. • Regularly visit bookshops.
find opportunities to read aloud to pupils for pleasure rather than as a tool for teaching?	• Always have a class book 'on the go' that you can pick up and read from at any time of the day. • Protect 'story-time', even if it is just for 15 minutes a couple of times a week, particularly for Key Stage 2 pupils.

Check your subject knowledge

Check your subject knowledge by providing definitions for the following terms. The definitions below are taken from the (non-statutory) glossary of terms in the National Curriculum.

Term	Guidance	Example
Grapheme	A letter, or combination of letters, that corresponds to a single phoneme within a word.	The grapheme 't' in the words *ten*, *bet* and *ate* corresponds to the phoneme /t/. The grapheme 'ph' in the word *dolphin* corresponds to the phoneme /f/.
Phoneme	A phoneme is the smallest unit of sound that signals a distinct, contrasting meaning. For example: • /t/ contrasts with /k/ to signal the difference between tap and cap • /t/ contrasts with /l/ to signal the difference between bought and ball. It is this contrast in meaning that tells us there are two distinct phonemes at work. There are around 44 phonemes in English; the exact number depends on regional accents. A single phoneme may be represented in writing by one, two, three or four letters constituting a single grapheme.	The word *cat* has three letters and three phonemes: /kæt/ [c/a/t]. The word *catch* has five letters and three phonemes: / katʃ / [c/a/tch]. The word *caught* has six letters and three phonemes: /kɔ: :t/ [c/augh/t].
Grapheme–phoneme correspondences	The links between letters, or combinations of letters (graphemes) and the speech sounds (phonemes) that they represent. In the English writing system, graphemes may correspond to different phonemes in different words.	The grapheme 's' corresponds to the phoneme /s/ in the word *see*, but ... it corresponds to the phoneme /z/ in the word *easy*.
Digraph	A type of grapheme where two letters represent one phoneme. Sometimes, these two letters are not next to one another; this is called a split digraph. A digraph can also be made up of two consonants that represent one phoneme. This is called a consonant digraph.	The digraph *ea* in *each* The split digraph *i–e* in *line* [The consonant digraph *sh* in *shed*.]
Trigraph	A type of grapheme where three letters represent one phoneme.	*high, pure, patch, hedge*

(Continued)

(Continued)

Term	Guidance	Example
Schwa	The name of a vowel sound that is found only in unstressed positions in English. It is the most common vowel sound in English. [Children and adults sometimes add an extra phoneme (schwa) when sounding phonemes out e.g. /h/a/m/ uh rather than saying the pure sounds h/a/m to read the word *ham*. This is unhelpful when blending the phonemes to read the word as they will read the word as *hammer* as that is what they have heard.]	*along* *butter* *doctor*

Further reading

To further develop your understanding of discussing books with pupils, this may be helpful:

Chambers, A (1993) *Tell Me: Children Reading and Talk*. Stroud: Thimble Press.

To further develop your knowledge of teaching systematic phonics and the Simple View of Reading, the following texts may prove useful:

Rose, J (2006) *Independent Review of the Teaching of Early Reading: final report* (the Rose Report). Nottingham: DfES.

Jolliffe, W and Waugh, D with Carss, A (2015) *Teaching Systematic Synthetic Phonics in Primary Schools* (2nd edition). London: Learning Matters SAGE.

Waugh, D and Harrison-Palmer, R (2013) *Teaching Systematic Synthetic Phonics: Audit and Test*. London: Learning Matters SAGE.

To help you to plan for developing comprehension based on oral language, the following may prove useful:

DfES (2005) *Understanding Reading Comprehension: 1*. Nottingham: DfES. Available at: **www.teachfind.com/national-strategies/understanding-reading-comprehension-1-%E2%80%93-what-reading-comprehension** (accessed 10 April 2014).

DfES (2005) *Understanding Reading Comprehension: 2*. Nottingham: DfES. Available at: **www.teachfind.com/national-strategies/understanding-reading-comprehension-2-%E2%80%93-strategies-develop-reading-comprehension** (accessed 10 April 2014).

DfES (2005) *Understanding Reading Comprehension: 3*. Nottingham: DfES. Available at: **www.teachfind.com/national-strategies/understanding-reading-comprehension-3-%E2%80%93-further-strategies-develop-reading-comprehension** (accessed 10 April 2014).

If you would like to know more about developing reading for pleasure, see:

Cremin, T, Mottram, M, Collins, F, Powell, S and Safford, K (2009) Teachers as readers: building communities of readers. *Literacy*, 43(1): 11–19.

Gamble, N (2013) *Exploring Children's Literature: Reading with Pleasure and Purpose*. London: SAGE.

To develop your understanding of reading interventions, this may be useful:

Brooks, G (2013) *What Works for Children and Young People with Literacy Difficulties? The Effectiveness of Intervention Schemes*. Bracknell: The Dyslexia-SpLD Trust. Available at: **www. interventionsforliteracy.org.uk/widgets_GregBrooks/What_works_for_children_ fourth_ed.pdf** (accessed 13 June 2014).

References

Bowker (2012) Understanding the children's book consumer in the digital age. Market research carried out by Bowker in the United States.

Britton, J (1970) *Language and Learning*. Coral Gables, FL: University of Miami Press.

Cliff-Hodges, G (2011) Textual drama: the value of reading aloud. *English Drama Media*, 19: 19–25.

Cremin, T. (2008) Teachers as readers: building communities of readers 2007–08 executive summary. Leicester: UKLA. Available at: **www.ukla.org/downloads/teachers_as_readers. pdf** (accessed 12 June 2014).

Cremin, T, Bearne, E, Goodwin, P and Mottram, M (2008) Primary teachers as readers. *English in Education*, 42(1): 1–16.

Cremin, T, Mottram, M, Collins, F, Powell, S and Safford, K (2009) Teachers as readers: building communities of readers. *Literacy*, 43(1): 11–19.

DCSF (2008) *Teaching Effective Vocabulary*. Nottingham: DCSF. Available at: **http:// webarchive.nationalarchives.gov.uk/20130401151715/http://www.education.gov.uk/ publications/eOrderingDownload/TEV_A4.pdf** (accessed 11 March 2014).

Department for Education (DfE) (2013) *The National Curriculum in England: Key Stages 1 and 2 Framework Document*. London: DfE.

DfE (2016) *National Curriculum Assessments at Key Stage 2: 2016 (interim)*. London: DfE. Available at: **www.gov.uk/government/statistics/national-curriculum-assessments-key- stage-2-2016-interim** (accessed 19 August 2016).

Department for Education and Skills (DfES) (2005a) *Understanding Reading Comprehension: 2*. Nottingham: DfES. Available at: **www.teachfind.com/national-strategies/understanding- reading-comprehension-2-%E2%80%93-strategies-develop-reading-comprehension** (accessed 10 April 2014).

DfES (2005b) *Understanding Reading Comprehension: 3*. Nottingham: DfES. Available at: **www.teachfind.com/national-strategies/understanding-reading-comprehension-3- %E2%80%93-further-strategies-develop-reading-comprehension** (accessed 10 April 2014).

DfES (2007) *Letters and Sounds*. Nottingham: DfES. Available at: **www.gov.uk/government/publications/letters-and-sounds** (accessed 17 April 2014).

Department of Education, Science and Training, Australia (2005) *Teaching Reading: Report and Recommendations. National Enquiry into the Teaching of Literacy*. Barton: Department of Education, Science and Training.

Gayan, J and Olson, RK (2001) Genetic and environmental influences on orthographic and phonological skills in children with reading difficulties. *Developmental Neuropsychology*, 20(2), 483–507.

Gough, PB and Tunmer, WE (1986) Decoding, reading and reading disability. *RASE: Remedial and Special Education*, 7: 6–10.

Johnston, R and Watson, J (2007) *Teaching Synthetic Phonics*. London: Learning Matters/SAGE.

MacKay, T (2007) *Achieving the Vision: The Final Research Report of the West Dunbartonshire Literacy Initiative*. Dumbarton: West Dunbartonshire Council. Available at: **www.nepes.eu/files/Tommy%20MacKay%20Literacy%20Initiative.pdf** (accessed 17 April 2014).

National Reading Panel (NRP) (2000) *Teaching Children to Read: An Evidence-Based Assessment of the Scientific Research Literature on Reading and Its Implications for Reading Instruction*. Washington, DC: US Department of Health and Human Services. Available at: **www.dys-add.com/resources/SpecialEd/TeachingChildrenToRead.pdf** (accessed 14 April 2014).

Organisation for Economic Cooperation and Development (OECD) (2002) *Reading for Change: Performance and Engagement Across Countries: Results from PISA 2002*. New York: OECD.

Rose, J (2006) *Independent Review of the Teaching of Early Reading: Final Report* (the Rose Report). Nottingham: DfES.

Shirley, VS, Smith, WG and Rasmussen, JO (1957) Conversion-electron and Photon Spectra of Gd 1 and Gd. *Nuclear Physics*, 4: 395–407.

Singleton, C (2009) *Intervention for Dyslexia*. Bracknell: The Dyslexia-Specific Learning Difficulties Trust.

Waugh, D (2013) Presentation to trainee teachers on systematic synthetic phonics. University of Cumbria, 11 October.

7 Fiction

Debbie Myers

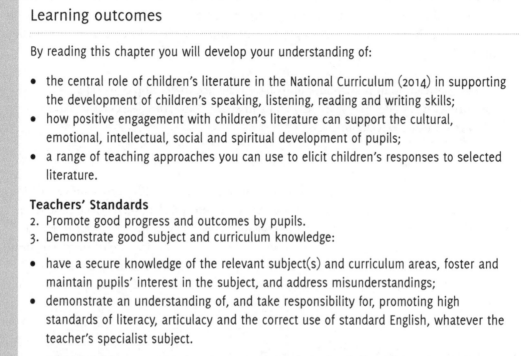

Learning outcomes

By reading this chapter you will develop your understanding of:

- the central role of children's literature in the National Curriculum (2014) in supporting the development of children's speaking, listening, reading and writing skills;
- how positive engagement with children's literature can support the cultural, emotional, intellectual, social and spiritual development of pupils;
- a range of teaching approaches you can use to elicit children's responses to selected literature.

Teachers' Standards
2. Promote good progress and outcomes by pupils.
3. Demonstrate good subject and curriculum knowledge:

- have a secure knowledge of the relevant subject(s) and curriculum areas, foster and maintain pupils' interest in the subject, and address misunderstandings;
- demonstrate an understanding of, and take responsibility for, promoting high standards of literacy, articulacy and the correct use of standard English, whatever the teacher's specialist subject.

5. Adapt teaching to respond to the strengths and needs of all pupils.

Introduction

Fern, a deputy headteacher working in the North East of England, recounted to her staff how, when visiting her neighbours, she was enthusiastically greeted by their pre-school child Mia, who pushed a picturebook into her lap crying, 'Talk to it, talk to it.' Mia was eager to share the wonders of her storybook with each adult she met by asking them to read it to her and with her. Mia would soon join her older siblings, all fluent readers, at the local primary school, fully inculcated into a world of reading and listening to stories. As Mia learns to read independently, she will begin to experience the attitudes, beliefs and values presented to her through the representational systems used in stories. Appleyard (1991) recognises children's literature has an important role to play as an instrument of socialisation, imparting civilising values, and communicating cultural and social norms of behaviour. However, these representations have to be recognised in order for readers to attribute meaning to them, and for those meanings to have significance. Ryan and Anstey (2003) assert: *All readers have an identity which is derived from their life experiences and which provides them with resources as a reader* (p11).

However, many children will enter school lacking such reading experiences. Research undertaken by the National Literacy Trust (2012) shows that children who read in their own time are more likely to be successful in the classroom and beyond school, including entering employment. The National Curriculum places engagement with children's literature at the heart of the 2014 primary English curriculum:

> Through reading in particular, pupils have a chance to develop culturally, emotionally, intellectually, socially and spiritually. Literature, especially, plays a key role in such development.
>
> (DfE, 2013, p13)

The role of the primary school is therefore pivotal in enabling children to achieve this long-term goal, but what can individual class teachers do to ensure that such development can take place? This chapter will enable you to consider how you can inspire in all pupils a love of literature and reading; how you can use fiction to contribute to children's cultural, emotional, intellectual, social and spiritual development; how fiction may be used to contextualise the study of topics and learning activities in a range of cross-curricular subject areas.

Traditional tales

In order to answer this question, it is helpful to reflect upon Fisher's (2000) observation: *In every language and in every culture, story is the fundamental way of organising human experience and understanding of the world* (p1). It is through the oral tradition of story-telling that cultural histories are passed down from generation to generation in the form of fairytales, folktales, fables, myths and legends to promote social cohesion. Storytellers construct a representation of reality that provides a mechanism for transmitting values and ideologies inherent in the words used throughout a narrative, perpetuating cultural reproduction. The inclusion of these tales in recent school curricula – the National Literacy Strategy and the National Curriculum (DfE, 2013) – confirms their continued role as an instrument of pedagogy. Children's literature has long been recognised as a very powerful medium through which to provide readers with a connection between real-life experiences and the imagined worlds of authors (Waugh *et al.*, 2016) and as a newly qualified teacher you will be in a unique and privileged position to support children's positive engagement with literature.

Children's literature

The National Curriculum emphasises the importance of developing children's comprehension skills through engagement with children's literature during Key Stages 1 and 2:

> Comprehension skills develop through pupils' experience of high-quality discussion with the teacher, as well as from reading and discussing a range of stories, poems and non-fiction.
>
> (DfE, 2013, p14)

Providing children with access to a wide range of genres, supported by activities to elicit their responses, is essential to achieving this long-term goal. By introducing children to a world of exciting, high-quality stories and poems, you will enable them to encounter a range of diverse and intriguing characters who will lead them on journeys of self-discovery and personal growth. The author becomes a perfect wizard, captivating readers in a spell whose ingredients include characters, settings, plots, themes and narrative voices (Figure 7.1).

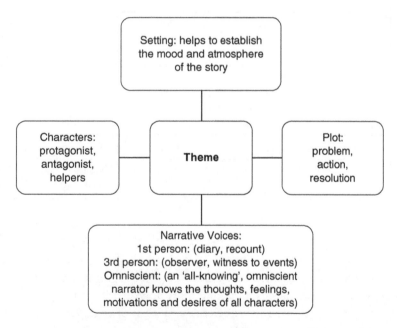

Figure 7.1 Components of a story

The possibilities to immerse young readers in new worlds of adventure in which they can explore ideas, and reflect on their attitudes, beliefs and understanding of human relationships are endless. Table 7.1 provides an overview of the genres that children should gain experience of reading and listening to, during their time in primary school.

Table 7.1 An overview of genres drawn from the Reading Comprehension Guidance of the National Curriculum (DfE, 2013)

Year 1	Year 2	Year 3	Year 4	Year 5	Year 6
Rhymes and poems Fiction	Contemporary and classic poetry Fiction	Poetry (free verse and narrative) Fiction	Poetry (free verse and narrative) Fiction	Poetry (free verse and narrative) Fiction	Poetry (free verse and narrative) Fiction
Fairytales	Fairytales	Fairytales	Fairytales	Traditional stories	Traditional stories
Traditional tales	Traditional tales	Myths and legends	Myths and legends	Myths and legends	Myths and legends
Stories from other cultures and traditions	Stories from other cultures and traditions	Stories from other cultures and traditions	Stories from other cultures and traditions	Modern fiction	Modern fiction
Non-fiction	Non-fiction	Play-scripts	Play-scripts	Fiction from our literary heritage	Fiction from our literary heritage
		Non-fiction	Non-fiction	Books from other cultures and traditions	Books from other cultures and traditions
		Reference books – e.g. dictionaries and textbooks	Reference and textbooks	Play-scripts	Play-scripts
				Non-fiction	Non-fiction
				Reference and textbooks	Reference and textbooks

Activity

- Can you think of a story that had a profound effect upon you as a child?
- Can you list the reasons this particular story appealed to you?
- How could you re-create this experience and sense of engagement for children?

Creating a teaching and learning resource

In answer to the questions above and in order to support the development of your professional knowledge and skills to teach reading comprehension, it will be helpful for you to create a Children's Literature Portfolio (Waugh *et al.*, 2016). This portfolio can be developed throughout your career to provide you with a teaching and learning resource of stories, poems, play-scripts and a range of teaching activities through which to build children's understanding of story structure, language patterns, word functions and narrative devices. If texts are organised chronologically from Early Years Foundation Stage through to Key Stages 1 and 2, they will provide users of the portfolio with a useful overview of genre development while demonstrating progression in themes, enabling you to identify a number of texts relating to a specific theme.

Using picturebooks with children

'And what is the use of a book,' thought Alice 'without pictures or conversation?'

Alice in Wonderland, Lewis Carroll

The picturebook is not a genre in itself but rather it is an effective choice of medium through which to deliver many genres (Lewis, 2001). Nikolajeva and Scott (2006, p20) categorise a picturebook as *an aesthetic whole* in which the recognition, deconstruction and interpretation of visual images and written text are all necessary for the communication of the primary narrative. Iser (1974) introduced the notion of the *implied reader*, asserting that a literary work is only brought to life when a reader engages in the act of reading. Readers are required to supply meaning to fill the gaps between what is written and what is implied but not explicitly written, through a process of anticipation and retrospection. Meek (1988) maintained that picturebooks enable a wide range of reading interpretations because gaps in the text may be informed by meaning drawn from the illustrations; conversely, the reader draws meaning from the text to fill in gaps, questions or dilemmas presented.

Activity: picturebook – *Come Away from the Water, Shirley*

Locate a copy of the picturebook *Come Away from the Water, Shirley* by John Burningham which is suitable for use with a Year 1/2 class.

1. Do the words and pictures in this text tell the same story or is there contradiction?
2. How could you use this picturebook to support the development of children's speaking and listening skills?
3. How could you use it to help children to understand the structure of the story?

(Possible answers can be found at the end of the chapter.)

Case study: *Handa's Surprise*

Yasmin, a Year 1 trainee, was asked to teach the topic of Africa to her Year 1 class during first placement. She chose to read *Handa's Surprise* by Eileen Browne because she felt it would enable her to meet a large number of learning goals by providing opportunities for speaking, listening, reading and role-play supported writing. A video animation of this story is available at **www.youtube.com/watch?v=XyIV_xYioas**.

Using a Big Book format to support the development of children's visual literacy and comprehension skills, she encouraged children to study the front cover to predict what the surprise could be. She asked children to justify their suggestions based on the visual information available to them and their own life experiences. After reading the back-page blurb to the children, Yasmin asked them if this new information had altered anyone's initial views of what the surprise might be. Several children replied that they now had more questions to ask. Yasmin explained the only way to answer these questions was to read the book – generating excitement and anticipation in her pupils.

In this story the main character Handa sets off to visit her friend Akeyo in a neighbouring village in Kenya, with a basket of delicious fruits. Unknown to her, a selection of animals steal fruits as she passes by. Near the end of her journey a tethered goat breaks free, charges into a tree and knocks a bunch of tangerines into the empty basket. Yasmin used the technique of hot-seating to enable children to question Handa about what might have happened to the original contents of her basket. This story progresses because Handa asks many questions throughout her journey; drawing on this feature of the narrative, Yasmin created a teaching focus around the use of question marks within speech bubbles and to show when dialogue occurred in the story. Children then wrote their own questions to an animal asking why they stole a fruit and what they did with it. Yasmin also asked the children to work in small groups to create three-dimensional maps of the story, including stick puppet characters to represent the animals so that they could map key events in the story and re-enact these to generate talk for learning (Dawes, 2008). Children created animal masks in preparation for a role-play supported writing task in which they would reply to the questions as if they were the animals. The children constructed simple fact files for a particular animal, naming and describing its appearance, habitat, preferred type of food and how it could escape from predators.

Curriculum link

The National Curriculum states:

6.3 Teachers should develop pupils' reading and writing in all subjects to support their acquisition of knowledge.

(DfE, 2013, p10)

Stories such as *Handa's Surprise* may be used to contextualise learning activities across a range of curricular subjects.

Numeracy Fruits from the story were sorted by colour and shape, then ordered according to size and weight. Pictograms were constructed to show the favourite fruits of children in class.

PSGE and Geography Yasmin used a map of the world and a globe to show children the locations of the African continent and Kenya relative to the United Kingdom. She introduced children to a new culture in which many children have a different way of life. Children considered how the hot climate provides habitats for physically different types of animals and fruits found in the story. The children considered how they could travel across great distances and how the animals had adapted to live in such a different place.

Science Yasmin took the opportunity to talk about healthy lifestyle, diets and exercise. She brought in a selection of featured fruits, enabling children to handle them and to generate sensory poems using their five senses to describe the appearances, smells, textures and tastes of each fruit. She then chopped the fruit in half so that children could undertake observational drawings of the resulting cross-sections. She also pointed out that Handa was physically active, walking everywhere each day and how important this is in maintaining physical health.

Technology: Children were able to create fruit salads and smoothies after looking at recipes online. This activity could contribute to children's experience of early enterprise.

Research focus: reading the pictures in stories

Sinatra (1986, p5 cited in Arizpe and Styles, 2003, p97) observes that as children's visual literacy skills develop, they have an increasing ability to engage in the *active reconstruction of past visual experience with incoming visual messages to obtain meaning*.

Additionally, Barthes (1974) identified a series of semiotic codes that readers have to learn to recognise in order to interpret and construct meaning from a text presented in printed or electronic format. These include textual or visual symbols used as clues to create a sense of anticipation and suspense, the presentation of dilemmas to be faced by characters, details of place and time in which the story is set, as well as metaphors and intertextual references creating links to other narratives.

Siegal (1995, 1996) proposed the notion of transmediation to explain the physical processes through which readers of picturebooks alternate their attention between verbal and visual sign-systems, presented as text and images, to construct, interpret and create integrated meanings from words and pictures (Figure 7.2).

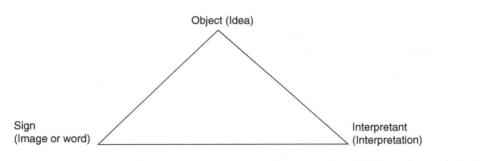

Figure 7.2 A simplified view of transmediation

This theory of transmediation supports social-constructivist theories of learning, exemplified by Vygotsky's (1986) observation that individuals construct understanding of their physical and sociocultural worlds through the development of language and the interpretation of shared, but sophisticated sign-systems.

Fairytales, fractured and subverted fairytales

Children's earliest encounters with literature may include listening to derivatives of classical folktales and fairytales. In EYFS and Reception, children are encouraged to engage with these tales through participatory pedagogies including oral retelling, role-play and play with puppets, enabling them to join in with repeated phrases and dialogue such as 'Once upon a time', and 'I'll huff and I'll puff and I'll blow your house down' and to sequence key events in these tales.

These activities will be extended during Years 1 and 2, enabling children to identify recurring literary language to create effects, to make predictions or to infer what might happen next; to write simple character profiles drawing on visual and descriptive evidence from the stories they are hearing, reading and interpreting. Children will also be invited to compare and contrast the behaviour of characters with their own responses to life experiences. As children progress through primary school, they will have opportunities to rewrite some fairytales from different perspectives and to subvert and transform the genre through their writing activities. Retellings of fairytales can be used with pupils to show how society's values and views change by providing a useful interplay between the already-given story, the contemporary narrative and the relationship between past and currently held beliefs, and attitudes held by members of that society.

Activity: traditional fairytale

Select a favourite traditional fairytale that portrays human characters. Look carefully at the illustrations, dialogue and the comparative adjectives used to describe the human characters.

- Which characters are active and which ones are passive?
- Which characters are strong, which ones are weak?
- How are binary oppositions used in this fairytale to create representations of gender stereotypes?
- What kind of ideology of gender is being promoted in this story?
- How could you address gender bias?

(Possible answers can be found at the end of the chapter.)

Case study: gender stereotypes

NQT Samantha decided to probe her Year 3 pupils' recognition of gender stereotypes using the story of *The Paper-bag Princess*. She wanted to see if children really do recognise and draw on the symbolism and codes identified by Barthes (1974) to help them to construct understanding of stories and the positioning of boys and girls. She asked children to create drawings of a princess before and after reading the story to them. She asked the following questions.

Before the reading

- If I said I was going to read a fairytale to you, what kind of characters would you expect to hear about?
- Can you name some of the characters from fairytales?
- Who would be brave? Why do you think this?
- Who would be strong? Why do you think this?
- Who would need help? Why do you think this?
- Can you all draw a labelled diagram of a princess?
- What kinds of adjectives will you use to describe her?

Introducing the story

- What do you predict will happen in this story?
- What makes you think this?
- How did the front cover help you to predict the events in the story?

During the reading

- Is this story as you expected?
- Why/why not?

→

- Do you think the words and pictures tell the story in the same way?

- Is Princess Elizabeth behaving as you expected? Please explain.

- What do you think about Prince Ronald's reaction to Elizabeth?

- What do you think about the last picture?

After the reading

- Did you enjoy the story?

- Did the story end in the way you expected?

- Has your view of a princess changed as a result of reading this story?

- Can you all draw a labelled diagram of a princess?

- What kinds of adjectives will you use to describe her?

Readers' responses showed that yes, both girls and boys were responding to the codes employed by the author/illustrator. However, they had all misunderstood the reasons why the Princess had been rejected by the Prince. Rejection occurred because the Prince was embarrassed at being rescued by a girl; the children all thought he rejected Princess Elizabeth because of her unkempt appearance, which may reflect contemporary society's preoccupation with image and appearance. Samantha made the following observations to share with her NQT mentor.

- **Hermeneutic code** Readers were able to answer questions drawing on the clues presented in the pictures and text to predict what the story might be about, what will happen next and how problems will be resolved. They were surprised when the story did not conform to the usual pattern of a fairytale.

- **Cultural code** The use of love heart motifs in the first double-page spread confirms marriage to be the Princess's destiny. However, expectations are challenged when a dragon kidnaps the Prince.

- **Semic code** Though the main character, Princess Elizabeth, wore a dirty paper-bag after her royal robes were destroyed during her battle with the dragon, the children continued to recognise her as royal because she always wore her crown – the symbol of royalty.

- **Proairetic code** The significance of Elizabeth's actions is revealed as the story ends. An adult interpretation recognises that she has gained her independence by subverting the usual pattern of fairytales – outwitting a fiendish dragon, only to be rejected by the Prince she rescued, who is embarrassed at this subverted resolution. She realises she can manage very well on her own. However, the children did not realise that gender

→

stereotypes were being deliberately subverted. They thought she was brave and clever, but had ended up looking a mess. They thought the Prince was unpleasant and should have said thanks for the rescue, but that it was okay for him to reject her if he didn't like the way she looked.

- **Symbolic code:** The usual pattern of binary oppositions (male/female, active/passive, rescuer/in need of rescue) is disrupted. Though the heroine, Elizabeth, discarded her crown and skipped off optimistically into an unknown future, young readers assumed that she had been rejected because of her appearance.

Activity: subverted fairytale

Several authors have attempted to subvert gender stereotypes and to challenge readers' expectations of fairytales.

- Map the key events in the traditional fairytale *Cinderella*.
- Read Laurence Anholt's *Cinderboy*.
- Compare how this author has attempted to reverse the usual pattern of this story.
- Can you use the features of a different fairytale to inform the creation of a subversion of a favourite fairytale or a new fairytale relevant to the concerns of a contemporary audience?

Research focus: ideology

Zipes (1997) identifies the presence of power and manipulation operating in children's literature resulting from the ideological preconceptions underlying the construction of the child reader as a literary child, despite its intention to give the child a sense of autonomy. More recently, Gruner (2009) has suggested: *one origin of children's literature is in didacticism, and learning and pedagogy continue to be important in much of the literature we provide for children today* (p216).

A reader's perceptions of reality may be influenced by the representational systems operating within the society from which they have emerged, such that the beliefs and attitudes towards a marginalised group become represented in an exaggerated or over-simplified way reducing them to stereotypes (Kortenhaus and Demarest, 1993). If equality is considered to be one of the most important founding principles of a democratic society, it is essential that its young citizens are explicitly taught to understand how and why texts are constructed in order for them to recognise the values and ideologies inherent in a wide range of reading materials and multi-modal media (Gilbert and Gubar, 1979).

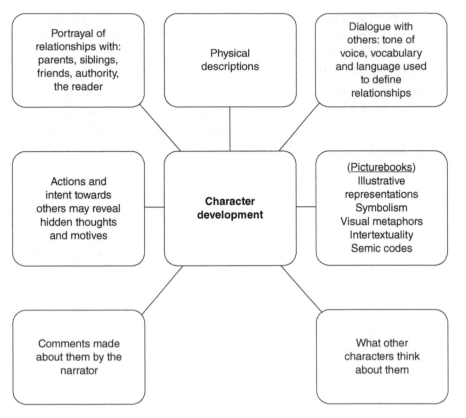

Figure 7.3 How characterisation is achieved in fiction and picturebooks

Building character profiles

How do real-life and fictional characters deal with issues? Authors and illustrators of stories and picturebooks employ a number of strategies to portray characters and to show their growth and development, as shown in Figure 7.3. As the case study below illustrates, supporting children to observe and deconstruct characters' responses to narrative events helps them develop critical literacy skills that enable them to recognise the presentation of stereotypical images, attitudes and behaviour.

Case study: difficult issues: prejudice-based bullying

Trainee Gareth was asked to plan a topic focusing on aspects of the Second World War in preparation for his second school-based training placement with a Year 5/6 class. He initially felt this topic provided opportunities to carry out enquiry-based learning to critically explore the issues of prejudice-based bullying that led to the Holocaust. In order to raise children's awareness of the ugliness of discrimination that fails to recognise the rich diversity of humanity, he focused on the historical persecution of peoples of differing faith, Judaism, race, ethnic origin, disability, age, gender and sexual orientation in Europe, by the Nazi regime, from 1938 to 1945, leading up to and during the Second World War.

He chose several texts to enable readers to appreciate the consequences of regime-led, prejudice-based bullying on the lives of people, including *The Diary of Anne Frank*, *The Boy in the Striped Pyjamas*, *Erika's Story* and *Rose Blanche*. *The Diary of Anne Frank*, which is of course not fictional, was central to the topic providing readers with evidence of first-hand experiences of the effects on a young schoolgirl's life in war-torn Europe. He asked the children to reflect on the statements: *Peace in our time* (attributed to Neville Chamberlain) – to explore the dangers of appeasing bullies – and *All that is needed for evil to triumph is for good men to do nothing* (attributed to Edmund Burke). Towards the end of the topic they revisited these statements to inform their preparation for a debate around Edmund Burke's statement.

Pupils developed research skills by using websites and archives to inform the creation of posters: 'It's Not Fair – We Are Human Too' outlining the consequences of the introduction of the Anti-Jewish Decree on children's lives. Pupils looked at bias and the use of propaganda in the media to present views that influence attitudes and encourage discriminatory behaviours. Pupils created their own newspaper reports of events such as book burning, 1933, Kristallnacht, 1938 and transportation to camps such as Westerbork and Auschwitz, using online newspaper archives and museum archives. Children were encouraged to respond to such events in a series of poetry workshops entitled 'Kristallnacht! Oh Night of Breaking Glass' and 'One Small Suitcase'. A hot-seating technique was used, with Gareth and his teaching assistant in role as Anne and Peter, to enable children to ask questions about real-life events. The class attended a special primary school screening of the film *The Boy in the Striped Pyjamas* that took place to commemorate Holocaust Memorial Day.

Computing

The software package Crazy Talk was used to create an animated avatar to express the viewpoints of Anne Frank. The children recorded their own narrative and embedded this into their own video-clips. Several children chose to animate images of the diary itself to give Anne's words their voices. Viewers of the resulting videos found them very moving.

Website links

www.annefrank.org

www.bbc.co.uk/annefrank/timeline.shtml

Additional texts

Gareth also used the story of *Rose Blanche* by Ian McEwan and Roberto Innocenti as a useful teaching instrument to show pupils an example of a fictional character who finds the courage to stand up to hatred. His topic research led him to discover the existence of The White Rose

$\longrightarrow$

Society – a group of German students who engaged in passive resistance to the Nazi regime – the literal translation of Rose Blanche is White Rose. He decided to link this to his topic to show children that even in difficult circumstances it is important to behave fairly if there is to be social justice for all and not just a dominant social group.

Stories that explore the effects of the Second World War on children in England from the perspective of evacuees include *Doodlebug Alley* and *Goodnight Mr Tom*.

Challenging prejudice-based bullying

Reading a text provides a safe *emotional space, which the child can inhabit largely on his or her own terms* (Stephens, 1992, p10). Stories can be highly effective in enabling the transmission of contemporary concerns about a range of issues to a young readership. O'Neill (2010) asserts that all forms of children's literature, from fairytales, traditional tales to post-modern picturebooks, function as cultural artefacts, facilitating the transmission of the attitudes and values of the societies that produce them. She observes that it is post-modern picturebooks and contemporary fiction that encourage young readers to *question the status quo* by enabling them to recognise those who are disadvantaged and marginalised and to promote social justice in contemporary society (O'Neill, 2010, p41). For example, an author may construct a plot and characters in which norms of behaviour are set in contexts to challenge readers' assumptions so that new insights are gained and fresh interpretations are drawn. It will, therefore, be your role as the guiding adult to help children to make sense of their reading experiences.

Research focus: new literacies

Surveys of young people's reading preferences outside of class were carried out by the National Literacy Trust (2012) in 2005, 2010 and 2012. The researchers reported that the proportion of children reading eBooks had doubled from 5.6 per cent in 2010 to 11.9 per cent in 2012; contributions to blogs remained steady from 16.1 per cent in 2010 to 17.1 per cent; visits to websites decreased from 63.8 per cent in 2005 to 53.2 per cent in 2012, and the numbers of young people using email fell from 52.3 per cent to 46.8 per cent in 2012. However, use of social networking sites increased from 48.8 per cent in 2010 to 51.1 per cent in 2012; text messaging increased from 61.0 per cent in 2005 to 68.4 per cent. These results suggest that young people spend a greater proportion of their own time using technology to communicate within their social groups rather than to read literature. Moreover, they have developed competence in the skills required to use the new literacies of blogging, text messaging, emailing, and Internet browsing not in their classroom environments but in their homes and sociocultural environments through peer observation and instruction, self-instruction and trial and error.

→

The increased emphasis learners place on communicating with others, in their lives beyond the classroom, presents teachers with new ways to develop collaborative, peer-based learning relationships that will support classroom-based learning through the production of new kinds of texts (Burnett *et al.*, 2006).

Case study: reading blogs

Jo, a Year 2 trainee, used an online blogging forum, hosted by her training school's learning platform, to facilitate collaboration between members of her Year 5 reading groups. This forum provided pupils with an online medium through which they could compare and exchange views about their home reading material. One group compared a selection of picturebooks by author Anthony Browne, including *Hansel and Gretel*, *The Tunnel*, *Into the Forest*, *Voices in the Park*, *Zoo* and *Gorilla*, while the remaining groups of six children compared the novel of a single author (e.g. Roald Dahl, Dick King-Smith, Jacqueline Wilson) to compare views via the reading blog instead of their reading journals. Pupils acknowledged that although they did not share their reading journals with each other, they did like to read each other's blogs. Jo was able to monitor children's comments and uploaded a post alerting children to the website below where they could 'Meet the Authors' and read the answers to a selection of questions posed to them by children: **www.bbc.co.uk/learning/schoolradio/subjects/english/meet_the_authors**.

Activity: reading blogs

Consider how you could introduce the use of reading blogs with your class to enhance children's engagement in reading.

How could they be used to support reading events or English activities throughout the year? (Identify some possible national/school events.)

(Suggestions can be found at the end of the chapter.)

Research focus

Whitehead (2002) observes that children *develop sophisticated abilities to read pictures, symbols and icons at an early age* (p43) in order to construct understanding as they engage in acts of interpretation in transaction with a variety of printed textual forms. When making meaning from printed text, the reader proceeds via a linear pathway, decoding and making meaning from the textual information presented. Users of on-screen information read images, graphics, symbols and text, and download sound-files and media-files as they click

→

in and out of links. Visual literacy skills dominate these multimodal texts that enable genre boundaries to be breached.

Reading and interacting with electronic textual forms whether on hand-held or touch-screen devices requires users to decode information presented in a variety of forms, to make meaning from this information and to manipulate and respond to a range of stimuli presented as a range of visual and audio semiotic codes: signs, symbols, alphabetical and numerical codes. Luke and Freebody (1999) proposed 'The Four Resources Model' to categorise the capabilities required to read multimodal texts, including decoding, meaning-making, using text functionally and text analysis. This model aims to provide a framework to support the identification of meaningful learning outcomes and to facilitate the integration of new literacies into classroom learning environments.

Whole school and class libraries

The National Curriculum states:

> 6.3 Pupils should be taught to read fluently, understand extended prose (both fiction and non-fiction) and be encouraged to read for pleasure. Schools should do everything to promote wider reading.
>
> They should provide library facilities and set ambitious expectations for reading at home.

(DfE, 2013, p10)

A study by Edmunds and Bauserman (2006) into what motivates children to read established five key factors. These were choice, personal interests, access to books, characteristics of books (illustrations, humour) and the active involvement of others (reading buddies, book groups, parents, supportive adults hearing reading in school). The development of school library facilities and a programme to support reading groups will facilitate such motivation.

As a result of reading this chapter, you should have developed a good understanding of the ways in which stories can be used with children to enable them to explore a range of ideas, views, attitudes and beliefs in a safe and stimulating learning environment.

You should also be able to appreciate how the use of stories provides an excellent medium through which to contextualise a variety of topic themes, to prepare a variety of teaching strategies that support the delivery and integration of three models of teaching and learning: experiential learning (Kolb, 1984), dialogic teaching (Alexander, 2008) and collaborative learning, enabling you to develop valuable professional knowledge, skills and experiences in accordance with the Teachers' Standards (DfE, 2011).

Learning outcomes review

You should now understand:

- the central role of children's literature in the National Curriculum (2014) in supporting the development of children's speaking, listening, reading and writing skills;
- how positive engagement with children's literature can support the cultural, emotional, intellectual, social and spiritual development of pupils;
- a range of teaching approaches you can use to elicit children's responses to selected literature.

Self-assessment questions
1. Why is it important to introduce children to a range of literary genres?
2. What is the value of picturebooks?
3. What is the place of new literacies in the primary classroom?

Possible answers to activities

Picturebook – *Come Away from the Water, Shirley*

1. This story uses counterpoint – disparity between what is said in the text and what the pictures reveal. This gives additional layers of meaning to children's reading experiences.

2. You can ask children to act out the story in small groups using simple props. This will stimulate talk for learning as children recount their understanding of the narrative. Observe the strategies children invent to show counterpoint. You can hot-seat characters, placing them in the spotlight so that they can be questioned. Sometimes the teacher can take on the role of a character if children are inexperienced, lacking confidence or knowledge.

3. You should develop knowledge of a range of strategies to help children to map the key events in a story. These can include creating storyboards, comic strips, a story road map or three-dimensional story map with puppets.

Traditional fairytale

You should help children to understand that in the past, flat, one-dimensional characterisation was deliberate to ensure an audience listening to the story or a child

(Continued)

(Continued)

reader could easily recognise which characters were good, bad, rich, poor, in need of help or capable of giving help.

You could ask children to retell the story, reversing some of the roles to represent a more democratic society in which girls help boys so that together they defeat threats and overcome challenges.

Reading blogs

Pupils can critically review some of the following:

- home-reading books;
- class novels;
- library book choices;
- texts used in class to support topics;
- reading group books.

In a reading forum children can contribute their responses to the stories they read as the plots twist and turn and the characters develop. To encourage participation, teachers can set a specific task – for example, some of the following ideas can provide an initial stimulus.

- Predict what might happen in the story before you begin reading. Then, half-way through, consider whether your expectations have changed.
- Write a description of the main character – their appearance, the way they talk, their behaviour and relationships with other characters.
- Write a diary entry from the perspective of a character, at a given point in the story.
- Write some advice to a character in trouble.
- Write a new blurb for the back cover.
- Write an entry evaluating the book for other readers.
- Write an alternative ending.
- Choose a descriptive passage and make a list of examples of vivid imagery – e.g. similes, metaphors, alliteration, personification, noun phrases, etc.
- List the words and phrases used to create a sense of atmosphere.
- Write down some words you had difficulty reading and had not met before. Find their meanings in a dictionary and record them.
- Write about your favourite part of a book and why you liked it.
- Write some questions you would like to ask the author.

Further reading

For chapters on several aspects of children's literature, see:

Waugh, D, Neaum, S and Waugh, R (2016) *Transforming Primary QTS: Children's Literature in Primary Schools* (2nd edn). London: Learning Matters/SAGE.

References

Alexander, R (2008) *Towards Dialogic Teaching*. York: Dialogos.

Appleyard, JA (1991) *Becoming a Reader: The Experience of Fiction from Childhood to Adulthood*. Cambridge: Cambridge University Press.

Arizpe, E and Styles, M (eds) (2003) *Children Reading Pictures: Interpreting Visual Texts*. London: Routledge.

Barthes, R (1974) *S/Z: An Essay*. New York: Hill & Wang.

Burnett, C, Dickinson, P, Myers, J and Merchant, G (2006) Digital connections: transforming literacy in the primary school. *Cambridge Journal of Education*, 36(1): 11–29.

Dawes, L (2008) *The Essential Speaking and Listening: Talk for Learning at KS2*. London: Routledge.

Department for Education (DfE) (2011) *The Teachers' Standards*. London: DfE Publications.

Department for Education DfE (2013) *The National Curriculum in England: Key Stages 1 and 2 Framework Document*. London: DfE Publications.

Edmunds, KM and Bauserman, KL (2006) What teachers can learn about reading motivation through conversations with children. *The Reading Teacher*, 59(5): 414– 24. Available at: **http://olms.cte.jhu.edu/olms/data/resource/4740/RT-59-5Motivation%20Edmunds.pdf** (accessed 13 June 2014).

Fisher, R (2000) Stories are for thinking: creative ways to share reading, in R Fisher and M Williams (eds), *Unlocking Literacy* (1st edn). London: David Fulton, pp1–14.

Gilbert, SM and Gubar, S (1979) *The Madwoman in the Attic*. New Haven, CT: Yale University Press.

Gruner, ER (2009) Teach the children: education and knowledge in recent children's fantasy. *Children's Literature*, 37: 216–35.

Iser, W (1974) *The Implied Reader*. Baltimore, MD: The Johns Hopkins University Press.

Kolb, D (1984) *Experiential Learning: Turning Experience into Learning*. Upper Saddle River, NJ: Prentice Hall.

Kortenhaus, CM and Demarest, J (1993) Gender role stereo-typing in children's literature: an update. *Sex Roles: A Journal of Research*, 28(3): 219–32.

Lewis, D (2001) *Reading Contemporary Picturebooks: Picturing Text*. London: RoutledgeFalmer.

Luke, A and Freebody, P (1999) Further notes on the four resource model. Available at: **www. readingonline.org/research/lukefreebody.html** (accessed 30 April 2014).

Meek, M (1988) *How Texts Teach What Readers Learn*. Stroud: Thimble Press.

National Literacy Trust (2012) *Literacy: State of the Nation: A Picture of Literacy in the UK Today*. London: National Literacy Trust.

Nikolajeva, M and Scott, C (2006) *How Picturebooks Work*. London: Routledge.

O'Neill, K (2010) Once upon today: teaching for social justice with post-modern picturebooks. *Children's Literature in Education*, 41: 40–51.

Ryan, M and Anstey, M (2003) Identity and text: developing self-conscious readers. *Journal of Language and Literacy*, 26(1): 9–22.

Siegal, M (1995) More than words: the generative power of transmediation for learning. *Canadian Journal of Education*, 20(4): 455–75.

Siegal, M (1996) Rereading the signs: multimodal transformations in the field of literacy education. *Language Arts*, 84(1): 65–77.

Sinatra, R (1986) *Visual Literacy Connections to Thinking, Reading and Writing*. Springfield, IL: C Thomas.

Stephens, J (1992) *Language and Ideology in Children's Fiction*. Harlow: Longman Group UK.

Vygotsky, L (1986) *Thought and Language*. Cambridge, MA: Harvard University Press.

Waugh, D, Neaum, S and Waugh, R (2016) *Transforming Primary QTS: Children's Literature in Primary Schools* (2nd edn). London: Learning Matters/SAGE.

Whitehead, M (2002) *Developing Language and Literacy with Young Children* (3rd edn). London: Paul Chapman Publishing.

Zipes, JD (1997) *Happily Ever After: Fairytales, Children and the Culture Industry*. New York: Routledge.

8 Poetry

Holly Dyer

Learning outcomes

By reading this chapter you will develop your understanding of:

- what children need to understand about poetry;
- what you need to know as a primary teacher in order to teach the 2014 English National Curriculum;
- some of the challenges you face when you teach poetry;
- some approaches to teaching poetry.

Teachers' Standards

3. Demonstrate good subject and curriculum knowledge:

- have a secure knowledge of the relevant subject(s) and curriculum areas, foster and maintain pupils' interest in the subject, and address misunderstandings;
- demonstrate a critical understanding of developments in the subject and curriculum areas, and promote the value of scholarship;
- demonstrate an understanding of, and take responsibility for, promoting high standards of literacy, articulacy and the correct use of standard English, whatever the teacher's specialist subject.

Introduction

For many teachers, poetry is a subject they would quite readily hide in a box at the back of the literacy cupboard and forget all about. However, the 2014 National Curriculum places a particular emphasis upon the teaching and learning of poetry in both Key Stages. Children are expected to read and write poetry, learn it by heart, recognise it in different forms, perform and read it aloud and, perhaps most importantly, enjoy it. Supporting the development of poetry in the classroom can be an overwhelming task for teachers, particularly when so many feel their own knowledge of poetry is limited. Teresa Cremin (Cremin *et al.*, 2009) has researched and written widely on the subject of teachers and poetry, and concludes that few teachers have sufficient knowledge and understanding to teach primary poetry effectively. An Ofsted report in 2007, *Poetry in Schools*, depicted a similar picture, and suggested that a key issue with primary poetry teaching was teachers' own lack of knowledge. In addition, it highlighted poetry teaching as the weakest aspect of the English curriculum in terms of teaching.

Despite this, Hughes (2007) suggests that effective use of poetry is highly beneficial for children's literacy development, since it *encourages an economy and precision in language that transfers to other types of oral and written communication*. Ofsted noted the important role poetry plays in demonstrating high-quality use of language and its importance in giving meaning to our experiences. Dymoke (2003) highlights two differing attitudes towards poetry in schools. She notes that while some teachers and critics believe poetry should be central to the curriculum, others treat it with suspicion, often arising from their own negative personal experiences of poetry in school.

This chapter aims to consider in more detail exactly why poetry is so important, and the benefits it has for children's literacy development. It will look more closely at the specific requirements of the curriculum in relation to poetry, and will explore some examples of how this can be put into practice. Additionally, you will be encouraged to consider what you need to know as a teacher in order to support development of poetry, and consider some approaches to the teaching of poetry.

The importance and value of poetry

Recent years have seen a huge emphasis on improving reading and a push for the development of phonics throughout Key Stages 1 and 2. For teachers in Year 2 and Year 6 there has also been pressure to focus on raising standards of writing in order to meet the high expectations of the new interim assessment frameworks. It might be suggested that these emphases have resulted in poetry being overlooked, despite its many benefits for learning. Teachers sometimes question why they must be expected to teach poetry, and often feel it is an additional unnecessary stress – just another tick-box on a never-ending list.

Ofsted argues that poetry is fundamental in developing children's literacy and is essential in demonstrating high-quality language at work. Poems are a tool for modelling effective use of language in a wide range of contexts, ranging from humorous, silly poems to more serious, meaningful expressions of life experiences. Poetry allows freedom of expression and creativity alongside the exploration of the technicalities of the English language, and allows children to be creative and explore the use of words in written language. When used effectively, it can be an engaging way of supporting a number of aspects of learning including:

- development of language and expansion of vocabulary;
- understanding of rhyme;
- development of phonemic awareness;

- development of writing;
- remembering of information.

Development of language and expansion of vocabulary

In order to progress successfully in literacy, teachers must support children in the development and expansion of their vocabulary. Waugh *et al.* (2016) assert that *poems are a wonderful way of meeting and experimenting with vocabulary* (p191). The National Curriculum has an expectation that children will acquire a wide vocabulary as they progress throughout Key Stages 1 and 2, and you have learned about vocabulary development in Chapter 3. Poetry is an excellent way of supporting this, and poems can be used in order to explore word classes and literary devices including similes and metaphors, and to demonstrate the use of rhyme. In order to employ these aspects of language successfully in their writing, children need models of how to use them effectively, and poems can be excellent tools for this.

Crystal (1998) highlights the importance of developing language and vocabulary through creative language play, and it is clear that poems give rise to opportunities to play with language as part of the creative process. Poetry comes in many forms, and allows room for creativity without too many restrictions. Poems can be long or short, humorous or serious, rhyming or non-rhyming, elaborate or simple. It is essential that children experience a range of types of poems in order to develop an awareness of the variety of ways in which language can be used. 'The Highwayman', by Alfred Noyes, is an example of an old poem which demonstrates the effective use of many aspects of language. Often, teachers choose humorous poems to share with children, including popular ones from Spike Milligan or Roald Dahl. Although these are excellent poems which have a place in poetry teaching, older poems such as Noyes's 'The Highwayman' or even Tennyson's 'The Eagle' can often challenge children to a deeper level in terms of vocabulary development, and additionally push children to look more closely at understanding the meaning of language. 'The Highwayman' is a complex poem, which must be carefully used, but the rich language and use of old-fashioned terms make it an excellent tool for demonstrating quality language at work. Older poems often use more archaic language which requires the reader to investigate more closely the meaning of the poem.

These two lines from Tennyson's 'The Eagle' can be used to draw attention to the power of using verbs and adjectives effectively in writing:

> He clasps the crag with crooked hands
>
> The wrinkled sea beneath him crawls

In order to progress in writing primary pupils must demonstrate an ability to use adjectives and teachers often repeatedly push them to achieve this. Whole lessons can be focused on using adjectives in writing. While it is important that children learn this, the exaggerated focus on adjectives can often lead to the overuse of adjectives, whereby the 'dark, shadowed figure' becomes the 'tall, dark, scary, handsome, shadowed figure', as children attempt to use every adjective they know to make their writing more interesting. Tennyson's poem uses adjectives carefully but effectively, and teachers can use this poem, and others, to demonstrate the importance of word choice.

Understanding of rhyme and development of phonemic awareness

Poetry is also an effective tool for developing children's understandings of rhyme and phonemic awareness. It is one of the first forms of language that young children experience, through nursery rhymes, and very young children are capable of responding to rhyme and rhythm through clapping and rocking long before they can articulate language (Waugh *et al.*, 2016). Research by Bryant *et al.* (1990) demonstrated a correlation between children's sensitivity to rhyme and successful acquisition of reading skills. With the recent push for phonics development, and the focus on improving the teaching of reading, poetry has seemingly faded in its significance in the classroom. However, poetry has enormous value in supporting children to learn to read, and the use of rhyming poems is particularly effective in supporting phonemic awareness (Bryant *et al.*, 1990).

Research focus: the link between understanding rhyme and successful reading and spelling

Early experiences of poetry support children's reading development, and research has demonstrated correlations between the understanding of rhyme and successful reading and spelling. Research has shown that there is a link between children's sensitivity to rhyme and the successful acquisition of reading skills.

A longitudinal study conducted by Bryant *et al.* (1990) investigated children's linguistic capabilities at age three and four, and later assessed their reading and spelling capabilities, aged six and seven. It has been argued that encounters with rhyme at a young age are beneficial in aiding the development of phonological awareness, and that children who have developed an awareness of sounds and the poetry of language are frequently more successful in reading, writing and spelling. Research by Goswami (1990) supports this notion that pre-reading rhyming skills can be a key indicator of reading development and acquisition of key reading skills. It is therefore important that poetry is used effectively throughout the primary curriculum, and especially significant that rhyme is used alongside the use of phonics to support reading development.

Development of writing

Goswami (1990) asserts that children who have developed an awareness of sounds and the poetry of language are frequently more successful in reading, writing and spelling. Poetry is therefore useful in supporting the development of writing. Writing poetry allows children to write expressively and, unlike many other forms of writing included in the curriculum, allows for creativity in writing. Allowing children to write expressively and creatively in the form of a poem gives purpose and meaning to writing. One of the key issues in teaching writing is motivating boys to write, and it has been suggested that an essential aspect of developing boys' writing is to encourage writing for purpose and audience (DfES, 2005).

The 2014 curriculum requires children to read poetry aloud and recite poetry, and encouraging children to write their own poems and then recite them may be an effective way of encouraging purposeful writing. Children then have a purpose for their writing: to perform it. This also gives them ownership of the poetry they are reciting. In addition, children can have the opportunity to employ techniques and use language they have previously explored in poems, and use the models of poetry they have experienced in their own writing.

Using poetry for remembering information

Rhyming poetry is an effective learning tool for memory. Waugh *et al.* (2016) discuss the everyday power of rhyme in remembering information. Rhymes can be used throughout the curriculum. For example, there are numerous rhymes used to support children in learning mathematical rules:

Hey diddle diddle, the median's the middle,

You add, then divide for the mean,

The mode is the one you see the most,

And the range is the difference between.

(Unknown)

Poetry in the National Curriculum

The National Curriculum (DfE, 2013) has specific requirements for the teaching of poetry. There are a number of key features which appear throughout Key Stages 1 and 2, including listening to and discussing poetry, reciting it by heart, performing it and writing it. Some examples of the expectations follow.

Children in KS1 should:

- listen to and discuss a wide range of poems;
- appreciate rhymes and poems, and recite some by heart;
- express views on poetry;
- write poetry.

In Year 2, they should continue to build up a repertoire of poems learnt by heart, and begin to recite some with appropriate intonation to make the meaning clear.

Children in lower Key Stage 2 should:

- listen to and discuss a wide range of poetry;
- develop understanding and enjoyment of poetry;
- recognise different forms of poetry;
- prepare poems and play-scripts to read aloud and perform, showing understanding through intonation, tone, volume and action.

Children in upper KS2 should additionally:

- read and discuss a wide range of poetry;
- read a wider range of poetry aloud;
- learn a wider range of poetry by heart;
- express views about a wide range of poetry;
- use knowledge of poetry to support reading and writing;
- recognise simple recurring literary language in poems;
- prepare poems and play-scripts to read aloud and perform, showing understanding through intonation, tone and volume so that the meaning is clear to an audience;
- write poetry.

The key themes which run through both Key Stages include listening and responding to a variety of poems, enjoying poetry, reciting some poetry and writing it. Children need to develop an ability to express their opinions and views on different poems, and explain why, and by the end of Key Stage 2 should be able to use their knowledge of poetry gained throughout the primary years in order to support the reading and writing of poetry.

Research focus: the need for teachers to know and understand poetry

Cremin (2011) researched teachers and reading, and questioned how many teachers read enough poetry, or possessed sufficient knowledge about poetry to teach it effectively. In 2008, Cremin *et al.* questioned 1,200 teachers about their reading habits, and less than 2.5 per cent claimed to read poetry for pleasure. She asked them about their childhood reading experiences and 1.5 per cent recalled choosing to read poetry for pleasure. Cremin argues that in order for children to develop as active readers, and consequently as writers, teachers must effectively model their own love of reading. If teachers are to teach poetry effectively and share a variety of poems with children, they must possess a good knowledge of children's poetry. Without this knowledge, teachers will be unable to share with children a variety of different types of poetry with children.

The teachers involved in the study were also asked to name six poets, but only 10 per cent could do this. Cremin's research has been reinforced by Ofsted (2007), who noted that teachers' lack of knowledge of poetry was a key underlying factor in the underdevelopment of poetry in schools. Cremin's research has shown that successful primary teachers are knowledgeable about children's literature. This must include poetry. The 2014 curriculum requires children to experience a range of types of poetry, and to listen to and discuss poetry. Unless teachers develop their knowledge of poetry and their awareness of a range of poets, children will continue to receive a limited diet of poets and types of poetry.

Activity: your knowledge of poetry

Write down the names of six poems and six poets. Ask yourself the following questions:

- Do you find this a difficult task?
- Does your list contain a range of types of poems, such as narrative poems, humorous poems, haiku, free verse?
- Could the poems in your list be used to challenge the children in your class and support their learning?
- How could the poems in your list be used to support children's literacy development?
- How could these poems be used outside of English lessons?

Challenge yourself to extend your knowledge of poems and poets. Continue to build up a collection of poems and poets you could use in teaching.

Case study: rhyme and movement

Barbara, a Year 1 teacher, wanted to explore rhyme and movement with her class. She decided to do this by using the poem 'Jump or Jiggle' by Evelyn Beyer.

Frogs jump

Caterpillars hump

Worms wiggle

Bugs jiggle

Rabbits hop

Horses clop

Snakes slide

Sea gulls glide

Mice creep

Deer leap

Puppies bounce

Kittens pounce

Lions stalk

But – I walk!

She began by reading the poem aloud to the children. She then read it a second time, but this time encouraged the children to listen to the words and make movements to imitate them. So, for example, at the first line 'frogs jump' the children jumped up and down.

After the children had explored the movements associated with each of the verbs in the poem, Barbara began to talk with them about rhyming words. The children discussed which words in the poem rhymed. The first pair of rhyming words in the poem was 'jump' and 'hump'. Barbara challenged the children to write down on their whiteboards as many words they could think of that rhymed with 'jump' and 'hump'. Some examples included 'bump', 'slump', 'plump'. She repeated this for a couple of other rhyming couplets. The children's phonics focus for the week had been /ee/ and Barbara noted the opportunity to bring this into the lesson. The children talked about other words which rhymed with 'creep' and 'leap' and the link with their phonics work was noted. One child noticed that leap and creep were spelt differently, and yet sounded the same, and Barbara was able to make a point of discussing and exploring this with the children. To end the lesson, she gave the children a chopped-up version of the poem, and challenged them to put the rhyming couplets back together.

→

This could be developed further, and the children could be challenged to learn some of this poem by heart. It is a simple poem which young children may be able to memorise and recite, particularly in addition to the actions.

Curriculum link

The National Curriculum requires children to listen to and enjoy poetry, and develop an understanding of rhyme. Children are expected to appreciate rhymes, and this approach to poetry teaching enables children to experience simple rhymes and link these to their phonics development. Additionally, the curriculum requires children in Key Stage 1 to learn some poetry by heart – and this is a simple poem which is easy for children to begin memorising.

Different types of poetry

Research from Cremin (2011) has shown that many teachers have had limited experiences of poetry, meaning they find it hard to provide children with a range of experiences of poetry. Poetry can be narrowly perceived, and many children believe that a prerequisite of poetry is that it rhymes. Although there is something attractive about a poem which rhymes, many forms of poetry do not rhyme. It is important that teachers and pupils alike are exposed to and are able to recognise some different forms of poetry. It is essential that you seek to expand your knowledge of forms of poetry. The National Curriculum Programme of Study maintains that children should experience a range of classic and contemporary poetry, and that they should recognise forms of poetry such as free verse or narrative.

Narrative poetry

Narrative poems tell a story and can often be very long. They often employ the use of different voices and include different characters. Narrative poems introduce a more complex element to poetry than simple humorous riddles and limericks and can be useful in engaging children through their story-like nature. Narrative poems employ many literary techniques in rhyming and can be far more descriptive than shorter forms of poetry. Examples include 'The Highwayman' by Alfred Noyes and 'The Listeners' by Walter de la Mare. Using these poems in class exposes children to different genres of poetry, and allows them to listen to and read a different form of poem. Additionally, the descriptive nature of narrative poems demonstrates the effective use of many literary techniques such as similes, metaphors, alliteration and rhyme. Poems such as 'The Highwayman' or 'The Listeners' can be used across units of work to explore a number of aspects of learning, both in English and in other subjects.

The following extract is from 'The Listeners' by Walter de la Mare:

'Is there anybody there?' said the Traveller,

Knocking on the moonlit door;

And his horse in the silence champed the grasses

Of the forest's ferny floor:

And a bird flew up out of the turret,

Above the Traveller's head:

And he smote upon the door again a second time;

'Is there anybody there?' he said.

But no one descended to the Traveller;

No head from the leaf-fringed sill

Leaned over and looked into his grey eyes,

Where he stood perplexed and still.

This poem can be used to develop speaking and listening skills with children, and to develop the use of expression when reciting poetry. On the BBC Learning Zone website you can find a clip of a young girl who recites the poem and demonstrates effective use of expression (**www. bbc.co.uk/programmes/p011szt3**). Children can be encouraged to consider the use of voice and tone when reciting or performing a poem such as 'The Listeners'.

The characters in the poem, including the Traveller, 'The Listeners' and the people the traveller came to see (known as 'them') can be explored with children. The poem does not give much description of the characters, and this poem can be useful in encouraging children to use their imaginations to support understanding of a text. Children can think beyond the text, and create character profiles for the different people in the story, write descriptions of how the characters may look, or even create 'Wanted' posters for 'The Listeners'.

The setting of this poem can also be explored with children. Exploration of the language used to describe the setting in the poem may be linked with an art lesson, and children can be encouraged to use the poem to create a painting or drawing. For example, children can explore the use of different art materials to create the look of the 'moonlit door', 'leaf-fringed sill' or 'faint moonbeams on the dark stair'.

This poem also demonstrates the use of rhyme, and the rhyming pattern can be explored with children. They can be encouraged to write an additional stanza for the poem, which fits the rhyming scheme. Alternatively, the language can be explored more closely, and children can look at the use of alliteration, selection of verbs, the use of imagery, similes and metaphors.

Free verse

Free verse is a form of poetry which has no set metre to it. It can be rhyming or non-rhyming. Free verse does not necessarily have to have a particular structure, although many poems written in this form have a structure of some kind. Free verse is a form of poetry which allows for freedom of expression, and does not confine its writer with structural restrictions. An example of a free verse poem can be seen below in 'Fog' by Carl Sandburg.

> The fog comes
>
> on little cat feet.
>
> It sits looking
>
> over harbor and city
>
> on silent haunches
>
> and then moves on.

In one Year 5 class, children drew on the style of Sandburg's poem and his use of metaphors to write their own free verse about weather. This included the following:

> Rain arrives
>
> A cascading waterfall.
>
> It waits for us
>
> As we unpack the picnic
>
> Lurking above
>
> And then pouncing.
>
> Snow blankets us
>
> With feathery flakes
>
> It lands softly
>
> Shedding its white feathers
>
> With a shiver
>
> Then flies away

Other examples of free verse include 'Free Verse' by Robert Graves and 'After the Sea-Ship' by Walt Whitman.

It is important that you familiarise yourself with these forms of poetry, and other less commonly used forms, in order to be able to share with children a wide range of poetry.

Activity: types of poetry

Read the poems below and identify the types of poetry they represent. Attempt to write your own poem in the style of one of these and aim to share it with your class.

Poem 1

From 'Custard the Dragon' by Ogden Nash

Belinda lived in a little white house,

With a little black kitten and a little grey mouse,

And a little yellow dog and a little red wagon,

And a realio, trulio, little pet dragon.

Now the name of the little black kitten was Ink,

And the little grey mouse, she called her Blink,

And the little yellow dog was sharp as Mustard,

But the dragon was a coward, and she called him Custard.

Custard the dragon had big sharp teeth,

And spikes on top of him and scales underneath,

Mouth like a fireplace, chimney for a nose,

And realio, trulio, daggers on his toes.

Poem 2

'There was an Old Man with a Beard' by Edward Lear

There was an Old Man with a beard,

Who said, 'It is just as I feared!

Two Owls and a Hen,

Four Larks and a Wren,

Have all built their nests in my beard!'

Poem 3

'Summer Lollipop', unknown author

Licking a lolly slowly,

sunlight lapping at the lazy lake.

Lovely evening,

lovely lolly,

lazy life.

(Answers to the types of poetry can be found at the end of the chapter.)

Case study: 'The Rime of the Ancient Mariner'

Andy, a Year 6 teacher, wanted to challenge his class with a poem which was different from their usual, much-loved diet of Roald Dahl's *Revolting Rhymes*. A colleague suggested he use 'The Rime of the Ancient Mariner' by Samuel Taylor Coleridge. Although initially hesitant at this suggestion, largely as a result of his own lack of confidence, Andy decided to give it a try.

The National Curriculum requires children in Upper Key Stage 2 to read and discuss a wide range of poetry, and also to express their views about different poems. Andy decided to use the poem to encourage the children to read aloud and then discuss the poem and their views of it. The poem is long, but has different parts, so he began by reading aloud Part I. Once the children had been given the opportunity to listen to the poem once, Andy asked them to take turns in reading parts of the poem aloud. Once the first section of the poem had been read aloud, Andy asked the children to write on their whiteboards any questions they had about the poem. The children had a number of questions about the meaning of certain words, or about the story. These questions were then shared, discussed and addressed. This was an opportunity for children to work on comprehension skills and to look at how to deduce meaning from unknown words.

After this, the children were split into mixed-ability groups for an activity. Andy wanted to use the poem to fuel discussion and to encourage the children to form their own opinions about the poem. Each group of children received a pack of cards which had questions written on them. Example questions included the following.

- What did you think of the poem?
- What did you like? Why?
- What did you not like? Why?
- Which part of the poem was your favourite?

$\longrightarrow$

- What was your favourite line in the poem?

- Can you find an example of alliteration/a simile/a metaphor in this part of the poem?

- What do you think will happen in the next part of the poem?

The children took turns within their groups to pick a question and then read it aloud. The children then shared, one by one, their responses with the group. The discussions among the children were surprising, and Andy observed different groups throughout the lesson. He questioned children where necessary in order to probe understanding or to challenge, and also used the opportunity to make notes for speaking and listening assessment. Some children noticed the use of alliteration or similes (something which had been previously covered in their literacy lessons) and this was noted by the teacher.

To end the lesson, children volunteered to share their opinions of the poem so far. Andy decided to continue using the poem in subsequent lessons, and was able to use further parts of the poem to support comprehension, and to look at sentence level work.

Curriculum link

The National Curriculum requires children in Upper Key Stage 2 to listen to, read aloud and discuss poems. Children are also required to develop their own views and opinions of a range of poems. Additionally, they must develop speaking and listening skills, and this is easily supported through group discussions.

Activity: 'Flannan Isle'

Read 'Flannan Isle' by Wilfrid Wilson Gibson (it can easily be found online).

Consider how you might use this poem in Key Stage 2. Think about how it could be used to support the following:

- development of comprehension skills;
- drama;
- writing activities;
- vocabulary development.

(Possible answers can be found at the end of the chapter.)

Although teaching poetry can be a daunting prospect – particularly when children are expected to recite poetry, know different forms of poetry, discuss opinions of poetry and enjoy poetry – the benefits of using it effectively are numerous. Although many teachers feel they do not have sufficient knowledge of poetry to teach it, this can be easily rectified through subject knowledge development. Poetry is everywhere, and an increased awareness of and recognition of its place and importance are necessary for successful teaching. It is important to develop an understanding and enjoyment of poetry in order to pass on a love and enthusiasm for it.

Poems are a wonderful way of expressing life experiences in an engaging and thoughtful manner, in addition to demonstrating high-quality use of language. Children love to explore language creatively, and engage with writing which allows for expression and creativity. Using poetry in the classroom should not be a chore but a joy, and children will reap the benefits of effective poetry teaching throughout their literacy education.

Learning outcomes review

You should now know:

- what children need to understand about poetry;
- what you need to know as a primary teacher;
- some of the challenges you face when you teach children poetry;
- some approaches to teaching poetry.

Self-assessment questions
1. In which Key Stage are children expected to appreciate rhymes and poems, and recite some by heart?
2. What is free verse?
3. What is narrative poetry?

Suggested answers to activities

Types of poetry

Poem 1 is narrative verse.

Poem 2 is a limerick.

Poem 3 is free verse and includes alliteration.

(Continued)

(Continued)

Flannan Isle

In Key Stage 2 this poem could be used:

- to develop comprehension skills by asking open-ended questions such as:
    o Why do you think people are fascinated by this story?
    o What do you think could have happened to the men?

Encourage children to look carefully at the text to justify their answers.

- as a stimulus for drama – ask children to imagine they have arrived at the deserted island. Encourage them to explore and to discuss what they find. Encourage them to speculate in conversations about the fate of the lighthouse keepers.
- in writing activities such as rewriting sections of the poem in prose, perhaps as a diary entry, a log book entry, or a newspaper article.
- in vocabulary development which might focus on some of the vocabulary which may be unfamiliar to your class, such as: *dwell*, *lee*, *swell*, *guillemot*, *threshold* and *flinching*. You could also look at the use of apostrophes to shorten words, including *look'd*, *o'er*, *untouch'd*. Talk about why the poet might have written in this way.

The poem has been the subject of an opera, a song and even an episode of *Dr Who*, so you may wish to explore some of these with children too.

Further reading

To find out more about what Ofsted discovered about poetry in schools, read:

Ofsted (2007) *Poetry in Schools: A Survey of Practice, 2006/07*. London: Ofsted. Available at: www.ofsted.gov.uk/resources/poetry-schools (accessed 16 June 2014).

For discussion about poetry and ideas for the classroom, see:

Waugh, D, Neaum, S and Waugh, R (2016) 'Poetry' in *Children's Literature in Primary Schools* (2nd edn). London: Learning Matters/SAGE, pp182–200.

References

Bryant, PE, MacLean, M, Bradley, L and Crossland, J (1990) Rhyme and alliteration, phoneme detection and learning to read. *Developmental Psychology*, 26(3): 429–38.

Cremin, T (2011) Reading Teachers/Teaching Readers: Why Teachers Who Read Make Good Teachers of Reading. *English Drama Media*, February: 11–18. Available at: **www.nate.org. uk/cmsfiles/edm/19/EDM%2019%2011-18.pdf** (accessed 16 June 2014).

Cremin, T, Mottram, M, Bearne, E and Goodwin, P (2008) Exploring teachers' knowledge of children's literature. *Cambridge Journal of Education*, 38(4): 449–64.

Cremin, T, Mottram, M, Collins, F, Powell, S and Safford, K (2009) Teachers as readers: building communities of readers. *Literacy*, 43(1): 11–19.

Crystal, D (1998) *Language Play*. Chicago: University of Chicago Press.

Department for Education (DfE) (2013) *The National Curriculum in England: Key Stages 1 and 2 Framework Document*. London: DfE Publications.

Department for Education and Skills (DfES) (2005) *Primary National Strategies. Improving Boys' Writing: Purpose and Audience*. London: DfES.

Dymoke, S. (2003) *Drafting and Assessing Poetry: A Guide for Teachers*. London: Sage, pp1–19.

Goswami, U (1990) A special link between rhyming skill and the use of orthographic analogies by beginning readers, *Journal of Child Psychology and Psychiatry*, 31: 301–11.

Hughes, J (2007) *Poetry: A Powerful Medium for Literacy and Technology Development*. Research Monograph # 7. Ontario: The Literacy and Numeracy Secretariat. Available at: **www.edu. gov.on.ca/eng/literacynumeracy/inspire/research/hughes.pdf** (accessed 27 April 2014).

Ofsted (2007) *Poetry in Schools: A Survey of Practice, 2006/07*. London: Ofsted. Available at: **www.ofsted.gov.uk/resources/poetry-schools** (16 June 2014).

Waugh, D, Neaum, S and Waugh, R (2016) *Children's Literature in Primary Schools* (2nd edn). London: Learning Matters/SAGE.

9 Non-fiction

Kirsty Anderson

Learning outcomes

By reading this chapter you will develop your understanding of:

- what children need to understand about non-fiction reading and writing;
- what primary teachers need to know to teach the National Curriculum Programme of Study for English;
- some of the challenges faced when teaching non-fiction reading and writing;
- approaches to teaching non-fiction reading and writing.

Teachers' Standards
3. Demonstrate good subject and curriculum knowledge:

- have a secure knowledge of the relevant subject(s) and curriculum areas, foster and maintain pupils' interest in the subject, and address misunderstandings;
- demonstrate a critical understanding of developments in the subject and curriculum areas, and promote the value of scholarship;
- demonstrate an understanding of, and take responsibility for, promoting high standards of literacy, articulacy and the correct use of standard English, whatever the teacher's specialist subject.

Introduction

When asked to teach non-fiction with Year 2 during a teaching placement, Louise, a third-year trainee, felt fairly confident that she would be able to do this well. Non-fiction is, after all, about factual experiences, which make up everyday life. The National Curriculum Programme of Study itself reminds us that non-fiction is essential in everyday life and being able to navigate the wealth of information around them supports pupil learning beyond English lessons. But consider how you would feel sitting in front of a class of expectant seven-year-olds who should be taught to develop pleasure in reading, motivation to read and understanding by *being introduced to non-fiction books that are structured in different ways* (DfE, 2013, p17). Can you enthuse about the further knowledge which can be gained from thoughtfully reading a non-fiction text? As teachers, you need to recognise and value the benefits brought by learning about and through non-fiction. You need to show, for example, that you are fascinated by the photographs in a newspaper or the animation used on a website, and encourage children to have the same response. This chapter introduces some useful strategies and ideas for teaching non-fiction in line with the National Curriculum expectations, but it begins by exploring the importance of non-fiction and some of the challenges teachers face.

Why is non-fiction so important?

Understanding how and why children benefit from using non-fiction is important as you develop as primary school teachers. The following aspects of learning are directly supported by non-fiction:

- moving from learning to read to reading to learn;
- developing interests;
- making sense of experiences;
- purposeful learning;
- purposeful communication.

When children have developed word recognition skills, as discussed in Chapter 6, they can access texts with greater independence. Essentially, reading to learn forms the basis of non-fiction reading; factual texts are read in order to find out more. As good teachers, you should ensure that when non-fiction texts are used with pupils these are matched to genuine interests. Children need to be excited about their learning and it is your role to scaffold this enthusiasm and support developing interests in order to introduce children to what the 2014 National Curriculum Programme of Study for English describes as *a treasure house of wonder and joy for curious young minds* (DfE, 2013, p5). It is important to take every opportunity to foster children's natural curiosity to support them in making sense of experiences they have. Your classroom should enable children to pursue their interests and find out more, like reading about life cycles in science after spotting the first butterflies of the year. When children are supported to read and write about their interests or to share their experiences, this is purposeful learning which engages them. Sharing learning through written texts, sharing news stories or giving formal presentations ensures purposeful communication is embedded in the classroom. When you teach using non-fiction both in English and across the curriculum, you are establishing a real love of learning in pupils which can link to pupils' own experiences.

Research focus: using experiences to write non-fiction

In their longitudinal research into cognitive processes involved in composing written texts, Bereiter and Scardamalia (1987) identified several areas which are important to children as they develop their writing skills: goal setting, planning, memory search, problem solving, evaluation and diagnosis. It is clear, then, that to write well in non-fiction children need to have enough information to conduct a 'memory search'. This information must come from meaningful and interesting real experiences which can be further enhanced through reading. When writing fiction, pupils use their imagination, in contrast with the accurate knowledge required for good non-fiction writing. Teachers must ensure that pupils have knowledge for the memory recall suggested by Bereiter and Scardamalia. Sometimes teachers use fictional knowledge as the basis of non-fiction writing. Children might be asked to write instructions for building a brick house based on *The Three Little Pigs*. Such genre transformation or text parodies are valid approaches to teaching non-fiction, especially given the amount of accurate information required. For non-fiction to be authentic, however, good teachers must endeavour to pursue other meaningful experiences which will lead to deeper knowledge, which can then be transformed into their written texts. Ofsted's report *Excellence in English* (2011) echoes this by identifying that excellent English teaching links English and real-life experiences. Planning these experiences for pupils is central to providing a scaffold from which non-fiction learning can develop and progress.

It is important to recognise that far from being simply dusty old textbooks, non-fiction includes websites, leaflets, forms and applications, which enable us to develop knowledge of ourselves and of other subjects. While this can seem obvious as you read this, non-fiction does not seem to have the same status as fiction. The 2014 National Curriculum aims ask schools to ensure that all pupils *appreciate our rich and varied literary heritage* (DfE, 2013, p4). It is important that the literary heritage is appreciated, but how many of the texts in our literary heritage are non-fiction? It is possible to suggest that Dahl's autobiographical *Boy: Tales of Childhood* (1984) or Shakespeare's historical plays are based on factual experiences, but on the whole these celebrated authors write fiction. Ask yourself the same question: which non-fiction authors do you know? Terry Deary's 'Horrible Histories' series of books and subsequent children's television programmes are possibly the most well-known non-fiction texts currently available for children, with the author's humorous style making history more accessible. Raising the status of non-fiction with your pupils is essential not only as a medium for teaching other subjects, but also to value their own non-fiction writing. Teaching pupils how to value non-fiction is only possible if appropriate texts are available. You may find this challenging as texts may not be age-appropriate or can include vast amounts of technical information which pupils need a great deal of help to explore. The Internet provides a wealth of materials, although this cannot always be relied on to be accurate, and you may find online materials are short-lived. Wherever you find appropriate information, talking about it is important as you teach how to respond to different texts.

Research focus: using talk to help children understand non-fiction

Talking about texts is central to the guidance for teachers offered by Aidan Chambers in his book *Tell Me: Children, Reading, and Talk* (1997), which is based on his own practical experiences. To engage with a text is not simply to read it, but to critically examine and interact with it. Chambers outlines how teachers facilitate text interaction through 'selection', 'reading' and 'response'. Response can be both formal and 'book gossip'. Book gossip is essential to encouraging talk about texts. It is divided into three categories – 'The Three Sharings'. Chambers explains these as 'sharing enthusiasm', 'sharing puzzles' and 'sharing patterns'. Chambers explains enthusiasms as the likes and dislikes about a text. Puzzles are difficulties the reader has with any aspect of the text. As a skilful teacher you will make use of questions which facilitate discussion about puzzles. For example, is a web page easy to navigate? Is the information fact or opinion? By sharing connections with other reading, readers can see the patterns in different text types. There might be similar features, like titles or diagrams, elements which are recognisable and can support the reader to make connections. By using talk as exemplified in Chambers's action research, you can help pupils to make sense of a text, which, with non-fiction in particular, can help them to make sense of the world.

Progression in non-fiction learning in the National Curriculum

Learning about and from non-fiction supports the purpose of study as set out in the National Curriculum. Pupils learn to communicate through speaking and writing to present factual information and experiences. They acquire knowledge about the whole curriculum from reading and embed the language skills essential to participate as a member of society.

It is essential to ensure that children recognise the differences between fiction and non-fiction as soon as they are introduced to texts. To understand non-fiction, pupils must be taught to recognise it as a way of finding out further information which supports and adds to prior knowledge and experience. You should introduce non-fiction texts with this in mind, stating clearly that listening to a non-fiction text will be different from listening to a story. It is important to remember that we have emotional responses to non-fiction texts and you should demonstrate these to pupils. The Research Focus below describes an effective teaching approach to non-fiction.

Research focus: the EXIT model

In 1992 David Wray and Maureen Lewis began a two-year curriculum development project. The EXEL project (Exeter Extending Literacy) resulted from concerns about standards in English teaching, teachers' knowledge of developments and the reliability of effective strategies to support learning. The aim of the project was to produce materials trialled by teachers which could support Key Stage 2 teachers with non-fiction. Wray and Lewis (1997) identified the key processes used by adults when interacting with non-fiction and developed a model for use by teachers: the EXIT model (Extending Interactions with Texts). The EXIT model strategies are described below. They can be applied in any order.

- Activating prior knowledge – asking questions about what pupils already understand facilitates further learning.

- Establishing purposes – knowing what you want to find from the text and why. Precision means learning is focused and has an end point.

- Locating information – making correct use of libraries, websites and books to tell you what you are looking for.

- Adopting an appropriate strategy – deciding if pupils should skim the text for key themes, scan for specific facts or close-read for revision or in-depth study.

- Interacting with the text – using different activities to explore the text – for example, resequencing a text or creating flow charts of key information which link pupil understanding to the writer's intention.

- Monitoring understanding – supporting pupils to check their learning by identifying the important themes in the reading and explaining how to check understanding.

- Recording – making key notes with a set or given purpose, often towards a final outcome.

- Evaluating information – teaching pupils to be critical about what they read and the value of the information. Does it give the answer they wanted?

- Assisting memory – by supporting interaction with the text you support children to make sense of it. This can be improved if children revisit a text.

- Communicating information – supporting children to clarify their understanding when they talk or write about their learning.

Making use of the EXIT model advances text interaction beyond initial discussions. Simply using a text for information can diminish the value and quality of the text, and can reduce children's interests in producing non-fiction writing. Moreover, when adults make use of non-fiction texts it is purposeful – checking train times, for instance. If you ensure there is purpose behind the retrieval, then learning is purposeful and memorable.

An understanding of what to expect from pupils in the different phases of primary school is useful as you develop as a teacher. Recognising when children learn the skills you use instinctively to approach non-fiction, like distinguishing fact from opinion or summarising key information from an email, can help you understand what to expect from your pupils. The following section outlines non-fiction learning in the different phases of the National Curriculum.

Non-fiction in Key Stage 1

In Year 1, non-fiction teaching focuses on broadening pupils' vocabulary. Children should be taught to make links between what they read and hear, and their own experience. In writing, pupils learn to organise ideas and sequence sentences to form short narratives. Although these can be their own stories or versions of familiar fictional texts, a narrative can also be a retelling or recount of their own experiences such as a visit to the beach.

By Year 2, children are reading and listening to information texts across other curriculum subjects. Comprehension develops alongside a growing vocabulary as children better understand the meaning of what they read. Pupils develop greater motivation for reading to learn through listening to and discussing texts which they might not be able to access independently. Teachers give guidance through background information, key vocabulary and questions to link prior knowledge with the information they read. Effective teachers will encourage children to ask relevant questions about the texts. Children will learn to write about real events and for different purposes, which may include explaining how something works, or giving instructions to play a game. The National Curriculum Programme of Study acknowledges that writing is more difficult than reading, so the texts you share are likely to be more difficult than those which children themselves produce. You need to ensure that pupils maintain high levels of confidence about their writing when this arises so that they *develop positive attitudes towards writing* (DfE, 2013, p20).

Case study: Key Stage 1 writing about experiences

Louise, a trainee in Year 2, decided to plan experiences to support her class writing independent instructions. The pupils were taught to *write for different purposes and about real events* (DfE, 2013, p20). Louise shared sets of instructions for board games with the class. They familiarised themselves with the rules and set about playing games independently. Louise let the children play for a short time in the lesson and then gathered the pupils back to read again. Louise paid close attention to the layout and language features of the rules. The class worked with Louise to highlight the use of titles, lists, numbered points and imperative verbs. During PE, the pupils learned traditional playground games, which they really enjoyed. Louise asked the class to write their experiences in a 'Big Book of Playground Games' to share with Year 1. Louise decided to demonstrate this process using a writing frame.

→

How to play ....

This is a game for ....

You will need:

....

....

....

....

Rules:

First ....

Next ....

....

Conjunctions you might use: *and, because, when, then, if, so*

The writing frame provided an outline and prompt for the independent writing. As Louise demonstrated writing instructions, she verbalised the reminder that each section of the writing frame gave: '"You will need", I think this section is reminding me to write a list of equipment. Do you think so? What did we use?' Louise's pupils learned what the text should look like from close reading, then how to write for real purposes from real experiences. Louise recognised that her pupils were engaged with the task because they enjoyed playing games. The children wanted to write instructions which would help younger children enjoy the games too; the purpose was not only clear instructions but also an emotional response to enjoy the game.

Curriculum link

Non-fiction reading and writing is central in all curriculum areas. In this case study, Louise made use of playground games to stimulate experiences for instruction writing. She could just as easily have linked this learning to Art lessons or D&T. What is central is that pupils are given the opportunity to familiarise themselves with both the real experience and the text type.

Non-fiction in Lower Key Stage 2

In Years 3 and 4 teachers need to give pupils opportunities to read age-appropriate non-fiction on a wide range of subjects across the curriculum using text and reference books. Pupils will build on retrieval skills introduced through discussions about texts in Key Stage 1 so that they can record this information. Children should be given access to text and reference books, and read information which is structured in different ways. This is an ideal opportunity to explore the layout of web pages and embed understanding of ways to retrieve relevant information. In writing, children learn to plan through sharing writing similar to their ideas, and make use of organisational devices like headings and subheadings.

Case study: Lower Key Stage 2 topic-based learning from texts

On a final placement in Year 4, student teacher Lee developed his skills teaching non-fiction through topic-based learning. The class were studying the topic 'Railways'. The main focus of the learning was history based, but Lee knew this was an excellent opportunity to contextualise English skills. At the beginning of the topic, which was planned to last for six weeks, the class visited a local transport museum. Pupils enjoyed seeing different forms of transport from the past, and watching black-and-white newsreels which included films of steam engines in use. Lee planned a sequence of English lessons to teach children to *understand what they read by asking questions to improve their understanding of a text and to retrieve and record information from non-fiction* (DfE, 2013, p26).

Lee recorded the children's prior learning, including their memories from the school trip, by jotting down notes in a KWL grid (What I know/What I want to know/What I have learned).

What I know	What I want to know	What I have learned
Stephenson invented the *Rocket* … Trains used steam to move … Trains used coal … I liked sitting in the wooden carriages …	When were they invented? Where did the trains go? Were they expensive? What was it like travelling on a steam train?	

Lee explained that it is important to make a record of what is known so that we can find out new information. He modelled some questions as a focus for reading and supported pupils to do the same. Before pupils read independently, Lee checked they could use the contents, index and glossary effectively and challenged the children to use encyclopaedias independently to search for the answers to their questions. When the pupils found the information, it was recorded on the grid. When some of the questions could not be answered, Lee was able to teach children to think critically about the usefulness of the text and to start considering more than one source of information.

Non-fiction in Upper Key Stage 2

By the time pupils are in Years 5 and 6, they should be reading widely for pleasure and information. You will have firmly established the idea that reading for information leads to learning, which, when purposeful and led by children's interests, is itself pleasurable. Children develop skills to present the information they have retrieved, and understand the differences between fact and opinion. They might, for example, look at newspaper reports of a football match, and compare these with a fan website about the same event. In writing, pupils need to have a good understanding of audience and purpose, and be able to plan, draft and edit their writing accordingly. Genre-specific organisational devices and features, such as diagrams in explanations, should be understood and used well by the end of Upper Key Stage 2, to ensure effective transition into secondary education where pupils continue to make use of English skills across the whole curriculum.

Case study: Upper Key Stage 2 independent research project

During a placement in a Year 6 class, Shelina was asked to work with a group of children who were developing their own independent research projects. Shelina's group were interested in charity posters they saw supporting Greenpeace. Shelina talked with the group about the poster first. She recognised that the pupils liked the images on the poster particularly, but did not have enough knowledge to respond to the information it provided about deforestation. Shelina used the Internet as an information resource and an opportunity to establish understanding of pupil responses to reading. She aimed to support pupils to *provide reasoned justifications for their views* (DfE, 2013, p35). She shared several charity posters she found online and asked pupils to rank them first according to the information included, then by impact. Next, Shelina decided to set a task of presenting information about the effects of deforestation on people and animals. She planned this because she wanted to ensure that the pupils responded emotionally to the information, especially given how far removed they were from the real experiences. The pupils then presented their research in slideshows and Shelina supported the pupils to *evaluate and edit by assessing the effectiveness of their writing*

⟶

(DfE, 2013, p38) by reflecting on the impact their presentations had on each other. The group presented their information as a slideshow of key images and facts, and used a voice-over adapted from the story *The Vanishing Rainforest* by Richard Platt and Rupert Van Wyk (2003). By telling the story as they presented the information, the pupils learned they could create even greater impact and link non-fiction with fiction.

Curriculum link

Linking non-fiction with fiction can be very powerful. Some children struggle to write narratives, so use of non-fiction can be a starting point. It is also valuable to explain to pupils that authors of fiction also research information for their writing, which can make writing experiences authentic for children.

Activity: features of non-fiction texts

List the features of an instruction text using the following headings.

- Audience
- Purpose
- Generic structure (think about what the layout might be)
- Language features
- Knowledge for the writer (clues which might help the writer).

Guidance can be found at the end of the chapter and at the archived National Strategies website: **www.nationalstrategies.standards.dcsf.gov.uk/**

The National Curriculum: teaching non-fiction

The National Curriculum objectives, which support teaching and learning of non-fiction in English, can be categorised into the following aspects which are explored with examples in this section.

- listening to and discussing information;
- retrieving and recording information;
- cause and effect;
- different structures of non-fiction texts;
- presenting information.

It is important to note that the National Curriculum Programme of Study for English objectives which can be taught in the context of non-fiction reading and writing do not always make an explicit link to non-fiction. You will need to make judgements which ensure there is a balance of fiction and non-fiction learning, and use objectives accordingly. For example, in Lower Key Stage 2 when teaching pupils to *understand what they read by checking the text makes sense to them, discussing their understanding and explaining the meaning of words in context* (DfE, 2013, p26), good teachers will recognise that this is applicable to both fiction and non-fiction, and should plan opportunities in both.

Listening to and discussing information

Children are naturally curious and ask lots of questions. They need to be taught to structure questions about detailed and complicated information and to listen carefully for answers. In Key Stage 1, for example, teachers can model the types of questions which yield further information when a visitor is in school. If the visitor is an expert on a particular subject – a dentist or a nurse, perhaps – the teacher might model the first few questions and let children ask the rest. A good idea would be to offer a simple structure to the questions such as who, what, where, when and why. Ensuring that there is an explicit purpose for the questions – to be able to write a job description about dentists, perhaps – can help children to ensure that their listening is active. Children can interact with texts and presentations by listening for the likes, dislikes, puzzles and connections, and by making their own notes on whiteboards to reflect on later. When pupils are older or competent at checking the relevance of the material they read or hear, strategies like *rainbow reading* can be used. Groups of children would work together but read separate texts about the same subject. After reading, pupils share a single set of questions which draw on all the reading, and this can support *active listening* and embed skills in discussion.

Retrieving and recording information

Children need to be taught how to find information and how they may record this. As teachers, you need to ensure that there is a specific purpose for the information. For example, pupils might find information about the Victorians to create their own museum for other pupils to visit. Pupils can work together to retrieve information from different sources using strategies like *jigsawing* or *snowballing*. To use jigsawing, groups are given a specific task such as finding out about Victorian schools. The group separates to find information from different places including textbooks, the Internet or encyclopaedias. The group then puts all the pieces of the 'jigsaw' together by sharing what they have found from the different sources. Groups might have different focuses. Snowballing is very similar in that pupils work in groups, but pupils move together from table to table building up their information. Pupils can record the information as they work by creating diagrams, flow charts or posters of their findings.

Cause and effect

With fiction texts, children learn to infer character behaviours by analysing speech and actions. In non-fiction texts, it is the *cause and effect* of particular events or actions from which complex inferential skills can be learned. In some non-fiction texts, cause and effect is much easier to identify. Explanation texts showing the results of a science experiment on reversible changes, for instance, would clearly show that, when heated, ice melts and becomes water. It might be sensible when teaching cause and effect to begin with genres in which the cause and effect can be easily recognised. As pupils learn to identify cause and effect, they can use activities like *sequencing* and *ranking* events or actions to show what the causes and effects were. Text reconstruction or transformation can be used to show understanding and recognition of key events. You might ask pupils to transform their knowledge about the Second World War into a diary of an evacuee or to write about the war in a story. Working in role also supports understanding of cause and effect. Using hot seating during a lesson, you may become a significant historical figure, like Winston Churchill, and talk about the effect of your speeches, for example.

Different structures of non-fiction texts

Children need to recognise how a text is organised and link this to their own writing. In the *Primary Framework* (DfES, 2006), teachers were given useful guidance documents for the six non-fiction genres which children should know. These are: instructions, recounts, non-chronological reports, and persuasion, discussion and explanation texts (see Web references). You should share different genres and ensure that children understand the purpose, audience, layout and language of each. To demonstrate their understanding, pupils could complete a quadrant to explain the Purpose, Audience, Language and Layout of the non-fiction text.

Name of text	
Purpose: What is it for? What is it supposed to tell you?	**Audience:** Who is likely to read it?
Language: What tense is it written in? Which conjunctions are used? Is the language formal or informal?	**Layout:** What does it look like? Are there diagrams/ arrows/bullet points?

You might ask children to show their understanding of text structure through strategies like reordering a text. After sharing examples of persuasion, for example, teachers could cut up a persuasive text and ask children to organise it into the correct order. Teachers support pupils becoming competent in this, using routines and external supports, which, for non-fiction especially, can include writing frames, as shown in the first case study. You need to use writing frames in your teaching as a bridge between oral support and independence. When you are teaching it is impossible to support all children at the same time. When you talk to pupils about their writing you might ask 'What comes next?' It is helpful to think of a writing frame as providing that same support for pupils working more independently. As teachers, you must first ensure that you model the use of writing frames so that children recognise the guidance they are being given.

Presenting information

By modelling the writing processes and carefully externalising the writer's internal dialogues you will help children to produce non-fiction writing. Pupils' own composition processes can be supported and skilful teachers will ask children to explain their choices, mirroring the thought processes they model. Organising ideas is particularly important when presenting information. Children can be encouraged to brainstorm all their knowledge, then categorise by grouping similar ideas together. Pie Corbett's *Talk for Writing* materials (Corbett and Strong, 2011) exemplify this 'boxing up' strategy in detail (see Further Reading for suggested resources). As teachers, you will find there are multitudes of ways to present information, some of which are suggested in this chapter. Two elements contribute to the presentation: ensuring the purpose is established before research begins and teaching children to plan, draft and edit the information they present. Thanks to advances in technology, this is incredibly easy to facilitate. Using a real Twitter feed, for example, will give your class a genuine purpose and audience for their presentation, and encourage editing because of the very challenging limit of presenting information in 140 characters (see Further Reading for inspiration).

Activity: using writing frames

Devise a writing frame for a non-chronological report on lions. A writing frame can include *sentence openers* (*Lions are enormous cats ...*) which are consistent with the tone of the writing, a list of possible *conjunctions* (*because, since, as,* etc.) and might include some of the *technical vocabulary* (*habitat, prey*) more likely to be used in non-fiction writing.

(Possible answers can be found at the end of the chapter.)

You need to be able to develop meaningful learning opportunities for your pupils. Teaching non-fiction offers you the opportunity to do this. There are challenges in teaching non-fiction but these are far outweighed by the benefits. When you teach non-fiction you support children to make sense of their experiences, widen their interests and develop critical thinking skills. It is important that you understand why it is important and how to use different approaches to teach non-fiction. Securing this knowledge is essential in ensuring that non-fiction is awarded the status it deserves in the classroom. While fiction can transport us to different worlds, non-fiction can secure understanding of place and purpose in the real world.

Learning outcomes review

You should now know:

- what children need to understand about non-fiction reading and writing;
- what we need to know as primary teachers;
- some of the challenges we face when we teach children non-fiction;
- some approaches to teaching non-fiction reading and writing across the primary phases.

Self-assessment questions

1. What is the difference between learning to read and reading to learn?
2. Why do pupils need a focus before attempting to retrieve information from a non-fiction text?
3. When do children learn some of the organisational devices associated with non-fiction (such as bullet points and parenthesis)?
4. Why is non-fiction useful across the curriculum?

Answers to activities

Features of non-fiction texts

Adapted from the National Strategies *Support for Writing* materials (DCSF, 2009).

Instructional/procedural		
Audience: People wanting to know how to do something		
Purpose: To ensure something is done effectively and/or correctly with a successful outcome for the participant(s)		
Generic structure	**Language features**	**Knowledge for the writer**
• Start with the goal or desired outcome. (How to make a board game.)	• Use of imperative verbs (commands). (*Cut* the card ... *Paint* your design ...)	• Use the title to show what the instructions are about. (How to look after goldfish.)
• List any material or equipment needed, in order.	• Instructions may include negative commands. (Do not use any glue at this stage.)	• Work out exactly what sequence is needed.
• Provide simple, clear instructions. Keep to the order in which the steps need to be followed to achieve the stated goal.	• Additional advice like good ideas or suggested alternatives.	• Decide on the important points you need to include at each stage.

(Continued)

(Continued)

• Diagrams or illustrations are useful and take the place of some text. (Diagram B shows you how to connect the wires.)		• Decide how formal or informal the text will be.
		• Present the text clearly using bullet points, numbers or letters.
		• Keep sentences as short and simple as possible.
		• Avoid unnecessary adjectives and adverbs or technical words.
		• Appeal directly to the reader's interest and enthusiasm. (You will really enjoy this game.)
		• Include a final evaluative statement. (Now go and enjoy playing your new game.)
		• Reread your instructions.
		• Use procedural texts within other text types.

Using writing frames

Lions: (This could be a question.)

Introduction: Lions are types of …

Description: (What does it look like and how does it behave?)

Habitats: (Where do you find them?)

Diet: (What do they eat? How do they get it?)

Conclusion: (Ask the reader a question)

Further reading

For practical guidance on book talk, which is explained through class-based experiences, see:

Chambers, A (1997) *Tell Me: Children, Reading, and Talk*. Stroud: Thimble Press.

Pie Corbett's successful 'Talk for Writing' approaches are exemplified with practical suggestions and activities to try in:

Corbett, P and Strong, J (2011) *Writing Across the Curriculum: How to Teach Non-fiction Writing 5–12 years.* Maidenhead: Open University Press.

For useful activities and suggestions for contextualised English learning, see:

Wray, D (2006) *Teaching Literacy Across the Primary Curriculum.* London: Learning Matters/SAGE.

For an inspiring exploration of Twitter in the classroom see:

Waller, M (2011) *Using Twitter in the Primary Classroom.* English 4–11, No. 39. London: UKLA.

Web references

DARTS (Directed Activities Related to Texts). DARTs activities encourage learners to engage with text in active ways that assist memorising and extraction of meaning. Available from this and other sites: **www.teachingenglish.org.uk**

Non-fiction text type guidance, including details on the audience, purpose and structure of different non-fiction texts, is currently available from the archived National Strategies at: **www.nationalstrategies.standards.dcsf.gov.uk/**

References

Bereiter, C and Scardamalia, M (1987) *The Psychology of Written Composition.* Hillsdale, NJ: Lawrence Erlbaum Associates.

Chambers, A (1997) *Tell Me: Children Reading and Talk.* Stroud: Thimble Press.

Corbett, P and Strong, J (2011) *Writing Across the Curriculum: How to Teach Non-fiction Writing 5–12 years.* Maidenhead: Open University Press.

Dahl, R (1984) *Boy: Tales of Childhood.* London: Puffin.

Deary, T (1993–2013) 'Horrible Histories' series. London: Scholastic.

Department for Children, Schools and Families (DCSF) (2009) *Support for Writing.* Nottingham: DCSF. Available at: **http://webarchive.nationalarchives.gov.uk/20100612050234/ nationalstrategies.standards.dcsf.gov.uk/primary/primaryframework/cpd/literacy/ support_writing** (accessed 17 June 2014).

Department for Education (DfE) (2013) *The National Curriculum in England: Key Stages 1 and 2 Framework Document.* London: DfE Publications.

Department for Education and Skills (DfES) (2006) *Primary National Strategy: Primary Framework for Literacy and Mathematics.* Norwich: OPSI. Available at: www.educationengland. org.uk/documents/pdfs/2006-primary-national-strategy.pdf (accessed 20 June 2014).

Ofsted (2011) *Excellence in English – What We Can Learn from 12 Outstanding Schools.* Manchester: Ofsted.

Platt, R and Van Wyk, R (2003) *The Vanishing Rainforest.* London: Frances Lincoln Children's Books.

Wray, D and Lewis, M (1997) *Extending Literacy: Children Reading and Writing Non-fiction.* London: Routledge.

10 Writing

Claire Warner

Learning outcomes

By reading this chapter you will develop your understanding of:

- the complexity of learning to write;
- the importance of balancing the technical and compositional aspects of writing;
- the teaching sequence for writing;
- the place of talk in becoming a writer.

Teachers' Standards
3. Demonstrate good subject and curriculum knowledge:

- have a secure knowledge of the relevant subject(s) and curriculum areas, foster and maintain pupils' interest in the subject, and address misunderstandings;
- demonstrate a critical understanding of developments in the subject and curriculum areas, and promote the value of scholarship;
- demonstrate an understanding of, and take responsibility for, promoting high standards of literacy, articulacy and the correct use of standard English, whatever the teacher's specialist subject.

Introduction

This chapter focuses in particular on how we can best help children to learn to write and see themselves as writers. Writing is, at its heart, about making sense of the world. As adults we write because we have something we want – or need – to communicate, whether this is information to convey, ideas and feelings to share, or stories to tell. The National Curriculum (DfE, 2013) states that the skills of language are essential to participating fully as a member of society. Being able to write is powerful and it matters for learning. When we write we can take the thoughts out of our heads to keep them. We can revisit them later, refine and shape our ideas, and take our thinking further. When we are teaching writing, we are, in a very real sense, teaching thinking.

Many children arrive at school knowing that writing is about communication and meaning. Observe young children in a well set-up classroom and you will often see them engaged confidently and purposefully in a range of self-directed writing activities, perhaps recording a phone call at the doctor's surgery, noting down the outcomes of a car service at the MOT stop, or writing down orders in a café. They have no doubt that the marks they make on the page convey important messages, and already know a little about the power of writing.

Fast forward a few years from the Foundation Stage and consider the range of responses to writing you have encountered. You may well have come across children who find the process of creating texts so daunting that the excitement of making meaning gets lost. 'It aches my arms ... ' a Year 1 child wrote recently, 'and I forget my full stops.' A number of research projects have found that children perceive writing to be a dull and complex physical activity (Bearne, 1998; Corden, 2000; Grainger *et al.*, 2003). Flutter's research (2000) suggests that Key Stage 1 children in particular may often be unclear about the purposes of the writing activities they are engaged with. She found that the overwhelming concern of many children was to make their writing neat and attractive. When children were asked what advice they would give to less experienced writers, the vast majority offered technical advice, frequently recommending that they make sure of 'capital letters and full stops', 'write neatly', 'join up', 'sound out', 'use correct grammar and spelling', 'use adjectives', use complex sentences', 'use a sharp pencil' or 'hold the pencil properly', and 'use a thesaurus' (Ings, 2009, p20). 'Writing can be a bit boring,' commented one Year 4 girl, 'because you need to remember to put in adjectives and remember everything in the (teacher's) checklist ... '. She went on to add, 'I've finally got out of the habit of doing small 't's so my writing is better now'.

Good writers have a range of skills. They can express their ideas and have the cognitive ability to do so. They can put their thoughts into written form and convey them in the way that is most appropriate for their reader, taking into account the purpose for the writing – for example, it may be to entertain or persuade. They know that written language is very different from speech and the ramblings of conversation, not least because the meaning they construct stands alone and needs to be read and understood later on. They are able to work out the spelling, use punctuation, coordinate fine motor skills and write legibly. It is little wonder that there is a general consensus that writing is the most difficult of the four language modes (speaking, listening, reading and writing), and we should not minimise the challenges it poses for children.

Research focus: motivation for writing

Research also shows that there is a clear link between writing well and being motivated to write. Bearne (2007) highlights the importance of attending to the emotions as well as the intellect. Other studies have shown that writing enjoyment, writing behaviour and writing attitudes have a positive relationship with writing attainment. Of the young people who do not enjoy writing at all, half write below the expected level, and two-fifths at the expected level.

→

Only 6 per cent of young people who do not enjoy writing at all write above the level expected for their age (Clark, 2012, p8).

Bereiter and Scardamalia (1987) talk about children's conditional competence. They suggest that children are capable of performing high-level mental activities when the task is of intrinsic worth to them. If children are given writing tasks that have no real purpose to them and no real audience beyond the classroom, it has been argued that all but the most committed pupils are likely to switch off (Ings, 2009).

The importance of composition

The English curriculum recognises the complexity of the writing process and organises it into two separate sections: transcription and composition:

> Writing down ideas fluently depends on effective transcription: that is, on spelling quickly and accurately through knowing the relationship between sounds and letters (phonics) and understanding the morphology (word structure) and orthography (spelling structure) of words. Effective composition involves forming, articulating and communicating ideas, and then organising them coherently for a reader. This requires clarity, awareness of the audience, purpose and context, and an increasingly wide knowledge of vocabulary and grammar. Writing also depends on fluent, legible and, eventually, speedy handwriting.
>
> (DfE, 2013, p5)

You may have noticed that transcription comes first. It has a significant emphasis and it is addressed in detail in other chapters of this book. As seen in Chapter 4, spelling words with accuracy and ease is integral to writing and without this skill, composition is often constrained (Alderman and Green, 2011). A lack of confidence in spelling can have a paralysing impact on writing, and result in an unwillingness to take risks with more adventurous vocabulary. Medwell *et al.*'s (2009) study found that handwriting was an important factor in the composition of Year 6 children and that low levels of handwriting automaticity was impacting on their composition.

This chapter is concerned with teaching the compositional aspects of writing, enabling children to convey meaning clearly and use an appropriate style and register to engage their reader. Composition, Barrs (1987) explains, is what drives the writing. Perhaps you have had the experience of children's writing that is technically correct, but of very little interest for the reader. As Myhill (2006) points out, perfectly spelled, perfectly punctuated and grammatically correct writing can not only be very dull, but it may also be completely inappropriate for communicating its message to its intended audience.

The children in our classes need to know what we see as being most important about writing. Ings (2009) suggests that *if writing is understood by a teacher as a largely mechanical process – getting spelling and punctuation right … then pupils will understand that this is what writing is and no more* (p20). Unless we address this, we run the risk of children seeing writing as production where they are 'doing writing' rather than being writers, and becoming disaffected and disengaged (Packwood and Messenheimer, 2003).

Activity: experiences of writing

Try asking some of the children you work with what they think good writing is like. You may like to use the questions below as a starting point, and reflect on the extent to which they perceive writing to be about accuracy, neatness and length.

- Can you remember a piece of writing you did when you were younger that you were particularly proud of? Why was that?
- What's the best piece of writing you've done recently? What was good about it?
- Is there anything you don't like about writing? (You may like to explore why they have answered in that way.)
- Are you a good writer? (Again, tease out the reasons for the answer given.)
- What advice would you give to someone in the year below you to help them get better at writing?

(Adapted from UKLA, 2009)

The content of the writing curriculum

Research focus: genre theory

Around 50 years ago the Plowden Report (DES, 1967) highlighted that children's experience of writing in school was often limited to personal expressive writing. Children were experiencing a very narrow diet, and when teachers did move beyond story writing, little attention was paid to the generic structure and language features of other kinds of texts.

Following the work of Australian genre theorists such as MAK Halliday, a limited number of key text types were identified as being particularly significant in the real world. They also demonstrated that pieces of writing that shared a common purpose tended to share a common structure. A genre-based approach to writing involves identifying the generic structure and language features of key text types and teaching these explicitly.

$\longrightarrow$

We usually think of writing in broad categories, such as fiction and non-fiction or narrative and non-narrative. The Primary Framework (DfES, 2006) mapped the previous curriculum and is still used by many schools. It listed and exemplified the key genres research identified as being significant. These were divided into three main genres: narrative, non-fiction and poetry, and each was further subdivided into a range of different text types – for example, narrative includes adventure, mystery, myths, science fiction and fantasy. Non-fiction texts were organised into six key genres:

- recount;

- non-chronological report;

- persuasion;

- explanation;

- instructional/procedural texts;

- discussion.

The current curriculum does not have a comprehensive list of the genres that children should be taught: the statutory framework for Key Stages 1 to 4 states that *the writing children do should include narratives, explanations, descriptions, comparisons, summaries and evaluations* (DfE, 2013, 6.3). This does not mean that there is no need to teach children how to write persuasive texts or that we shouldn't spend time writing mystery or fantasy stories, of course. Nor does the lack of emphasis on digital literacy negate the importance of our curriculum, taking into account the wide variety of forms of communication such as multimodal texts, digital texts online and moving image media. Writing for a wide range of purposes using a diverse range of media matters. Indeed, unless we address this, the gap between cultural practices at home and at school will widen as technology advances.

We need to go back to the aims of the current English curriculum to get to the heart of what is intended. These make clear that children need to write clearly, accurately and coherently, and adapt their language and style *for a range of contexts, purposes and audiences* (DfE, 2013, p5). As we will see in Chapter 13, this has the potential for schools to design a broad and balanced writing curriculum that makes strong links with other subject areas and offers a broad and rich writing repertoire which will offer children the opportunity to become successful writers who can confidently experiment with different kinds of writing. What it does indicate is just how important it is that children select their material, and shape the language and style of their writing according to the context, purpose and audience: writing should not be an exercise in learning a text type where success is determined by the inclusion of particular features.

Critics of genre theory have worried (perhaps with good reason) that reducing types of writing to specific identifiable characteristics can lead to 'instrumental' teaching (Barrs, 1991; Wyse and Jones, 2001). Writing is far more than a list of features and techniques, and good writers play around with genre, often merging and blending different types of text. As experienced readers and writers, you will regularly come across these. Historical recounts may be written from the viewpoint of a fictional individual – for example, the diary of a child living in Victorian London. A non-chronological report about the life of a penguin can be written in a poeticised way, or be constructed to subtly persuade you about the importance of conservation. However, it seems logical that knowing the expectations of different kinds of writing will offer young writers a good foundation for starting to play with hybrid forms of their own.

There are, of course, implications for our own subject knowledge if we are going to teach a broad range of texts confidently. The good news is that there are well-written, accessible resources to support this. The example below formed part of the Primary National Strategies (2008) *Support for Writing* materials, and these are readily available online (www.teachfind. com/national-strategies/primary-framework-literacy-text-types). While there are references to terminology that is no longer used (in the example below you will see the use of the word 'connective'), they nonetheless provide a useful starting point.

Non-fiction – Explanatory texts

Explanatory texts generally go beyond simple 'description' in that they include information about causes, motives or reasons. Explanations and reports are sometimes confused when children are asked to 'explain' and they actually provide a report – e.g. what they did (or what happened) but not how and why. Although some children's dictionaries do include an encyclopaedia-like explanation, others are inaccurately categorised as explanation texts when they simply define a word's meaning. Like all text types, explanatory texts vary widely and are often found combined with other text types.

Purpose: To explain how or why – e.g. to explain the processes involved in natural/social phenomena or to explain why something is the way it is		
Generic structure	**Language features**	**Knowledge for the writer**
• A general statement to introduce the topic being explained. (In the winter some animals hibernate.) • The steps or phases in a process are explained logically, in order. (**When** the nights get longer … **because** the temperature begins to drop … **so** the hedgehog looks for a safe place to hide.)	• Written in simple present tense. (Hedgehogs wake up again in the spring.) • Use of temporal connectives – e.g. first, then, after that, finally. • Use of causal connectives – e.g. so, because of this.	• Choose a title that shows what you are explaining, perhaps using why or how. (How do hedgehogs survive the winter? Why does it get dark at night?) • Decide whether you need to include images or other features to help your reader – e.g. diagrams, photographs, a flow chart, a text box, captions, a list or a glossary. • Use the first paragraph to introduce what you will be explaining. • Plan the steps in your explanation and check that you have included any necessary information about how and why things happen as they do.

(Continued)

(Continued)

Generic structure	Language features	Knowledge for the writer
		• Add a few interesting details. • Interest the reader by talking directly to them. (You'll be surprised to know that … Have you ever thought about the way that …?) or by relating the subject to their own experience at the end. (So next time you see a pile of dead leaves in the autumn … .) • Re-read your explanation as if you know nothing at all about the subject. Check that there are no gaps in the information. • Remember that you can adapt explanatory texts or combine them with other text types to make them work effectively for your audience and purpose.

Activity: different types of writing

Try writing down all the different kinds of writing you have done over the last two weeks, from notes left on the fridge to assignments. Think about the purpose and who you wrote them for. How did this influence the way that you wrote? Would all of these different kinds of writing have high status in the classroom?

Reflect on some of the decisions you have had to make. Consider the form the text took, the level of formality and how you organised the material.

Teaching writing: contexts, purpose and audience

Teaching and learning English is at its richest, an energising, purposeful and imaginatively vital experience … at its poorest English teaching and learning can be a dry didactic experience, focussed on the instruction of assessable skills …

(Cremin, 2009, p1)

Teaching writing well will involve developing knowledge, skills and understanding through meaningful and interesting contexts and experiences. Given the challenges considered earlier, we need children to be interested and actively engaged. 'Real' experiences often offer a highly effective stimulus for writing. In a Year 4 classroom, the appearance of a large, old, rusty key on the classroom floor provided immediate excitement and great speculation about the door it might open, and what might be behind it. Writing linked to a class text that is being read aloud often offers the context for a wide range of writing, with children taking on the role of a character, writing a letter at a critical part of the story, or imagining and predicting future events. Making strong links to other curriculum areas can also provide engaging contexts. For example, in one class studying the Great Fire of London as part of a history topic on Tudor England, the children were involved in drama activities that led to the writing of reports, diaries and poetry.

Case study: engaging boys in writing

Shabina was teaching a Year 2 class with a significant number of boys who seemed to be very reluctant to write. She knew she needed to find a way of engaging them with the writing process.

One morning, the children came into the classroom to find a large box on the carpet. On top was a label on which she had written 'Only to be opened by Class 2'. This was just enough to excite the children's imaginations. After an animated discussion about where it might have come from and what might be inside, they carefully opened it to find a nest, three enormous eggs, and a note that simply read 'please take care of these dragon eggs'. Immediately the children expressed their delight and amazement. They began to speculate about how the nest had got there, when the eggs might hatch and what they would need to do when this happened.

The experience provided the opportunity for Shabina to teach or revisit many different kinds of writing. Over a period of half a term, children took on the role of reporters and investigators, using special notebooks and enormous glasses to help them to look closely. They wrote letters to persuade the headteacher to let them keep the eggs, compiled a report for the other children in the school, and asked a fictional dragon expert for advice through an email account Shabina had set up. Later, they wrote an instructional text about how to look after a dragon safely and put together a training manual – dragons could, after all, cause considerable damage if untrained.

At the start of each piece of writing, Shabina provided the children with a stance from which to select and organise their material. She made sure that her children had a clear purpose and an authentic, if not real, audience for their writing. The children knew who they were writing for and what they were trying to achieve, and this helped them to think about the tone, how to organise the content, and best language choices to make.

Some weeks later, the children came into the classroom to find that the eggs had hatched – all that was left was a thank you note for the care the class had provided. The children wrote imaginative stories about the young dragons' adventures. These were published in a class book that soon took pride of place in the book area.

Curriculum link

The English curriculum states that children should *write clearly, accurately and coherently, adapting their language and style in and for a range of contexts, purposes and audiences* (DfE, 2013, p5). Of course, it is not always possible to find 'real' readerships beyond the classroom and children respond well to writing opportunities where there are imaginative authentic audiences as in the example above. They will readily suspend disbelief. The audience will sometimes be the community of writers within the class, or indeed you as the teacher, but in each case we need to help the children to think clearly about the impact they want their writing to have on their reader.

Writing for an audience

The children in Shabina's class knew their material well: they were writing as experts. The experience, the reading and the discussion allowed them to have something to say, and the authentic purposes and audiences combined with focused teaching allowed them to shape their writing and find the best way of saying it.

If we are going to help children to see that writing is about thinking and making choices, it can be helpful for them to get used to asking themselves some key questions as they start to collect together and try out ideas for their own writing.

- Who am I writing for? What is the purpose of the writing?
- From whose viewpoint am I writing this?
- What will happen?
- What do I want my reader to think and feel?
- What choices do I have?
- What kinds of techniques will help?

It is also worth considering whether children always need to write for someone else. How often do you provide opportunities for personal writing? Graham and Johnson (2003) described the benefits of writing journals and giving children time and space to write about things that matter to them or that they are interested in. Try asking children about their preferences when they write at home. Reluctant writers at school will sometimes surprise you by talking enthusiastically about what they write when they can choose for themselves. A small-scale research project by the Primary National Strategies (2011) found that almost all the children interviewed wrote at home. One boy referred to the 'fluffy notebook' he kept in his bedroom for all his special writing; another was writing sequels to *Captain Underpants*, while others talked about the imaginative stories they composed just for themselves or sometimes 'for my mum'. Outside school, many children are experienced users of a range of digital formats and can use these confidently to produce digital texts. Having ownership of writing and allowing children to choose for themselves often allows their voices to come through particularly strongly, and it is worth considering how to foster choice and make connections between writing at home and at school.

Research focus: teaching writing – the importance of reading

Meek (1991) describes the powerful literates as those who have a kind of confident knowing that they will be able to cope with written language, however unfamiliar. If children are going to be able to tackle a wide range of texts successfully, they need to achieve competence in all the skills that underpin composition. So how do we teach different kinds of writing?

The starting point for writing is reading: it makes sense that good writers are also good readers. The experience of hearing texts read aloud and reading them for themselves allows children to have a growing awareness of the sense and shape of different kinds of texts, and start to become familiar with the features of the language. *The Reader in the Writer* project (Barrs and Cork, 2001) investigated the influence that reading quality literature had on children's writing. It clearly showed that reading aloud, extensive discussion of themes and issues, and strategies such as the use of drama, impacted on the quality of the language used by the children in their own writing. It also influenced the range and appropriateness of sentence structures, and the children's ability to sustain a clear narrative voice. Barrs explains that when we come to know books well through reading and rereading, we absorb their characteristic tunes and patterns. Writers, she says, have a large number of tunes and structures in their heads.

A sequence for teaching writing

The model for teaching writing in Figure 10.1 has reading as its starting point. It came out of the research project *Raising Boys' Achievements in Writing* (PNS/UKLA, 2004) and is well established in many classrooms across the country. It offers a flexible but structured sequence to teaching writing that goes through three main stages:

- **reading**: familiarisation with the genre or text type;
- **planning**: capturing ideas for the children's own writing;
- **writing**: scaffolded writing experiences, leading to independent written outcomes.

Familiarisation with the genre or text type

One of the most important things we do as teachers of writing is to make the implicit explicit. Although some good writers seem to pick up the vocabulary and sentence structures of the texts they read and use them in their writing almost naturally, to be effective writers all children need to read, discuss and analyse good examples of the kind of text that they will be writing for themselves. It makes sense that we let children in on the secret of how an explanation text is structured before they write their explanation of how to trap a troll (and allow the Billy Goats Gruff to cross the bridge), and that we look at the kinds of language that is used by experienced writers of this kind of text. The key question is: *how has this writing been created?*

But we also want to reflect on why particular choices have been made. If you are reading an effective description of a character you will want to explore how this was done. What did the author want us to be thinking here? How did they create this effect? With older children you may well want to look at several texts – for example, if you are focusing on how to convey a strong sense of atmosphere through the setting, you could look at how EB White describes the barn in *Charlotte's Web* and the way that Angela McAllister uses language to create the sense of magic in *Leon and the Place Between*. There will be similarities but also differences that will help children to see writing as a creative and active process that requires choices to be made.

Choose your model text(s) carefully. This will, of course, depend on the text type of the final outcome and the learning needs of the children. Very short stories (picture books and short novels), for example, can be particularly useful when looking at plot structure; extracts from familiar novels, especially those currently or recently read as part of your planned read-aloud programme, will allow you to look at particular aspects of narrative – for example, how dialogue is used or how tension is built up; if you are exploring the features of different non-fiction writing: the model texts in *Talk for Writing Across the Curriculum* (Corbett and Strong, 2011) may provide a useful starting point.

Familiarisation starts by making sure there is ample time for the class to read and enjoy the text you have chosen. They need to have the opportunity to talk, discuss and respond to it as readers first and foremost. Sometimes you may want to learn part of the text together and retell dramatically with the help of actions or props. Talking like a book in this way can be particularly effective for internalising language patterns that may be new: don't be surprised if you see similar patterns replicated in the children's writing.

Once children have enjoyed the experience that the text has to offer, it can be revisited selectively, perhaps looking at key sections close up from a writer's perspective. This kind of attentive reading will help the children identify and collect together information about the text's organisational, structural and language features so that they understand how the writer created it and what makes it effective. This offers a good opportunity to contextualise and revisit grammar knowledge – as we make visible what experienced language producers know and do, we show children how to control grammar to express increasingly complex ideas (see Chapter 5).

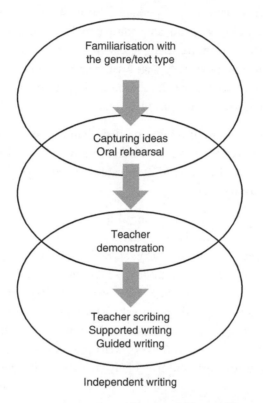

Figure 10.1 The teaching sequence (PNS/UKLA, 2004, p7)

You will want to make sure that the learning from such rich discussion isn't lost. One highly effective approach is to identify, collect together and display the organisational, structural and language features on large sheets of flip-chart paper and pin them on your working wall – or hang them on 'washing lines' across the classroom. It matters that the learning is visible. Writing places a high demand on young writers' working memory and the flip-chart sheets provide reminders and resources for children that can lighten the cognitive load when they are composing themselves. The Transforming Writing Project (Rooke, 2013) suggests calling these toolkits so that children understand they are suggestions (to write a good character description you could …) rather than fixed success criteria which can be unhelpful. Children need to know good writing is not made by cramming in or replicating a set list of structures and language features. Writing journals can be a helpful way of collecting and keeping features of good writing. Encourage children to 'magpie' ideas, vocabulary and turns of phrase, and keep examples for their own writing.

Capturing ideas for the children's own writing

This phase focuses on capturing ideas ready for the writing the children will be doing for themselves in Phase 3. They need to know what they are going to write, so this phase is likely to include planning out their own version, perhaps creatively imitating on the bare bones of a model text, creating a story map, or using a co-constructed writing frame that allows them to play with the order of their writing. Inexperienced writers are less likely to know where their writing is going, so making sure that they have a sense of the whole is important. You may well have read writing that begins well, but fades into rambling middle sections and abrupt endings ('I woke up and it was all a dream'). Talking their text to a partner can be very supportive.

Alongside discussion as a class and in smaller groups, drama activities such as hot seating, freeze framing and thought tracking can be powerful strategies for taking children right inside their writing, trying out new ideas, extending vocabulary and ways of talking, as well as an understanding of characters and plot.

This is also the time to rehearse specific writing skills for the kind of text being written. Young writers need regular opportunities to have a go at crafting relevant short pieces of writing – for example, a setting, a persuasive paragraph, or a few sentences building up tension: all of these could be based on visual images. Daily word and language games can provide excellent opportunities to broaden and deepen vocabulary, try out and practise ideas and techniques, revisit and re-create grammatical patterns, and manipulate language to make sure it suits the given purpose and audience. Research shows that explicit attention to relevant grammatical constructions within the context of writing produced significant improvements in the writing of secondary students, and it is likely that this is also true in the primary years (Myhill *et al.*, 2011).

All this important preparatory work means that by the end of this second phase children will have models and content that can be drawn on throughout the independent writing process.

Scaffolded writing experiences, leading to independent written outcomes

Case study: *Leon and the Place Between*

Simon had a class of Year 3 children. The focus of his unit of work was narrative, and more specifically fantasy worlds. Simon noticed that the children tended to write 'rushed' narrative. Although their writing often started off well and they had plenty of ideas, text structure tended to be weak and many children wrote one event after another sometimes in a rather

→

random order. This informed his choice of text, *Leon and the Place Between*, a beautifully written story by Angela McAllister and illustrated by Grahame Baker-Smith, with a very strong structure that the children would be able to use as a model for their own writing.

Before reading the text, and to engage the children, he put tickets for a show on each table that simply read 'Admit One' together with an artefact relating to the text – a set of playing cards, a top hat, a magic wand, a cape and the question 'Dare you step into the place between?' After some initial speculation, Simon introduced the book itself. Simon knew that the children's ability to write well was dependent on their understanding of how this kind of text worked. He read the text aloud, and together the children enjoyed and discussed it as readers. He used drama and role play to help the children imagine themselves right inside the story.

They then went on to examine the text structure in detail and used story maps to outline the plot. Together, they began to identify organisational, structural and language features, collecting these together on large sheets of sugar paper that were pinned on his working wall. This provided the children with a visual reminder that they could refer to when they were doing their own writing, but also enabled them to agree the success criteria together.

The children were invited to write their own version of the journey to 'The Place Between'. They used the features of the text and the success criteria to plan their writing and Simon supported the writing process by modelling at each stage. He had prepared this earlier, and had what he was going to write on a post-it note at the top of the flip-chart just as an *aide-memoire*. Over the three-week unit of work, he was able to demonstrate all aspects of the writing process, writing and redrafting in front of the children in real time, thinking aloud as he wrote.

The importance of modelling

Simon's emphasis on modelling has its basis in research and is an essential part of what we know makes an effective teacher of writing. This is a powerful pedagogy and involves making visible what you do when you write. The voice we model is so important for shaping the voice that we want children to have and use in their own heads when they are writing. Simon was learning to talk his thoughts aloud to himself as he wrote, so that the children could see the decisions he was making.

> The children were able to see that ideas don't just come straight to me, Simon commented, and that I am sometimes hesitant and change my mind. They saw that I needed to choose from different words and phrases rather than writing the first thing I thought of. This really helped them to see me as a writer and to realise that writers have choices to make.

As he did this he was building up a meta-language with the children for talking about writing, using terms that everyone was able to understand and modelling the running commentary they might use. By taking over the spelling and handwriting, Simon enabled the children to focus exclusively on how composition worked and see the process close up, focusing all the time on the impact and effect he wanted to have on the reader. Just as important was the opportunity to observe first-hand the behaviours of an experienced writer.

Research focus – teachers as writers

Modelling writing in this way can seem daunting as it demands significant teacher knowledge and not all of us are confident writers, particularly when writing in front of others. However, it is worth persevering. We know that teachers who write teach writing better, and that this can impact constructively on their roles as teachers of writing in the classroom. Cremin and Baker (2010) have shown that in order to enhance the teaching of writing, teachers and student teachers need real opportunities to write at their own level and reflect upon the process. Ofsted (2009) found that teachers who were confident as writers themselves, and who could demonstrate how writing is composed, taught it effectively. As we demonstrate 'writerly' behaviours and make explicit our own compositional challenges, children will benefit as writers themselves.

Shared writing, supported composition and guided writing

We have seen that an important part of our role as teachers of writing is to make the whole process explicit and to scaffold writing experiences so that children are able to write well independently. One way of thinking about this is to see our role as one that changes.

Modelled writing – watch me: demonstrating the writing process.

Shared writing – take part with me: scribing the children's thoughts.

Supported composition – experimenting together: trying out language, vocabulary and sentence structures.

Guided writing – have a go with my support: scaffolded independence.

Independent writing – over to you: applying learning independently.

Shared writing involves collaboration with the children, asking for ideas, accepting some but not all, extending vocabulary and shaping the writing to fit the purpose and audience. This approach temporarily removes some of the problems of orchestrating writing skills, provides opportunities for partner talk and discussion, and helps children to clarify their ideas.

Supported composition can offer closely scaffolded support. You might, for example, ask the children to work in pairs or individually to orally rehearse or write a phrase or sentence linked to the learning objective. Year 1 children are expected to say out loud what they are going to write about and compose a sentence orally before writing it. This allows them to rehearse the flow, fluency and feel of their words (Cremin, 2009) and transfer the patterns, structures and cadences of the text into their spoken, and then written, language. This can be done on mini whiteboards, perhaps followed by the 'show me' strategy where children hold up their suggestions. This allows you to make an immediate assessment and to identify and share some of the good examples produced.

Guided writing provides an additional supported step between modelled and shared writing and independent writing. It can take place at any point during the teaching sequence and is where you draw together a group of writers with similar learning needs. A guided writing session might support a group of children who are finding it hard to capture ideas for their writing or might focus with another group on the use of more precise vocabulary. At a later stage, children might be supported to self-assess and review their writing. This is explored in more detail below.

Supporting children at the point of writing in this way is far more productive than distance marking at the end of the process and is why guided writing can be so powerful – it is another opportunity to think through the process of writing aloud with the children, 'there and then' at the table, making sure children are going back to their writing, reading it, and checking that it makes sense with an audience to help them. It is not about children being in fixed groups – it is about responding to their needs at the right time.

Finally, children need enough time and space to write for themselves. Independent writing provides children with the opportunity to use all the skills and understandings they have learned throughout the teaching sequence, and the toolkits you created earlier will provide a helpful scaffold.

Drafting and rereading

The National Curriculum has a strong emphasis on the writing process – that is, children learning to:

- plan their writing;
- draft and write;
- evaluate and edit;
- proofread for spelling and punctuation errors;
- read aloud their own writing.

The notion of writing as a process was recognised by Smith (1982) and Graves (1983) who were concerned that children had to write one-off pieces of writing, with the occasional opportunity to write out 'a neat copy'. As writers ourselves, we know that we are unlikely to get everything right first time. Few of us would hand in the first draft of an assignment and expect to receive a high mark.

From Key Stage 1, children are expected to draft and reread to check that their meaning is clear, and as children progress into Key Stage 2 they are expected to do this as the writing develops. Real writers are constantly looping back on what they have just written to assess its likely impact and quality, and how far the writing is meeting the intended writing goals. The drafting and rereading process for many adult writers is recursive – we often go back, reread and revise as we write, perhaps making a final check for meaning, spelling and punctuation at the end. If children only go back and review their writing when they think they have got to the end of the task, this can be met with dismay. However, you may have noticed that although you invite children to reread and 'correct' their work and give them time to do this, they will very often offer you the same writing with very few revisions. One of the reasons for this is that we simply do not see the errors in our own writing. The first draft of this chapter was returned from the editors with inaccuracies that should have been obvious. We read what we think we have written.

One approach that supports the drafting process is to invite children to read their work aloud to a partner. This provides an immediate audience for their writing, and allows the words to be lifted off the page. It will also help children to develop a greater awareness of the impact and effect of their writing on the reader. Missing words, incomplete sentences and parts of the text that need further thought will often surface. Children will, of course, need be shown how to talk about writing with a partner. Try modelling this using a visualiser and a 'real' piece of writing. It goes without saying that it is essential to have their permission, and to have developed a learning environment where children are happy to share their work publicly. This will not be successful if they are fearful of peers' judgements.

You may find it useful to provide highlighters to help the children identify aspects of writing that have gone well or that need improvement. This can allow them to identify their own good writing explicitly while at the same time having ownership of the particular sections of the writing that would benefit from the most attention. Teachers in the Transforming Writing Project (Rooke, 2013) found that this elicited a higher quality assessment response, perhaps because it inverted the usual teacher evaluate – child responds to practice; the teacher was responding in part to the child's priorities for improving their writing. This can be helpful for identifying the level of complexity that children believe they can work at.

Learning outcomes review

Becoming a writer is, as we have seen, highly complex, and our role as teachers is critical. It requires explicit and focused teaching within meaningful and motivating contexts. You should now know:

- why learning to write is complex;
- the importance of balancing the technical and compositional aspects of writing;
- the teaching sequence for writing;
- the importance of talk for becoming a writer.

Self-assessment questions
1. Can you now explain the difference between transcription and composition?
2. What are the key elements of the teaching sequence for writing?
3. Why do you think that reading is so important for writing?

Answers to activities

There are no specific answers for the activities in this chapter as your response will depend upon your personal experiences.

Further reading

For a detailed look at creative approaches to teaching writing, read:

Cremin, T (2009) *Teaching English Creatively*. London: Routledge.

For practical approaches to embedding talk throughout the teaching sequence for writing, explore the Primary National Strategies materials:

Primary National Strategies (2008) *Talk for Writing*. Nottingham: DCSF. Available at: **http://webarchive.nationalarchives.gov.uk/20110809101133/nsonline.org.uk/node/163592** (accessed 27 June 2016).

To explore ways of embedding formative assessment in writing, read:

Rooke, J (2013) *Transforming Writing: Interim Evaluation Report*. London: National Literacy Trust.

References

Alderman, G and Green, S (2011) Fostering lifelong spellers through meaningful experiences, *The Reading Teacher*, 64(8): 599–605.

Barrs, M (1987) *Learning to Write: Language Matters 2 and 3*. London: Centre for Literacy in Primary Education.

Barrs, M (1991) *Thinking about Writing: Language Matters 1*. London: Centre for Literacy in Primary Education.

Barrs, M and Cork, V (2001) *The Reader in the Writer*. London: Centre for Literacy in Primary Education.

Bearne, E (1998) *Making Progress in English*. London: RoutledgeFalmer.

Bearne, E (2007) 'Writing'. *ITE English: Readings for Discussion*. Available at: **www.ite.org.uk/ite_readings/writing_20071130.pdf** (accessed 1 October 2012).

Bereiter, C and Scardamalia, M (1987) *The Psychology of Written Composition*. Hillsdale, NJ: Lawrence Erlbaum Associates.

Clark, C (2012) *Young People's Writing in 2011: Findings from the National Literacy Trust's Annual Literacy Survey*. London: National Literacy Trust.

Corbett, P and Strong, S (2011) *Talk for Writing Across the Curriculum*. Maidenhead: Open University Press.

Corden, R (2000) *Literacy and Learning Through Talk*. Birmingham: Open University Press.

Cremin, T (2009) *Teaching English Creatively*. London: Routledge.

Cremin, T and Baker, S (2010) Exploring teacher–writer identities in the classroom, *English Teaching: Practice and Critique*, 9(3): 8–25.

Department of Education and Science (DES) (1967) *Children and their Primary Schools* (Plowden Report). London: HMSO.

Department for Education (DfE) (2013) *The National Curriculum in England: Key Stages 1 and 2 Framework Document*. London: DfE.

Department for Education and Skills (DfES) (2006) *Primary National Strategy: Primary Framework for Literacy and Mathematics*. Norwich: OPSI. Available at: **www.educationengland.org.uk/documents/pdfs/2006-primary-national-strategy.pdf** (accessed 20 June 2014).

Flutter, J (2000) *Words Matter: Thinking and Talking about Writing in the Classroom*. Slough: National Foundation for Educational Research.

Graham, L and Johnson, A (2003) *Children's Writing Journals*. Leicester: United Kingdom Literacy Association.

Grainger, T, Goouch, K and Lambirth, A (2003) Playing the game called writing: children's views and voices. *English in Education*, 37(2): 4–15.

Graves, D (1983) *Writing: Teachers and Children at Work*. Portsmouth: NH Heinemann.

Ings, R (2009) *Writing is Primary*. London: Esmée Fairbairn Foundation. Available at: **http://esmeefairbairn.org.uk/news-and-learning/publications/writing-is-primary** (accessed 22 June 2014).

Medwell, J, Strand, S and Wray, D (2009) The links between handwriting and composing for Y6 children. *Cambridge Journal of Education*, 39(3): 329–44.

Meek, M (1991) *On Being Literate*. London: The Bodley Head.

Myhill, D (2006) Designs on writing: Part 1, *The Secondary English Magazine*, October.

Sheffield: National Association for the Teaching of English.

Myhill, D, Jones, S and Bailey, T (2011) *Grammar for Writing? The Impact of Contextualised Grammar Teaching on Pupils' Writing and Pupils' Metalinguistic Understanding*. Swindon: Economic and Social Research Council.

Ofsted (2009) *English at the Crossroads: An Evaluation of English in Primary and Secondary Schools 2005–8*. London: HMSO.

Packwood, A and Messenheimer, T (2003) Back to the future: developing children as writers, in E Bearne, H Dombey and T Grainger (eds), *Classroom Interactions in Literacy*. Maidenhead: Open University Press.

Primary National Strategies (2008) *Support for Writing*. Nottingham: DCSF. Available at: **http://webarchive.nationalarchives.gov.uk/20100612050234/nationalstrategies. standards.dcsf.gov.uk/primary/primaryframework/cpd/literacy/support_writing** (accessed 22 June 2016).

Primary National Strategies (2011) *Tackling the Key Stage 2 Reading–Writing Gap*. Nottingham: DCSF. Available at: **http://wsassets.s3.amazonaws.com/ws/nso/pdf/ ef05102f69387399f7fafcccffe4554b.pdf** (accessed 22 June 2016).

Primary National Strategy and United Kingdom Literacy Association (PNS/UKLA) (2004) *Raising Boys' Achievements in Writing*. London: PNS/UKLA.

Rooke, J (2013) *Transforming Writing: Interim Evaluation Report*. London: National Literacy Trust.

Smith, F (1982) *Writing and the Writer*. London: Heinemann.

United Kingdom Literacy Association (UKLA) (2009) *Support Materials for ECAW*. London: UKLA. Available at: **www.ukla.org/resources/view/every_child_a_writer_ecaw_surveys/** (accessed 22 June 2016).

Wyse, D and Jones, R (2001) *Teaching English, Language and Literacy*. London: RoutledgeFalmer.

11 Multimodal Texts

Claire Norcott

Learning outcomes

By reading this chapter you will develop your understanding of:

- what multimodal texts are;
- how multimodal and digital texts can be used to motivate pupils to write;
- how multimodal texts can be used to engage pupils, especially boys.

Teachers' Standards

3. Demonstrate good subject and curriculum knowledge:

- have a secure knowledge of the relevant subject(s) and curriculum areas, foster and maintain pupils' interest in the subject, and address misunderstandings;
- demonstrate a critical understanding of developments in the subject and curriculum areas, and promote the value of scholarship.

4. Plan and teach well-structured lessons:

- promote a love of learning and children's intellectual curiosity;
- contribute to the design and provision of an engaging curriculum within the relevant subject area(s).

Introduction: what are multimodal texts and digital literacies and why are they important?

A multimodal text is described as *the strategic use of two or more communication modes to make meaning, for example image, gesture, music, spoken language, and written language* (**https://creatingmultimodaltexts.com**). While the assumption might be that multimodal must include some form of digital media, this is not the case. A multimodal text can be:

- **paper** – such as books, comics, posters;
- **digital** – from slide presentations, e-books, blogs, e-posters, web pages, and social media, through to animation, film and video games;
- **live** – a performance or an event.

https://creatingmultimodaltexts.com

To become multimodal literate, we need to be able to make meaning through

> the reading, viewing, understanding, responding to and producing and interacting with multimedia and digital texts. It may include oral and gestural modes of talking, listening and dramatising as well as writing, designing and producing such texts.

(Walsh, 2010: 213)

These skills may need to be explicitly taught. Bhojwani (2015, p145) based on Kress suggests the following model as a way of understanding the four main modes of a multimodal text.

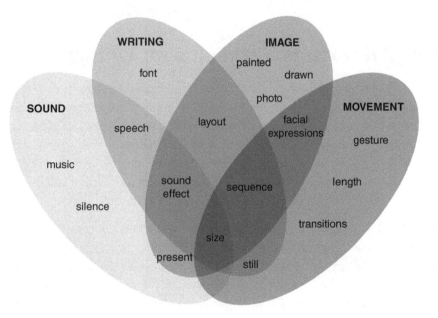

Figure 11.1 Understanding the four main modes of a multimodal text

As children now grow up in an environment where communication is often a mixture of words, images, movement and sounds, the need to understand and interpret these messages by combining the media is paramount. Along with this, we now have a wide range of new methods of communication available via the Internet, emails and presentations (Bearne and Wolstencroft, 2007). As teachers, we must therefore explore and embrace these new ways of communicating to ensure that children are equipped for a future where technology and digital communication will surely continue to grow. The National Curriculum (2013) stresses the importance of developing children's understanding of *inference*, allowing pupils to access and understand a range of texts and to understand features of such texts. While a variety of novels and storybooks might be traditionally selected to achieve these outcomes, digital texts can also be used to ensure that the objectives are met and that pupils are also engaged while doing so.

Although digital literacies are not specifically mentioned within the National Curriculum, visual literacy and digital literacies have received attention recently (Savage and Barnett, 2015). The skills required to read, interpret and understand digital texts – for example, websites and online presentations – are vastly different from those required to enjoy and understand a novel.

Activity: considering forms of reading and their skills

Consider the forms of reading you have completed today, along with the purpose, and make a list. Now list the skills that you needed to read, understand and engage with the media you have listed.

Using digital texts as a stimulus for writing

While print-based reading has always been multimodal, requiring an understanding and interpretation of how features such as space, layout and font choice interact and affect the reader, image has become more dominant than the word in a variety of texts (Jewitt, 2005). Therefore, children will arrive in the classroom with an expectation of engaging with more than just text-based novels. We need to ensure that we have the resources and skills required to teach successfully using digital methods as, if our teaching uses digital and multimodal approaches well, literacy standards can rise noticeably (UKLA, 2009).

We know that many children use their own experiences of a range of visual texts such as graphic novels, computer games, picture books and even films to inspire their writing (Bearne and Wolstencroft, 2007), yet this can lead to written narratives which are incoherent and do not flow. Often, this is because the ideas generated by the varying stimuli can be too complicated to transfer into words. There might be aspects of characterisation or movement, for example, which do not transfer from image or digital format to text. Therefore, allowing children to create texts digitally opens up new, creative avenues. Children today possess the digital mindsets, and necessary cultural and cognitive tones, to adopt and apply their technological skills (UKLA, 2009) as they are routinely exposed to computers, mobile phones, emails and other technologies in their daily lives (Smeda *et al.*, 2014), and this should be embraced and celebrated. Using digital technology allows the visual element to become more obvious, with language being extended, enhanced or even replaced, reflecting how images are now reflected in day-to-day life (Matthewman *et al.*, 2004).

Digital storytelling is not a new concept, but recently the development of new technology has allowed more creativity and flexibility in our approaches to teaching reading and writing. There is not one set definition of digital storytelling, yet *the majority emphasise the use of multimedia tools including graphics, audio, video and animation to tell a story* (Smeda *et al.*, 2014).

If we consider the teaching sequence we usually follow when asking pupils to write, we can look at how digital texts can be used in a similar manner to increase motivation and engagement.

Activity: using digital texts

Watch the following short video clip: **www.youtube.com/watch?v=V31_oo1jybw**

It is possible to critically analyse this short film in the way we would when we introduce a new genre. Consider and note your responses to the points below.

- How were you able to infer certain elements and predict what could happen next? Were there any visual clues?
- How did you respond to the character?
- Just as in written texts when we would discuss aspects of composition, we can also do that here. How does the lighting, shot of angle, sound, timing and focus of camera affect the quality of the film?
- Develop a short personal response to the film.

Research focus

Lobello (2015) recognised that some primary aged pupils lack the motivation to write using traditional methods. She studied the difference in both motivation and attainment of 9-year-old pupils when writing traditionally and when using digital methods. Within Lobello's research, Ormrod (2008) explores the issue of motivation and discusses how pupils who are presented with a task they *want* to do will be more persistent, even if they face challenges, and will therefore complete the task successfully. To foster this motivation, Bruning and Horn (2000) recommend four factors of motivation-enhancing conditions for writing:

1. Nurturing functional beliefs about writing.

2. Fostering student engagement through authentic writing goals and context.

3. Providing a supportive context for writing.

4. Creating a positive emotional environment.

They go on to suggest the following as ways of developing factor two:

- having students create examples of different kinds of writing;

- encouraging students to write about topics of personal interest;

- having students write for a variety of audiences.

By allowing digital writing to be incorporated into the classroom, we can develop engagement and also aim to improve pupils' perceptions of their writing ability. A survey in 2009 (National Literacy Trust) discovered that only 13 per cent of pupils questioned believed themselves to be 'very good' at writing, with 33 per cent stating that they 'could be better'. Alongside this the survey also discovered that 49 per cent of those questioned stated they thought writing was 'boring'. It would appear, therefore, that motivation, engagement and performance are linked. Regarding writing format, the survey examined which writing formats were engaged in at least once a month. The top five responses were as follows.

1. Text messages – 81.9 per cent.

2. Notes in class or for homework – 77 per cent.

3. Instant messages – 73.1 per cent.

4. Emails – 67 per cent.

5. On a social network site – 62.5 per cent.

This supports the discussions of Rosen (2011, p. 1), who maintains children born into the so-called iGeneration:

> expect technology to be there, and they expect it to do whatever they want it to do. The smartphone, the internet, and everything technological are not 'tools' at all—they simply are. Just as we don't think about the existence of air, they don't question the existence of technology and media.

This constant involvement with the world of technology means that we must not 'teach with technology' but use technology to convey content more powerfully and efficiently. For example, using iPads, which are often used for pleasure, can instantly create a sense of 'fun' (Lobello, 2015) and therefore increases motivation. Lobello found that students who are motivated spend more time on and are more persistent at tasks. She also found that the use of digital storytelling was a successful way of intrinsically motivating and engaging students. We must find ways to ensure our pupils are intrinsically motivated to write. The outcomes for the students were increased levels of satisfaction, confidence and enjoyment with writing.

Case study: digital writing

In a Lower Key Stage Two class within a challenging school, Sarah was seeking ways to engage her pupils with the writing process. She selected the app 'Zooburst' as a creative and multimodal way to ensure that pupils would be motivated to fully engage with writing. Due to the moving images and flexibility of the app, the children felt they had more control over

→

their writing and were less pressured to produce written text in the more traditional sense. All pupils produced work which showed progression and enthusiasm levels in the class were raised. The fact that the books were written for a purpose and could be published added a greater sense of context and authenticity to their work, something which the children valued when they were asked about using the app.

By using a range of digital methods to produce both fiction and non-fiction texts, we motivate and engage more pupils in writing tasks. There is still a clear process to follow, just as if we were asking pupils to physically write. Bearne and Wolstencroft (2007, p32) suggest a Multimodal Planning and Teaching Sequence, which has been shortened below.

Familiarity with the text type Read and categorise text, explain how design, layout and organisation of text create effect.

Capture ideas Explore ideas using drama and role play. Record ideas through drawings, story maps. Capture ideas using digital audio.

Plan Demonstrate how to choose modes which are best for the task. Model designing layouts.

Draft Demonstrate making changes to the text, how to add or remove elements. Show how to use drawings to engage the reader.

Revise Ask response partners to review and respond using agreed criteria. Show how to use software to reorganise sections of text.

Proofread Check visual text for colour, layout and effects. Check auditory elements for sound effects and timings. Check written text for accurate grammar.

Present Discuss decision about final presentation. Model how to evaluate final copy. Publish using chosen method.

Within each of these stages there should be examples of Teacher Modelling leading to Children's Independent Learning before the sequence continues.

This process of creating digital texts still requires pupils to *think* as writers; the difference lies in the way they present their work and the tools they are using. A benefit of presenting digitally is that pupils can have a clear audience in mind and tailor their presentation for that audience more easily (Savage and Barnett, 2015). Writing for a purpose assists with motivation, as pupils have a clear sense of *why* they are writing and *who* they are writing for. This also helps with the construction of the text, as when they have an audience in mind the tone, language and prevention can be adapted accordingly. Alongside this is the ease of sharing a digital presentation, something which pupils can do instantly in many digital forms. The appeal of engaging with visual and auditory texts rather than purely written pieces will be of benefit to most people.

Multimodal texts, digital texts and visual literacy – getting the boys engaged

Research focus

Historically, girls have outperformed boys in reading attainment at both primary level and secondary level, not just in the UK but worldwide (DfE, 2015; OECD, 2014). Alongside this, there is also a clear gap in the *enjoyment* of reading between genders, with more girls than boys saying they enjoy reading (NLT, 2012). This study also showed that the gap appears to be widening with comparisons to data from 2005. The report explores how teacher knowledge about literature could be an issue, as Jarrett maintained.

> I think there is an issue of subject knowledge, particularly in primary schools. Understandably, because they are not specialists, too few teachers in primary schools have a detailed knowledge of literature, either classic or contemporary children's literature. I think this makes it more difficult for them to choose the right kinds of text to share with children, and also how to recommend books individually to boys that they might read outside of school.

(NLT, 2012, p13)

A further report by the National Literacy Trust in 2015 stated that children spent more time reading materials online than they did reading a book (NLT, 2015, p8). The gap between girls and boys is still evident yet has reduced slightly, perhaps suggesting a link between the growth of online reading compared to reading books alone. Within this report explanations were sought as to why they might read outside of class and some interesting responses were as follows.

- Technology makes reading more accessible.

- More reading is done via social media.

- Because I can choose what I want to read.

(NLT, 2015, p11)

Yet while boys engage in reading online, they still do this considerably less than girls, with blogs, for example, being read by 29.1 per cent of girls compared to 14.9 per cent of boys. Conversely, the study showed that comics are read by 34 per cent of boys compared to 19.3 per cent of girls. As teachers, it is vital that we understand the range of literature available to us and maintain a knowledge of what will engage and motivate our pupils.

Exploring types of multimodal texts

As discussed in the Introduction, multimodal texts combine modes of sound, movement, images and writing. Picture books are a type of multimodal text as are comics, both of which will be explored. When young children first experience picture books they engage with pictures solely for the purpose of enjoyment; there is no seeking out meaning from the pictures. However, as children become more able readers and picture books become more sophisticated, we can begin to explore the purpose of illustrations within text. Are they there purely to engage the reader and to reduce the number of words on the page or is there more to the illustration? Do they add extra meaning to the text and allow us to understand the author's intent in a deeper way?

Case study: using picture books with Year 5

Over the course of a six-week period, Emma, a trainee teacher, utilised a picture book to engage a very reluctant Year 5 class. The class consisted of 32 children (21 boys and 11 girls) from low socioeconomic backgrounds.

The picture book *Queen of the Falls* by Chris Van Allsberg allowed her to adopt a more multimodal approach by using images, music and videos to elicit engagement from the children. This particular text was successful as the illustrations depicted such emotion that from the images alone you could really step into the characters' shoes. Instead of having the book read to them, they could see, hear and feel what the characters were feeling.

One particularly successful approach was when the image of Niagara Falls was combined with the text and a sound clip of the falls in order for the pupils to describe a setting. The vocabulary, imagination and structure of the writing from the children greatly improved. More importantly, the children were engaged, motivated and therefore learning.

Adopting this multimodal approach enabled Emma to very quickly see its effectiveness in engaging the boys and other reluctant learners within the class. The progress pupils had made with their writing, following the six-week topic was also very clear.

Activity: using comics

Using information from this chapter, explore how you could use comics to engage children as readers and also to teach aspects of writing.

Learning outcomes review

You should now have a clear understanding of what a multimodal text is and the range which is available to you as a teacher to use in the classroom. It should be clear how using digital texts (as well as other multimodal texts) can help to engage and motivate both boys and girls to read and write, thus improving attainment and enjoyment of English.

Self-assessment questions
Select a picture book which you feel would engage your choice of age range of pupils.

1. How do the pictures interact with the text?
2. Which elements of the book would you wish to emphasise to the pupils?
3. Consider ways you would use the book to develop and promote writing.

The following are some picture books you might like to explore.

Madeline by Ludwig Bemelmans

The First Slodge by Jeanne Wilis and Jenni Desmond

Slug Needs a Hug by Jeanne Willis and Tony Ross

Mikki by Stephen Mackey

Through the Magic Mirror by Anthony Browne

Sam's Sandwich by David Pelham

A Monster Calls by Patrick Ness

It's a Book by Lane Smith

Leon and the Place Between by Angela McAllister

The Something by Rebecca Cobb

Varmints by Helen Ward and Marc Craste

Explore the range of digital apps and technologies which are available for producing digital texts. Some to start with are: Comic life, iBooks Author, Night Zoo Keeper.

1. Use your idea for developing writing from the picture book you selected to produce a digital text using Bearne and Wolstencroft's sequence (2007).

2. Consider the challenges you faced and how you might help pupils overcome these in the classroom.

References

Bhojwani, P (2015) 'Multimodal literacies can motivate boys to write' in Waugh, D, Bushnell, A and Neaum, S (eds) *Beyond Early Writing*. Northwich: Critical Publishing.

Bearne, E and Wolstencroft, H (2007) *Visual Approaches to Teaching Writing*. London: Sage.

Bruning, R and Horn, C (2000) Developing motivation to write. *Educational Psychologist*, 35(1): 25–37.

Department for Education (DfE) (2015) *National Curriculum Assessment at Key Stage 2 in England*. Available at: **www.gov.uk/government/uploads/system/uploads/attachment_ data/file/456343/SFR30_2015_text.pdf**(accessed 9 August 2016).

Jewitt, C (2005) Multimodality 'reading' and 'writing' for the 21st century, *Studies in the Cultural Politics of Education*, 26(3): 315–31.

Lobello, C (2015) The impact of digital storytelling on fourth grade students' motivation to write. *Education and Human Development*. Master's theses, paper 573.

Matthewman, S *et al*. (2004) What does multimodality mean for English? Creative tensions in teaching new texts and new literacies. *Education, Communication and Information*, 4(1).

National Curriculum (2013) *Programme of Study for English*. London: DfE.

National Literacy Trust (2009) Writing survey. Available at: **www.literacytrust.org.uk/ assets/0000/0226/Writing_survey_2009.pdf** (accessed 8 August 2016).

National Literacy Trust (2012) Boys' reading commission. Available at: **www.literacytrust. org.uk/assets/0001/4056/Boys_Commission_Report.pdf** (accessed 9 August 2016).

OECD (2014) PISA 2012 results: What students know and can do: student performance in mathematics, *Reading and Science* (Vol. 1).

Ormrod, J.E. (2008). How motivation affects learning and behavior [online]. Excerpt from *Educational Psychology: Developing Learners*: 384–386. www.education.com/reference/article/ motivation-affects-learning-behavior/ (accessed 28 December 2016).

Rosen, L (2011) Teaching the iGeneration. Available at: **www.steveclarkprincipal.com/ uploads/1/6/5/2/16527520/teaching_the_igeneration.pdf** (accessed 8 August 2016).

Savage, M and Barnett, A (2015) *Digital Literacy for Primary Teachers*. St Albans: Critical Publishing.

Smeda, N *et al*. (2014) The effectiveness of digital storytelling in the classrooms: a comprehensive study. *Smart Learning Environments*, 1(6).

UKLA (2009) I know what to write now! Engaging boys (and girls) through a multimodal approach. Available at: **https://ukla.org/shop/details/i_know_what_to_write_now_ engaging_boys_and_girls_through_a_multimodal_** (accessed 2 August 2016).

Walsh, M (2010) Multimodal literacy: what does it mean for classroom practice? *Australian Journal of Language and Literacy*, 33(3): 211–39. Available at: **www.alea.edu.au/documents/ item/63** (accessed 26 July 2016).

12 Is There a Place for Drama?

Eve English

Learning outcomes

By reading this chapter you will develop your understanding of:

- what children need to understand about drama;
- what we need to know as primary teachers in order to teach the 2014 English National Curriculum;
- some of the challenges we face when we teach children drama;
- approaches to teaching drama.

Teachers' Standards
3. Demonstrate good subject and curriculum knowledge:

- have a secure knowledge of the relevant subject(s) and curriculum areas, foster and maintain pupils' interest in the subject, and address misunderstandings;
- demonstrate a critical understanding of developments in the subject and curriculum areas, and promote the value of scholarship;
- demonstrate an understanding of, and take responsibility for, promoting high standards of literacy, articulacy and the correct use of standard English, whatever the teacher's specialist subject.

Introduction

At primary stage drama has never been a discrete subject in the National Curriculum. It has found its place within the English Programme of Study and its importance has changed from curriculum to curriculum and from strategy to strategy. In the National Curriculum for England (DfE, 2013), the Spoken Language section of the English Programme of Study states:

> All pupils should be enabled to participate in and gain knowledge, skills and understanding associated with the artistic practice of drama. Pupils should be able to adopt, create and sustain a range of roles, responding appropriately to others in role. They should have opportunities to improvise, devise and script drama for one another and a range of audiences, as well as to rehearse, refine, share and respond thoughtfully to drama and theatre performances.

(p13)

It is a short paragraph, but as Woolland (2010) maintained:

> Teachers who regularly use drama in primary schools do not need specific clauses
> in curriculum documents or educational reports to convince them of the rich
> and profound learning opportunities that drama can create, of its great value in
> delivering other aspects of the curriculum.

> (pxv)

This chapter will consider those learning opportunities within literacy teaching and other areas of the curriculum. It will look at the most recent requirements and also explore areas for using drama where there is no explicit mention of it.

The importance of drama

Drama is about pretence, but that pretence can be very real when children, and indeed adults, are fully involved. Within the safe boundaries set by the drama, children can examine issues and let their imaginations flourish. Drama often begins with stories where the narrative and characterisation can be explored in depth. By using very simple techniques (see below) the emotions and motives of characters can be probed. This enables children to empathise with others and delve into situations that they may not experience first hand. They also learn to question motives and examine different perspectives. All areas of the English curriculum can be enhanced by the use of drama. Speaking and listening skills are developed as children speak more confidently in role than they do when they are simply themselves. At a surprisingly early age, children learn to use different registers depending on their role. Reading comprehension improves as the text is probed in a drama activity and writing, whether in role or alongside role, can be enhanced by providing an audience and purpose that is almost as good as the real thing.

Children also benefit from the social situations that drama provides. They learn to work with others and to value their views. Clipson-Boyles (1998) describes how drama motivates children to learn and how new knowledge is retained in the long-term memory because of the interactive nature of drama. Baldwin and John (2012) stress the importance of socialisation for children:

> Human brains are wired to be social. Children need to socialise, to become
> part of groups, to belong, to make sense of lived experience with and alongside
> other people.

> (p20)

As with many aspects of English teaching, drama in education has changed its focus over the years and this has led to debates and controversies in terms of both pedagogy and content.

A long-standing argument has been between drama as theatre (performance) and drama as education and a process of development. The term 'process drama' is often seen as being synonymous with 'drama in education' and describes the interaction between pupils and teacher as the drama develops. Fleming (1994, p15) quotes the very influential Way (1967) on the subject of drama versus theatre:

> 'theatre' is largely concerned with communication between actors and an audience; 'drama' is largely concerned with experience by the participants, irrespective of any function of communication to an audience.

This distinction is still often made today, although writers on drama would suggest that it is often difficult to separate the two aspects. As Fleming (1994, p15) states, pupils may not always perform on stage but they are often performing to their classmates when involved in what is deemed to be educational drama.

Another ongoing debate is the place of drama in the curriculum. Should it be a vehicle for teaching other subjects or should it be seen as a subject in its own right? Again, in the modern primary school classroom there is room for both and a balanced view is emerging (Clipson-Boyles, 2012).

Activity: concerns about drama

Many teachers are reluctant to use drama in the classroom. Why do you think this may be? For example, you may worry about losing control of the class or think that you need a lot of experience.

(Suggestions can be found at the end of the chapter.)

Drama throughout the primary stage

In this section, drama techniques will be described, with suggestions and case studies, as a way of showing how drama can be taught throughout the primary stage.

Role-play areas

Role-play areas or home corners are very common in the Early Years setting, but are also evident throughout Key Stage 1. Often they are linked to the topic being studied. So, for example, you will find fire stations, pirate ships, garden centres, post offices and castles. What is important is that after these areas have been created, then dramatic play should be developed. It is tempting to leave the children to freely explore these areas, but a little teacher intervention can move the drama on and develop children's skills.

Hot seating

Hot seating can be used throughout the primary stage and beyond. It is well within the grasp of Key Stage 1 children. The term 'hot seating' describes exactly what the activity is. Someone is put into the *hot seat*, in role, and other children in the group ask questions, often to find out the motivation of the characters in the hot seat. The role is usually a fictional character but can be a character from history or an official who has to answer questions from journalists or concerned villagers, for example. Teachers should be prepared, at least initially, to be the ones in the hot seat. The following case study demonstrates how a role-play area and hot seating can be used with Year 1 pupils.

Case study: *Goldilocks and the Three Bears*

In the corner of a Year 1 class a simple cottage was set up for the three bears of the fairy tale. Anna, a Year 3 BA student, had gone to great trouble creating the cottage with a table and chairs, small camp beds and, of course, bowls for porridge. The children knew the story very well. They would spend time putting on the bears' masks and making endless bowls of porridge and cups of tea. On one occasion, Anna asked a child to go to sleep in one of the beds while no one else was in the cottage. Anna was delighted when the next group of children entered the cottage and immediately went into role as the bears seeing Goldilocks in the bed. Nothing was said to them; they simply knew that the sleeping child was Goldilocks and the drama followed, unprompted.

Anna also developed the children's understanding of the story by hot seating children as the three bears and inviting the rest of the class to question the bears after they had discovered the chaos Goldilocks had wreaked. Anna was ready to intervene with questions if necessary but found that the children, who were all 'journalists' at a press conference, asked appropriate questions. 'How did you feel when you came through the door and saw the mess?' 'What do you think should happen to Goldilocks?' 'Who was supposed to lock the door?' (This latter question resulted in a little argument between daddy and mummy bear.)

Goldilocks was then hot seated and the journalists asked questions such as: 'Have you ever done this before?' 'How do you think baby bear felt when his porridge was eaten and his chair was broken?' 'How would you feel if that happened to you?'

The questions posed by these young children required responses that went beyond literal understanding. The Spoken Language Programme of Study (DfE, 2013) requires children to *use spoken language to develop understanding through speculating, hypothesising, imagining and exploring ideas* (p17).

Freeze frame

This technique is also sometimes known as 'tableau'. Three or four children work together to freeze a significant part of a narrative. An example of this would be the freezing of characters at the Mad Hatter's Tea Party in Lewis Carroll's *Alice's Adventures in Wonderland*. A 'voice-over' works very well with freeze frame. By choosing a scene to freeze frame, the children have to study the text carefully in a way that they perhaps would not if simply reading the text.

Thought tracking

Thought tracking gives those in role a chance to voice their thoughts and, again, this means they have to think carefully about the text and the characters. In the example of the Mad Hatter's Tea Party where the Dormouse, the Mad Hatter and the March Hare are frozen in a tableau, the teacher could ask them what they were thinking as Alice approached.

Conscience alley

This is quite a sophisticated technique and is used when children become more confident with drama. It is a way of debating an issue or exploring a dilemma. The children are divided into two lines, facing each other. One child has to walk down the middle of these lines. As he or she does so each person in the line has to make a comment. Those on one side support one argument and those on the other side give the opposite viewpoint. In Wallace's story, *Chin Chiang and the Dragon's Dance*, a young boy, Chin Chiang, is preparing to dance the dragon's dance for the first time. He has looked forward to it for most of his life but instead of being excited he wants to 'melt into his shoes'. Using conscience alley, Chin Chiang would make his way slowly between the two lines of children while, one at a time, those on one side would make a single comment about why he should not do the dance and those on the other side would say why he should. At the end Chin Chiang would make his decision.

Conscience alley is a technique that has to be handled with care. Although it may seem to be very useful for dealing with issues such as bullying, it must be remembered that the child walking down the alley might feel very exposed.

Mantle of the expert

Mantle of the expert is an approach developed by Dorothy Heathcote in which the children take on the role of experts. Their expertise is often based on research they have undertaken or their knowledge of a fictional situation. An example would be the Mayor of Hamelin asking an expert group of rat catchers to help him get rid of the town of rats. The children would have read Browning's *The Pied Piper of Hamelin* and know the outcome, but could have a lot of fun suggesting other ways in which the rats could be exterminated. The teacher would take on the role of the mayor, as it is usually the case when using this technique that the teacher is the one who needs advice. A case study in the section on Drama and Writing below exemplifies the mantle of the expert technique where the pupils were experts on earth and space, and were called upon to help the Science Museum with a problem they had.

Teacher in role

Teacher in role is at the heart of process drama. When the teacher is working alongside the children, he or she is able to respond to the children's drama and challenge where appropriate from within the role. Baldwin and John (2012) describe how, when in role, the teacher can *stimulate, inspire provoke and/or challenge thinking, speaking, emotion and/or action* as well as being able to *organise and ensure focus and structure* (p29). The role adopted by the teacher could be high status where he or she can be more in control, or it can be low status where the teacher may need advice from the children. To avoid confusion as to whether the teacher is in or out of role, it is a good idea to use a small prop – a hat, for example – to indicate when the teacher is in role.

A closer look at the curriculum

Drama, speaking and listening

The Spoken Language Programme of Study in the National Curriculum (2013, p17) includes as statutory requirements that pupils should be taught to:

- listen and respond appropriately to adults and their peers;
- ask relevant questions to extend their understanding and knowledge;
- use relevant strategies to build their vocabulary;
- articulate and justify answers, arguments and opinions;
- give well-structured descriptions, explanations and narratives for different purposes including for expressing feelings;
- maintain attention and participate actively in collaborative conversations, staying on topic and initiating and responding to comments;
- use spoken language to develop understanding through speculating, hypothesising, imagining and exploring ideas;
- speak audibly and fluently with an increasing command of standard English;

- participate in discussions, presentations, performances, role play, improvisations and debates;

- gain, maintain and monitor the interest of the listener(s);

- consider and evaluate different viewpoints, attending to and building on the contributions of others;

- select and use appropriate registers for effective communication.

Drama offers a wide variety of experiences for children to develop their speaking and listening skills. They have to listen very carefully to others speaking in order to continue the drama and act upon what they have heard. It is active listening because they need to make sense of what they hear. Children's speaking skills improve as they take on different roles, selecting the most appropriate register. When young children play, they almost instinctively adopt the voice and language of the character they are playing, whether it is their favourite action hero or their teacher.

Activity: spoken language

Think about how the following statements from the statutory requirements of the Spoken Language Programme of Study (2013, p17) could be taught using the drama techniques already described:

- articulate and justify answers, arguments and opinions
- ask relevant questions to extend their understanding and knowledge

(Suggestions can be found at the end of the chapter.)

Drama and reading

The acting out of favourite stories gives young children a curiosity about books even before they begin to read and thus motivates them to want to read. Drama is usually seen as being most effective in developing reading comprehension, but McMaster (1998) describes how it can also be used to address decoding. She describes an activity where pupils match up consonant digraphs and trigraphs (onsets) with appropriate word endings (rimes) and then act out the word. On the board are written the onsets of words, e.g. *gr*. The teacher has a bag containing rimes e.g. *in*, *ab*, *oan* and *ow*. The children match onsets with rimes and act out the word, *thus providing a visual, aural and kinesthetic memory cue for the word* (McMaster, 1998, p577). Reading fluency also develops through the reading of playscripts. This is particularly effective in guided reading sessions.

Research focus

Larkin (2001) describes a strategy called 'Readers' Theatre' in which a group of children practise reading different parts in play-scripts. The children begin by highlighting their parts. They read their parts over and over again until they are fluent and can add expression. The lines are not learned but are delivered with feeling and expression, often to the rest of the class. Sloyer (1982 cited in Larkin, 2001, p479) describes Readers' Theatre as:

> not a play. There are no stage sets, no elaborate costumes, no memorised lines. It is not ordinary reading with dull word by word reading. Readers' Theatre is an interpretive activity for all the children in the classroom. Children bring characters to life through their voice and gesture.

Larkin found that children's motivation and reading skills improved, particularly those of struggling readers. The repeated readings, in particular, enhanced fluency.

Larkin also describes how the children's comprehension improved as they reread the scripts. Drama really comes into its own in the development of comprehension. Play-scripts can be useful but many of the more participatory activities described above can enhance understanding. Getting meaning from text is what reading is all about. This comprehension can be at different levels, including literal understanding, reorganising text, projecting oneself into situations and predicting what might happen. Gungor (2008) describes how, by being involved in a drama activity, children *not only read what is in a text but actually 'live' in it* (p3). McMaster (1998) reviews research into the effects of drama teaching on reading comprehension and reports how children develop:

> an understanding and ability to express the details of the plot, characters, sequence of events, cause-and-effect relationships, word meanings, motivations and main events of the story.

> (p582)

By freeze-framing a scene from a story pupils are forced to examine the text closely. By introducing hot seating and thought tracking the motivation of characters is explored and by using the technique of conscience alley dilemmas presented in texts can be examined.

Drama and writing: fiction and non-fiction

The importance of children writing for a real purpose and a real audience has become central to the teaching of writing. Real contexts and purposes, however, are not always readily at hand. This is where drama steps in. Being engrossed in a drama activity allows the children to become so involved with the situation or characters that they write as if for a real purpose. Children will write 'in role' where the writing is part of the drama or 'alongside role' where they come out of the drama but with a deeper understanding of the purpose for writing. In Oscar Wilde's *The Selfish Giant* the children, banished from the garden, could be asked to put together a letter begging the giant to allow them back into the garden where they have played so happily, or they could write diaries describing the events. The children will do this while they are still in role. If the giant is hot seated to explore his motives, then pupils will write alongside or after the drama to explain why the giant acted as he did.

When children are engrossed in drama there are many opportunities for writing in different non-fiction genres. In Early Years and Key Stage 1 role-play areas children write out prescriptions in a doctor's surgery, take down an order in a café, address letters in a post office.

Grainger (2001) writes about using drama to increase the quality of non-fiction writing. The opportunities to write to prepare for a role, write in role, write alongside role are seen by Grainger to be as effective for non-fiction writing as for fiction. Chamberlain (2016) describes how children can become engaged with a particular period in history, research the period and then use drama techniques, such as hot seating or mantle of the expert to explore events. Drama can be used to teach the children about different non-fiction genres. Persuasive writing can emerge from, for example, a meeting called to discuss the abolition of a community centre where the children are in the role of concerned villagers. The teacher in role will chair the meeting and will ask the villagers to voice their opinions and try to persuade local councillors to think again. A persuasive letter will be written. This is shared writing but with a purpose and a specific audience. 'Decision alley' (sometimes known as 'conscience alley') can be used to encourage discussion.

Research focus

Grainger (2001) (now Cremin) looked at the opportunities that drama offered for writing across different genres. One of the interesting aspects to emerge was what she called 'seizing the moment' where children were encouraged to write appropriately when the moment arose in the drama. This was contrasted with a more planned approach to using drama to teach about specific genres. Cremin *et al.* (2006) developed this idea in a paper that reported on research that compared pupils' writing responses when drama was planned with a particular genre in mind and when the drama developed intuitively (i.e. when the children 'seized the moment'). Both approaches were reported as motivating the children to write, but the 'seize the moment' approach was seen as being more engaging.

$\longrightarrow$

Relevant details were included, a clearer point of view was established and the choice of language, whilst frequently appropriate in both approaches, was more adventurous and inventive in 'seize the moment' writing. The children seemed to write with greater urgency when they chose their form, content and viewpoint and settled more quickly to the business of putting pen to paper when their writing had a purpose in their imaginary world.

(Cremin *et al.*, 2006, p277)

Cremin *et al.* recognised that this approach demands skill and intuition from teachers, especially when they are used to working to tight objectives. They recommend that the rewards, however, are such that professional development would be very worthwhile.

Case study: mantle of the expert

Kirsty, an experienced teacher, was teaching a Year 5 class which that year was particularly 'boy-heavy'. The class consisted of twenty boys and eight girls. Writing was a particular challenge with this class, especially for ten boys whose abilities ranged from level 3C to level 3A. Given that this was Year 5, significant progress was needed.

Kirsty had tried out different ways of writing in role in the past. The children had written as if they were characters from a story, written diary entries and letters as if they were historical figures such as Henry VIII, but these had been 'one-offs'. Kirsty wanted to try something with a greater purpose to try to encourage 'real' writing. Through university contacts she found out about Dorothy Heathcote's 'mantle of the expert' and decided to try this with her class.

The pupils were learning about Earth and Space through a topic approach. She asked the children to 'buy-in' to the idea that they were experts on Earth and Space. Some were reluctant at first, but once their peers were joining in, and the expert teams were decided and established, everybody played a full part. The experts received a made-up email from the Science Museum outlining a predicament: the Science Museum's resident expert was on a mission to the Moon, so could the Year 5 experts help with the latest exhibition? It would need posters, publicity and information leaflets: carefully planned opportunities for non-fiction writing.

The pupils took on their roles with gusto, dividing up jobs, researching key information, and working as a very effective team. There were daily whole-team meetings, and anybody not pulling their weight was in danger of dismissal. They worked to deadlines and took responsibilities very seriously. For three weeks (afternoons only) the pupils learned through this mantle. There were times when she worried that some teams were working on diagrams rather than writing (which had been the initial reason for this enquiry-based drama) but she

→

223

overcame that with different emails from the Science Museum, asking for written reports from all staff. Pupils particularly enjoyed the daily team meetings, which gave them a chance to talk about what they were doing and to get feedback from each other.

Using a drama approach like this had a significant impact on pupil writing. The pupils believed they were writing for a real purpose, which was sustained. In a short period, all pupils improved their writing attainment by at least one sublevel, often more. Most significantly, pupils believed they could write and enjoyed doing it.

The statutory requirements for writing (composition) for Years 5 and 6 state that:

Pupils should be taught to plan their writing by:

- identifying the audience for and purpose of the writing, selecting the appropriate form and using other similar writing as models for their own.

(DfE, 2013, p47)

Kirsty's pupils believed in their audience and purpose, and produced writing that was appropriate to the task as well as being of a higher quality than they usually produced.

Drama across the curriculum

We saw earlier in this chapter that there has been some debate about whether or not drama should be used as a learning medium for different areas of the curriculum. However, it is seen by most educators as in no way detracting from drama if it is used as a vehicle for teaching about other subjects. *You cannot have drama which does not refer to other curriculum areas. All drama has to have content; it has to be about something.*

In order to enhance understanding of knowledge in different curriculum areas, Woolland (2010) describes how drama is best taught actively – i.e. where the children make their own decisions in the drama. The case study below is an example of how a trainee teacher used drama actively to teach the children about aspects of a topic on Australia.

Case study: Aboriginal legends

Chris, a PGCE student, used drama to access the topic for his placement, Australia. He planned a series of lessons for his Year 2 class on Aboriginal legends, covered over several subjects, including art, geography, history and music.

→

Chris used drama in one particular lesson because while he believed the children understood and enjoyed the legends, he did not think they appreciated the stories' historical distance. A lot of Aboriginal stories deal with the creation of the natural world, including parts of our solar system such as the Sun and the Moon. They often have a human element to them, man being imagined as the creator of various aspects of our universe through one means or another.

Chris used the Aboriginal legend of how the Sun was made in his drama lesson. In brief, the story deals with a girl who runs away from her tribe because she is not allowed to marry the man she loves. Her life becomes endangered in the wild and she is rescued by her ancestors and taken into the sky. When she sees her tribe miserable and cold, she builds a huge camp fire in the sky to keep them warm. This fire becomes so big that it becomes the Sun.

Chris used a hot-seating activity after reading this story with the children, having them take the character either of the young girl, her young love, the tribe elders who prevented the marriage, the tribesmen who hunted her after she left, or the ancestors who saved her. By taking the roles of the characters, Chris hoped the children would sympathise with the characters' feelings and relate to the themes and ideals in the story of loyalty and love, while understanding the strong link in Aboriginal legends between man and the natural world.

This was the first time the class had done a hot-seating activity, so Chris modelled the role playing first. Overall, the children worked well in the activity. The questioning from the children ranged from simple questions directly from the text about how the character felt when something happened, to ones they had inferred from the text, or ones asking characters to predict what was going to happen next. The children taking on the roles equally had a range of responses, from simple answers such as 'I was sad' or 'I was angry' to whole dialogues with the questioner about their question. Some children strayed from the topic at hand by asking or answering about things not relevant to the story or the historical context (for example, 'What games consoles do you have?'), but Chris's questioning about whether they thought these were relevant refocused the children.

The children's questions were mainly to do with the characters and their relationships with each other. While this was fine for the children's understanding of the characters' feelings, Chris had to question the children to meet the lesson's objective of understanding the link between man and the natural world in Aboriginal legends.

The children enjoyed being in role and everyone who was chosen to be in the hot seat assumed their character and were not afraid or embarrassed. The activity allowed the low-attaining children to access a text away from any formal writing or worksheets, and some of them excelled, performing at a level above their average for other aspects of literacy.

The children effectively used the hot-seating activity to imagine what life for an Aboriginal must have been like. Questions about how the characters lived, what food they ate, why they needed a camp fire, and tribe culture sometimes startled the children, having never considered the cultural and historical differences.

The National Curriculum Programme of Study for History requires children to:

> know and understand significant aspects of the history of the wider world; the nature of civilisations; the expansion and dissolution of empires; characteristic features of past non-European societies; achievements and follies of mankind.

> (DfE, 2013, p188)

Drama and inclusion

Peter (1994) emphasises the value of drama education, both for mainstream teachers who want to include and develop the skills of those children in their classes who have special educational needs and for teachers in special schools. She looks at the accommodations that might be needed to meet the needs of all the pupils in the class, including management issues. Among the points that she develops in her discussion relating to the value of drama for pupils with special educational needs she includes: enabling children to become independent learners, giving pupils opportunities to demonstrate their skills in less pressurised contexts than the more traditional ways, and serving cross-curricular learning.

One of the challenges Peter describes is motivating children with special educational needs. This, of course, is a challenge for teachers of all pupils, but there are particular difficulties when children have, for example, limited ability in terms of concentration, language ability, etc. One piece of advice she gives (1994, p47) is to present tasks in a simple way by limiting the amount of listening required.

Case study: Vikings

As a second-year BA (Ed) student, Alex had a teaching placement at a special school in the North East of England that caters for pupils with emotional and behavioural difficulties (EBD). The pupils lacked motivation, especially when asked to write, so it was decided

$\longrightarrow$

to use drama as a way of encouraging them. The school follows a creative curriculum that allowed Alex to develop drama through the topics they were studying. Through looking at Vikings they were able to re-enact events such as the Lindisfarne battle. The use of the drama not only enabled pupils to gain a better understanding of what they were learning about, but become more interested and better engaged in their learning. The use of process drama allowed pupils to develop their own ideas and take more ownership of their learning. This type of drama involves the children using their imagination through unscripted and spontaneous scenes. Process drama was chosen as it gave the children the chance to choose how they wanted to explore the issues and what direction to take it. The drama activity involved the children re-enacting the monks of Lindisfarne seeing the Vikings coming across the sea to invade. Teacher and pupils began the lesson by discussing what the characters would be feeling and looked at what weapons the monks may have had. They then used process drama to explore the terror the monks would feel seeing the Vikings coming across the sea. They finished the session with the children writing as monks in first person narration, seeing the Vikings coming to invade. The learning objective was 'To be able to write an accurate first person account of what it was like to be a monk in Lindisfarne during the Viking invasion'.

The children enjoyed the drama and it showed through their writing, which was more imaginative, descriptive and longer than usual, as pupils had a desire to write about what they had performed. Drama was chosen to be employed as the children had previously struggled to 'get into another character's shoes' when they wrote from the Viking perspective. The writing produced from the drama far outweighed work previously done from the Viking perspective and Alex believes that it was because of drama that the writing became more accomplished. In addition, the pupils, many of whom were usually very reluctant to work, found the drama activity and the writing 'alongside role' motivating and enjoyable.

The National Curriculum includes a section on inclusion, which states that 'teachers should set high standards for every pupil' (DfE, 2013, p8). By using drama Alex was able to engage the pupils and help them to reach their full potential.

At the beginning of this chapter, you saw how drama has only a small mention in the 2014 National Curriculum. However, this chapter has shown how drama is important in all aspects of English teaching and, indeed, all areas of the curriculum. Techniques and different approaches have been described throughout the chapter that should allay concerns about the teaching of drama that may have been highlighted in the first activity. Some concerns relate to classroom management, but by using hot seating, mantle of the expert or teacher in role, the situation is controlled within the drama. Children are very motivated by drama activities and their imaginations can soar, leading to increased understanding and achievement in every area of the curriculum.

Learning outcomes review

You should now know:

- what children need to understand about drama;
- what we need to know as primary teachers in order to teach the 2014 English National Curriculum;
- some of the challenges we face when we teach children drama;
- a range of approaches to teaching drama.

Self-assessment questions

1. How can drama be used to teach reading comprehension?
2. Can drama be used in different areas of the curriculum?
3. Is drama a useful activity for working with children who have special educational needs?

Answers to activities

Activity: concerns about drama

You were asked to think about concerns that teachers might have about teaching drama. This chapter has shown that you can start off in a very small way and do not need a lot of experience. Worries about classroom management can be solved by giving the children roles that they know something about and leading the drama by using subtle prompts as 'teacher in role'. You will find that children are often more involved and better behaved when in role than when they are themselves. The use of large spaces can also be seen as being daunting. Suggestions for activities such as hot seating demonstrate that drama can happen when the children are sitting in their own seats and only their minds are in role.

Activity: spoken language

Hot seating is a drama activity where children ask appropriate questions to gain greater knowledge of a character's actions and motivations. In conscience alley different points of view are put forward. Using the mantle of the expert, pupils will form opinions and have to justify their choices.

Further reading

As the titles of the following books suggest, they are full of very good ideas for drama in the classroom with very clear explanations.

Clipson-Boyles, S (2012) *Teaching Primary English through Drama*. Abingdon: Routledge.

Cremin, M and Grainger, T (2001) *Resourcing Classroom Drama: 5–8*. Sheffield: National Association for the Teaching of English.

Cremin, M and Grainger, T (2001) *Resourcing Classroom Drama: 8–14*. Sheffield: National Association for the Teaching of English.

Ideas and approaches are discussed alongside many practical ideas and there is a section on integrating drama into different areas of the curriculum in:

Woolland, B (2010) *Teaching Primary Drama*. Harlow: Pearson Education.

References

Baldwin, P and John, R (2012) *Inspiring Writing Through Drama*. London: Bloomsbury.

Chamberlain, L with Kerrigan-Draper, E (2016) *Inspiring Writing in Primary Schools*. London: SAGE.

Clipson-Boyles, S (1998) *Drama in Primary English Teaching*. London: David Fulton.

Clipson-Boyles, S (2012) *Teaching Primary English through Drama*. Abingdon: Routledge.

Cremin, T, Goouch, K, Blakemore, L, Goff, E and Macdonald, R (2006) Connecting drama and writing: seizing the moment to write. *Research in Drama in Education*, 11(2): 273–91.

Department for Education (DfE) (2013) *The National Curriculum in England: Key Stages 1 and 2 Framework Document*. London: DfE.

Fleming, M (1994) *Starting Drama Teaching*. London: David Fulton.

Grainger, T (2001) Drama and Writing. *The Primary English Magazine*, April: 6–10.

Gungor, A. (2008) Effects of drama on the use of reading comprehension strategies and on attitudes towards reading. *Journal for Learning through the Arts*, 4(1): 1–30.

Larkin, BR (2001) Can we act it out? *The Reading Teacher*, 54(5): 478–81.

McMaster, JC (1998) 'Doing Literatur' using drama to build literacy. *The Reading Teacher*, 51(7): 574–84.

Peter, M (1994) *Drama for All*. London: David Fulton.

Way, B (1967) Development through drama, in M Fleming (1994) *Starting Drama Teaching*. London: David Fulton.

Woolland, B (2010) *Teaching Primary Drama*. Harlow: Pearson Education.

13 Planning for Delivery

Kate Allott

Learning outcomes

By reading this chapter you will develop your understanding of:

- why schools need to plan their English curriculum;
- the different levels of planning involved;
- the factors that need to be considered when developing long-term, medium-term and short-term plans for English.

Teachers' Standards

2. Promote good progress and outcomes by pupils:

- be accountable for pupils' attainment, progress and outcomes;
- plan teaching to build on pupils' capabilities and prior knowledge;
- guide pupils to reflect on the progress they have made and their emerging needs;
- demonstrate knowledge and understanding of how pupils learn and how this impacts on teaching;
- encourage pupils to take a responsible and conscientious attitude to their own work and study.

4. Plan and teach well-structured lessons:

- impart knowledge and develop understanding through effective use of lesson time;
- promote a love of learning and children's intellectual curiosity;
- set homework and plan other out-of-class activities to consolidate and extend the knowledge and understanding pupils have acquired;
- reflect systematically on the effectiveness of lessons and approaches to teaching;
- contribute to the design and provision of an engaging curriculum within the relevant subject area.

5. Adapt teaching to respond to the strengths and needs of all pupils:

- know when and how to differentiate appropriately, using approaches which enable pupils to be taught effectively;
- have a secure understanding of how a range of factors can inhibit pupils' ability to learn, and how best to overcome these;

- demonstrate an awareness of the physical, social and intellectual development of children, and know how to adapt teaching to support pupils' education at different stages of development;
- have a clear understanding of the needs of all pupils, including those with special educational needs; those of high ability; those with English as an additional language; those with disabilities; and be able to use and evaluate distinctive teaching approaches to engage and support them.

Introduction

Hannah is eleven years old and about to leave primary school. She speaks confidently and fluently on a range of topics, in formal situations and in informal group discussion. She is a keen reader, who discusses her favourite authors with enthusiasm, and reads critically and thoughtfully. Her writing, in a range of genres, is lively, well structured and technically accurate. Harry is almost four, and about to enter the nursery of Hannah's school. He is a shy child who talks most freely with familiar adults. He loves being read to but as yet does not show much interest in print or in mark-making. He recognises the letters H, M and D.

What does the school need to do over the next eight years to ensure that Harry leaves primary school with the skills, knowledge and attitudes that Hannah demonstrates? Planning is a vital part of the answer to this question. Throughout the years, in every English lesson, the long-term goal needs to be kept in mind. Planning for English is more complex than for many other subjects – in part, simply because it takes up so much time in the teaching week; the recommendation of the National Literacy Strategy (DfEE, 1998) was that about 7 to 7½ hours of the week, a third, should be devoted to English, but many schools and teachers spend even more teaching time on the subject. Planning is also complex because unlike maths, which typically is taught in one focused lesson each day, English teaching often consists of different elements spread across the day and the week – whole-class English teaching, guided reading sessions separate from this, separate phonics teaching, reading to the children, spelling and handwriting sessions, drama lessons. Cross-curricular planning increases the complexity, with lessons having two or more subject focuses, including English.

This chapter will look in turn at long-term, medium-term and short-term planning for English, since this is how the planning process in schools works.

Long-term planning

Curriculum planning is a process which starts with whole-school, long-term planning and then works down through one or more levels to lesson planning. Everyone involved in English teaching, including teaching assistants and student teachers, needs to be aware of the whole-school picture, which is set out in the English policy. The jigsaw pieces of individual lessons, intervention programmes, resources, and so on only make complete sense when seen in that context, and every tiny piece either contributes to progress towards the long-term goals or does not. Consider, for example, the teaching assistant who is asked to support a writing group. A child asks for a spelling. The assistant's inclination may be to give the spelling; after all, he is there to help. But this will not help the child as a speller, and indeed if done on a regular basis will simply serve to make the child dependent and conceal from the teacher when marking what could be useful evidence of the child's knowledge about spelling. Awareness of the school's spelling policy, however, might lead the teaching assistant to ask the child to have a go at the spelling and check it later, or to use a dictionary to look it up, or the assistant might use the opportunity to teach a common spelling pattern (read Chapter 4 for more guidance on teaching and supporting spelling).

Activity: aims of the English curriculum

Many school policies include their vision or long-term goal for children. What do you feel the English curriculum should aim to achieve with pupils?

Summarise your ideas in five key points, and then read the introduction to the 2014 National Curriculum Programme of Study for English (DfE, 2013, pp10–11) to compare your ideas with the aims set out there.

(Possible answers can be found at the end of the chapter.)

The school's policy and long-term planning are based on its own values and aims for its pupils, and also on the statutory curriculum – the National Curriculum. The policy sets out what the school aims to achieve and how it intends to do it. While it is likely that this will be broadly similar in most schools, there is an opportunity for schools to emphasise aspects of the curriculum which they feel are particularly important – for example, the opportunities English can offer for creativity. The National Curriculum has a particular focus on reading for pleasure, while in contrast its focus in writing is on competence rather than enjoyment.

The long-term plan, or scheme of work, sets out what will be covered in each year. The 1999 National Curriculum provided a programme of study organised by Key Stage, while the 2014 National Curriculum sets out a programme of study for Year 1, Year 2, Lower Key Stage 2 and Upper Key Stage 2, and many schools have also used the Primary National Strategy's Literacy Framework (DfES, 2006), which set out learning by year group, including the Reception year. In developing these documents into a long-term plan, schools need to consider their own particular context.

Case study: planning in a small school

In a small village school with only two classes, 4–7-year-olds and 7–11-year-olds, staff worked to devise rolling three and four-year programmes, to ensure children encountered a wide range of text types without gaps or unintended repetition during their time in the school.

Three-year rolling programme for Reception and Key Stage 1

Year A			
Fiction	Stories with familiar settings	Traditional tales	Stories from other cultures	Author study
Non-fiction	Instructions	Information texts	Non-chronological reports	
Poetry	Using the senses	Pattern and rhyme	Poems on a theme	
Year B			
Fiction	Stories with familiar settings	Traditional tales	Fantasy stories	Author study
Non-fiction	Recounts	Information texts	Explanations	
Poetry	Patterned poetry	Really looking	Nonsense poems	
Year C			
Fiction	Stories with familiar settings	Fairytales	Stories from other cultures	Author study
Non-fiction	Instructions	Information texts	Alphabetically ordered texts	
Poetry	Poems on a theme	Playing with language	Traditional rhymes	

Four-year rolling programme for Key Stage 2

Year A			
Fiction	Stories with familiar settings	Traditional tales, myths, legends	Adventure stories	Author study
Non-fiction	Biography	Instructions	Explanations	Information texts
Poetry	Performance poetry	Poetic style	Classic poetry	

→

Year B			
Fiction	Stories with historical settings	Stories from other cultures	Author study	Plays
Non-fiction	Recounts	Newspapers	Persuasive writing	Non-chronological reports
Poetry	Shape poems, calligrams	Power of imagery	Language play	
Year C			
Fiction	Stories which raise issues	Fables, myths, legends	Classic fiction	Author study
Non-fiction	Autobiography	Instructions	Argument	Information texts
Poetry	Choral poetry	Poetic style	Narrative poetry	
Year D			
Fiction	Science fiction	Stories from other cultures	Author study	Plays
Non-fiction	Recounts	Newspapers	Persuasive writing	Non-chronological reports
Poetry	Exploring form	Creating images	Nonsense poems	

The Primary National Strategy provided in its Framework (DfES, 2006) and planning guidance not only learning objectives to be met each year, but also the range of text types to be studied, in order that children left primary school familiar with key text types in fiction, non-fiction and poetry, and revisited them over the primary years in order to develop their understanding of each type. The 2014 National Curriculum leaves schools to determine this for themselves, but they will continue to need to plan for a wide range of text types, and to use their long-term plan to ensure that there is a balance of non-fiction, fiction, poetry and plays, and that within these there is further balance – for example, that time is given to non-chronological reports as well as instructions, and that children do have the opportunity to read historical fiction and science fiction, haikus and ballads.

Resourcing is also relevant to long-term planning; decisions about how much to spend on books can have a significant impact on learning, as children are more likely to want to read if they are provided with a wide range of high-quality materials, in good condition, than if the book corner consists of two shelves of old and tattered books. Decisions about funding also affect the number of children who can be supported by literacy intervention programmes, but there also need to be decisions made at school level about when to intervene – early intervention usually being more successful – and which programmes and staff to deploy.

Curriculum targets were introduced in the early days of the National Literacy Strategy, as a way of improving attainment (QCA, 1999). Schools reviewed children's progress – for example, were they doing better in maths or in English? Reading or writing? Fiction or non-fiction writing? – and set targets to address those curriculum areas which the evidence showed were not as strong. A school might, therefore, decide to target non-fiction writing, and would put in place an action plan to address the target. Long-term planning might be adjusted to ensure that curriculum targets would be met.

How might decisions made as part of long-term planning affect Harry, the three-year-old whom you met at the beginning of this chapter, in his progress through school? A curriculum target focused on improving non-fiction writing might mean that in the nursery staff have ensured that there are opportunities to write in a range of forms in every provision area, and many models of non-fiction writing, including books, are available and shared with children. This might develop Harry's interest in mark-making. A small group phonics intervention programme in Year 1 might help Harry to catch up, if he has had a shaky start in phonics in the Reception year. The school's emphasis on non-fiction writing might mean that as well as meeting authors of fiction, Harry might meet a series of writers of non-fiction as he goes through school – a journalist from the local paper, a writer of non-fiction books for children, a cookery book author – who inspire and inform him about writing. The carefully planned range of texts over the years would ensure that Harry reads many authors he would not have come across outside school, and acquires some new favourites, and perhaps a taste for science fiction which will last into adult life. Finally, a carefully planned drama programme could give Harry the confidence and skills in speaking that he needs to overcome his early shyness.

Medium-term and unit planning

Planning for English is likely to be more extensive than many other subjects because of the time that schools devote to it. Planning is likely to consist in the first place of a plan for the year, or medium-term plan, in which decisions are made about how much time is to be given to non-fiction, fiction, poetry and plays, how much time to individual units and what these are to be, and in what order they will be taught, and also unit plans, which cover a block of work focused on one text type and lasting anything from one to four or five weeks.

Medium-term planning

Some schools continue to use the Primary National Strategy literacy units (DfES, 2006), which made these decisions, but many have already used this guidance flexibly to make it more appropriate to their needs, and some have chosen to start afresh. In any case, medium-term plans need to be based on the National Curriculum Programme of Study, and while the Primary Strategy materials were all linked to the 1999 National Curriculum, schools' medium-term plans based on the 2014 National Curriculum need to show how the Programme of Study will be broken down into a sequence of coherent and interesting teaching units.

A number of decisions have to be made when writing a medium-term plan:

- Number of weeks to be allocated to fiction, poetry, etc. over the year, and following on from that, time given to each unit. Pupils' existing knowledge, skills and understanding need to be taken into consideration. If, for example, there is a unit on instructions, the length of time allocated to it should depend on how much the children already know about this text type.

- Whether to teach longer blocks on one text type or shorter, more frequent units – for example, one five-week unit on persuasive writing or two shorter units, one in the autumn term and one in the summer;

- Balance of fiction, poetry and non-fiction – whether there should there be a balance within each term and even half term, or simply over the year as a whole;

- How learning objectives will be matched to text types – for example, where particular aspects of grammar would be relevant;

- Cross-curricular links – whether there are meaningful links to be made with other subjects, which might influence when particular units are taught (e.g. a unit on historical fiction at the same time as a history unit).

Activity: constructing a medium-term plan

A scheme of work for Year 5 indicates that the following text types will be taught.

- Fiction and plays – stories by significant authors; myths and legends; stories from other cultures; older literature; film narrative; dramatic conventions.
- Non-fiction – instructions; reports and explanations; persuasive writing.
- Poetry – classic narrative poems; choral and performance poetry.

Draw up a medium-term plan for the year, based on three 12-week terms and considering all the issues listed above.

(Possible answers can be found at the end of the chapter.)

Unit planning

Once a medium-term plan is in place, more detailed planning of each unit can be done. The medium-term plan is likely to indicate:

- the text type which is the focus of the unit;
- the learning objectives for reading, writing, speaking and listening;
- the length of time given to the unit.

The first question to ask when planning a unit of work is: what do the children already know about this text type and, by the end of the unit, what will they have learned? Without clear answers to both these questions, there is a danger that children revisit text types without ever making real progress – that there is revision but not development of their learning.

Case study: 'cold' assessment

Sophie was planning to teach a unit on non-chronological reports to a Year 3 class. In order to know what her starting point should be, she carried out a 'cold' assessment activity, using a set of information books linked to a geography topic with a guided reading group. She found that though the children were confident in using the contents page and index to locate information, they were surprised to find that different books included different information and that some did not seem to agree. She then asked the children to write about what they had learned. They included relevant information, and used an appropriate style, but on the whole did not structure their writing into sections or include an introduction and conclusion. Sophie therefore decided to focus her teaching in the unit on drawing information from a range of sources and structuring reports appropriately.

Although it may seem odd, an early decision to be made in planning an English unit is what the outcome should be. This will often be a written outcome, but it does not need to be; it could be a debate, or a story-telling, or performance poetry. This back-to-front focus is to ensure that enough time is given to the final outcome to ensure success. Children may need several days to plan, draft, redraft and edit a piece of writing, and although not every piece of writing done in the classroom needs to be brought to a polished outcome, a main written outcome from a whole unit of work should be. The planning and thinking about the unit then focuses on what needs to be put in place in order that children can produce a successful outcome.

The Primary National Strategy emphasised a teaching sequence within units, described in detail in Chapter 10, which started with reading, in order to familiarise children with a text type, and then led to analysis of the text type in order that children could understand how it worked and what its key features were. Teaching then moved on to writing, where children were at first given support through whole-class shared writing, with teachers modelling, then drawing on children's ideas and scribing, then into more independent writing, with some support given, perhaps by an adult in guided writing or by use of a writing frame, to the point where children had mastery over the text type and could work completely independently. (See Chapter 10 for a diagram of a teaching sequence for writing.)

While this model has great value, it does need to be used flexibly. Particularly for younger children, it can work better to introduce elements of writing much earlier in the unit, so there are several cycles of reading into writing rather than just one. This works well when children have tried out a writing task with mixed success; going back to look again at what other writers have done is much more meaningful when children have encountered difficulties themselves.

Case study: linking reading and writing

Farrida, a second-year trainee, was planning an author study unit for her Year 2 class, and had chosen David and Ronda Armitage, authors of the 'Lighthouse Keeper' series. Her first idea was for the children to create a fact file about the authors, but then she realised that this would not really connect with the stories themselves. She decided instead to focus on a comparison of the stories, and then discovered that the Armitages had written other books beside the series. Farrida collected as many as she could of the texts, and used these not only for shared reading in English lessons, using a document reader to enlarge the text, but also at story time, and for independent reading. The children generated a range of questions about the books – which had been written first? How many had the Armitages written? etc. They created two comparison charts – of the series books and of the other books. They wrote reviews of the books they read for each other, and at this point Farrida realised she needed to build in some reading of book reviews, as the children were unfamiliar with the text type. The children then began to plan and write their own 'Lighthouse Keeper' stories, which were produced in illustrated book form by the end of the unit. Reading and writing were closely linked throughout the unit.

Curriculum link

The setting of the 'Lighthouse Keeper' stories is important to the narrative, and Farrida made meaningful links with her geography and history topic, the seaside. She also read the children other stories set by the sea, including Mairi Hedderwick's 'Katie Morag' series, and Antonia Barber's *The Mousehole Cat*.

English Pupils explain and discuss their understanding of books.

Geography Pupils should understand geographical similarities and differences through studying the human and physical geography of a small area of the United Kingdom.

History Pupils should be taught about changes within living memory.

Text selection

Text selection is a crucial element of successful unit planning, not only because we want to introduce children to high-quality texts that interest and challenge them, and that they are unlikely to know already, but because those texts are likely to need to provide a model for the children's own writing. It is useful always to have this in mind when reading: some poems are wonderful and well worth sharing with children, but simply do not work as models for the children's own writing, while finding a story set in a period being studied in history, which is also appropriate for the age group in terms of readability and content, can be a real challenge. It goes without saying that the text also needs to be one the teacher can show some genuine enthusiasm for, as without this it is unlikely that the children will be enthused.

Case study: fantasy fiction

Paul, a trainee teacher, used his own reading interests when planning a unit on fiction for a Year 5 class. He wrote about his initial thinking:

I'm teaching a three-week block on extended narrative [choose your own adventure-style writing] after the half term. The guidance is rather dry and technical. It will be fun to make it interesting and engaging. We've been doing a shared read of a *Fighting Fantasy* game book in spare minutes here and there in preparation. The children have all designed elemental superheroes in the *manga* style in art who will form their characters. The class teacher has suggested that a whole day is spent creating maps of a world for the adventure to take place in, with the children working in threes. They read *The Hobbit* last term and were really taken with the maps. I think I might find a few more fantasy maps and explore those with them and think how features of them could affect the narrative. I'm getting excited thinking about it! Finally, all those fantasy and science fiction novels I've read will serve a purpose!

Curriculum link

Paul's links from his English unit to art and geography (map making) arose naturally from the children's previous experience and Paul's own interests. The best curriculum links work in this way, providing meaningful and genuine connections between areas of learning.

Developing a pathway through a unit

Unit plans are likely to show what is to be covered each day, including learning objectives and an indication of the main teaching input, independent activity and plenary focus. If more detail is included at this level of planning, lesson planning may be easier, but there does also need to be some flexibility as on a day-to-day basis planning must respond to the children's needs, as evidenced through assessment.

When planning a unit, therefore, the following decisions need to be made:

- How will children be 'hooked in' to the learning?

- Which texts will be used?

- What will the main outcome (written or spoken) be?

- How will reading and writing be balanced and linked through the unit?

- How will reading and writing skills be modelled and supported in the unit?

- How will speaking and listening be integrated in a meaningful and purposeful way?

- Is sufficient time being given to allow children to complete a polished piece of writing? This may well not be one long session, but shorter sessions over several days, allowing children thinking time and not making unrealistic demands of their writing stamina.

Planning a lesson

The session plan is drawn from the unit plan. Some teachers choose to add detail at the unit plan and work from that rather than writing a detailed session plan. Trainee teachers, however, will need to write a detailed plan to ensure they are quite clear about what they are trying to achieve and how they will do it. Planning at this level is really a rehearsal for the lesson – what will I say and do? How might the children respond? What am I hoping to achieve, and how will I know if I have succeeded? How will the lesson appear from the children's point of view? What resources will I need? How will I make sure that the lesson is genuinely inclusive?

Considerations when planning a lesson include the following:

- **Learning objectives** – What is the key learning objective? Having a number of learning objectives may make the teaching unfocused and then children are less likely to make progress. Of course, there may be continuing objectives (referred to by some teachers as ALF – Always Looking For) such as punctuation, but both teacher and children should have a clear view as to what the main focus is. We do not want children to think that remembering capital letters, full stops and 'finger' spaces matters as much as writing something of interest to the reader.

- **Success criteria** – How will you know if the children have achieved the learning objective? Success criteria can be difficult to identify if the aim is, for example, to create a character. Including physical characteristics, personality attributes and some biographical details could result in a lively and interesting pen-portrait or a dull one which simply does not bring the character to life. There is a danger that we select features which are easy to identify rather than being important. For example, it is possible to write instructions which have numbers and time connectives (and do we really need both?), imperative verbs and appropriate layout, but which do not give enough information to make sense and allow the reader to follow them successfully. It is important to try to pin down what constitutes success, and this should be based on the analysis of examples of the text type which has already taken place. If children have already read, analysed and performed several play-scripts, they are in a good position to decide what makes for a successful one. Success criteria are best arrived at through discussion before children embark on the task, and more discussion afterwards, rather than simply being presented to them (although teachers will have thought carefully about what they will be looking for).

- **Inclusion** – How will all children be successfully included? Some tasks are naturally inclusive: a five-year-old who has just learned to write independently, a ten-year-old and an adult could all write a story, and could all be challenged by the task and experience success in it. Reading tasks are more likely to need to be differentiated. While a high-quality, rich text is likely to allow readers at all levels to gain something from it, in terms of understanding and response, it may simply not be accessible to some children whose word-reading skills are not well developed. When planning, there are several approaches that could be taken. The text could be read to the children, but this denies them the independent reading experience which they need in order to become better readers. They could be provided with a modified text – shorter, simpler in terms of words used and sentence structure. They could read the text with an adult before the session to help sort out any difficulties and ensure that their familiarity with the text gives them a head start.

- **Use of other adults** – How will adults be deployed throughout the lesson? If teaching assistants are present, what is their role during whole-class teaching, and when children are working independently, do they usually work with low-attaining pupils? If so, why and what is the impact? Are they simply helping children to do a task which is too difficult for them? Are they 'keeping children on task' and, if so, what is it about the task which has not engaged the children? If they always work with the same group, do these children start to feel they cannot – or do not need to try to – work independently? What is the teacher's role during independent work? Working with a group and a real teaching focus is more likely to be useful than moving around monitoring progress and intervening in an unplanned way.

- **Engagement** – How will children be engaged and interested in the lesson? This is perhaps the most important consideration of all. If children are not engaged, there is unlikely to be any learning.

Research focus: keeping children on task

Powell *et al.*'s research (2006) into why children go off task in American primary class-rooms suggested that children were much less likely to be engaged when literacy was taught through scripted programmes. Children were more likely to be engaged in the lesson when the tasks were open-ended rather than closed tasks such as worksheets. Other factors which affected children's motivation and engagement included opportunities to make choices and have some control over what they were doing, an appropriate level of challenge, opportunities to work collaboratively, and tasks which were purposeful and meaningful to the children.

Case study: writing for a real purpose and audience

Naomi had taken her Reception and Year 1 class on a trip on a steam train. She planned that each day following the trip she would work with a different writing group on a recount of the trip. As the days went by, the children – perhaps unsurprisingly – became increasingly reluctant to engage with the task. Naomi realised that she needed to provide a clear audience and purpose for the writing. She had displayed large numbers of photographs from the trip, and she explained to the children that visitors to the classroom would not know what the photographs were of and that captions were needed. She selected photographs for each child in which they appeared, and asked them to write about what was happening. She referred constantly to what visitors might want to know and would be interested in. Children in these groups wrote at greater length and included more interesting details than children in the earlier groups. Naomi asked the headteacher and other members of staff to visit the classroom, read the captions and comment on them to the children.

English lessons often consist of a basic three-part structure – introduction, independent work and plenary, with possibly a lively starter activity in addition.

Lesson introduction

There may be a starter or warm-up activity as happens in maths lessons, to introduce a concept or skill in an active and playful way. The main teaching input is likely to focus on text work – either reading or writing. Shared reading was an approach introduced in England by the National Literacy Strategy; it was seen as a *step between reading to children and independent reading by children* (DfEE, 1998, Module 1, p6) which for younger children gave valuable practice in applying decoding skills in a supportive context, and for all ages provided opportunities for discussion of texts.

Independent work

Trainee teachers sometimes worry about planning independent activities for children who are not yet reading or writing independently. An important principle to remember is that the priority then should be developing the skills they need to be independent readers and writers. Providing adult support to read or scribe for them may seem to be a solution, and indeed might be an appropriate solution in another lesson, but in English lessons it is a wasted opportunity. Texts for reading can be simplified so that the children can tackle them with support; adult support for writing can focus on teaching children whatever it is they find difficult – composing a sentence, segmenting words and matching graphemes to phonemes, and so on.

Plenary

As in any subject, the plenary is used to revise and consolidate learning, to deal with misconceptions and difficulties, and to look ahead to the next lesson. Plenaries in English lessons are often used to review children's writing: this can be either a powerful opportunity for learning or a time when a child reads out their work, none of the class gain a clear idea of it, and any assessment, whether by peers or the teacher, does not really provide useful feedback from which anyone can benefit. It is important to select the work to be shared carefully; it is not simply about celebrating achievement, but also about identifying features in the work which provide useful learning points. It is very useful for the whole class to be able to see the writing – for example, by using a document reader, or even copying some of the work on to a whiteboard or flip-chart. Reading a text is very different from listening to it, and the text can then be used to model redrafting. The child herself may have suggestions, or other children could contribute ideas. It is a valuable way of showing that writers do often rework their writing to improve it, and that this is a characteristic of good writers rather than poor ones.

Research focus: effective planning

Ofsted's report, *Moving English Forward* (2012), which drew on evidence from inspections of 133 primary schools, found that English teaching was effective when planning was clear and realistic about what learning could be achieved in a lesson, and tasks were meaningful, with real audiences and purposes wherever possible; where teaching was flexible rather than always sticking rigidly to the plan; where planning ensured all groups within the class were appropriately challenged and supported; and where pupils were given enough time to work independently. The report suggested that while the basic three- or four-part lesson structure is helpful, teachers needed to be creative and adventurous in their planning, matching lesson

→

structure to content, avoiding too many short activities and allowing pupils to engage fully in independent work before being asked to review and evaluate it. Ofsted commented that schools sometimes required very detailed plans, which risked the loss of a clear focus. The report recommended that *Lesson plans should be simplified to encourage teachers to consider the central question: what is the key learning for pupils in this lesson and how can I bring it about?* (Ofsted, 2012, p47).

Planning for reading

Children's reading improves the more they do. Planning for English therefore needs to ensure that children have many opportunities to read at school, and particularly those children who do not read much at home. These will include the following:

- **Shared reading in English lessons** – Reading texts to children does not give them practice. In the early stages, shared reading where the class reads the text together is an experience which challenges and supports developing readers. Older children should in general be expected to read the text silently to themselves.

- **Guided reading** – Regular group guided reading sessions, with children (and texts) matched by attainment. Children should not be reading around the group, but reading the text independently to themselves, to maximise the benefit of the experience.

- **Independent reading** – Children should have many opportunities to read to themselves, whether in other curriculum areas or in dedicated reading times (known in some schools as ERIC, or Everyone Reading In Class).

- **One-to-one reading** – This is a very time-consuming way of supporting reading, although reading volunteers can provide this experience, and this can be particularly valuable where children do not have so much support at home. For teachers and teaching assistants guided reading is usually a better use of time.

- **Reading conferences** – Held on a termly or half-termly basis, in which the child discusses what they have been reading with the teacher.

Planning for phonics, spelling and handwriting

The nature of phonics, spelling and handwriting means that they need to be planned for as stand-alone elements of English teaching. Although teachers may make incidental links to them in English lessons (noting a newly learned grapheme during shared reading, for example, or a word containing a spelling pattern the class has been discussing) and they will, of course, gain very valuable assessment evidence for phonics and spelling from the children's reading and writing, it is not necessary to try to integrate the planning and teaching any more closely. Schools are likely to be following a phonics programme which is already carefully planned to ensure progress. Spelling needs the same sort of systematic planning for skills and knowledge. Both are likely to be taught in short discrete sessions, rather than as part of English lessons. The learning is then applied in all the children's reading and writing, across the curriculum. These skills will, of course, not be taught throughout the primary years: phonics teaching is likely to be concentrated in the Reception year and Year 1, with spelling teaching largely replacing it from Year 2 onwards, while handwriting teaching is likely to be a priority in the Reception year and at the point where the school introduces a joined script.

Phonics is likely to be planned over a week. In its Letters and Sound guidance (DfES, 2007), the Primary National Strategy recommended a daily four-part lesson, already encountered in Chapter 6, consisting of the following:

- **Revisit and review** – A quick revision of previously learned grapheme–phoneme correspondences (GPC), typically through showing children a series of graphemes and asking them to give the matching phoneme.

- **Teach** – A new grapheme–phoneme correspondence is introduced.

- **Practise** – An activity which allows children independently to practise the new GPC, through reading or writing words containing it.

- **Apply** – Putting the new learning into the context of whole texts, through (typically as a whole-group activity) reading or writing a sentence or two which includes words containing the new GPC. This reminds children every day why they are learning phonics.

The approach is based on some important principles. Pace is important; there is new learning every day in order that children quickly acquire the skills and knowledge they need to read and write independently. Even if a child does not remember a GPC learned on Monday, they may remember Tuesday's one, and meanwhile what has been taught previously is constantly revisited. Pace in the session is important; little and often is the key to learning of this nature, and time given to phonics needs to be balanced against time given to all other aspects of English, and of other curriculum areas, so ten minutes of fast, simple and varied activities is better than twenty minutes of more leisurely and complicated activities. Children must have opportunities for independent practical tasks; over-reliance on whole-group interactive whiteboard-based activities may mean children are fairly passive and that some do not really engage at all.

Planning for grammar, punctuation and vocabulary

Grammar, and punctuation which is closely connected to it, is much more effectively taught in the context of reading and writing than through decontextualised exercises. Children's attention can be drawn to grammatical features and punctuation in the context of shared reading in a meaningful way: this is the analysis phase of the reading into writing model. Use of those features can then be explicitly modelled in shared writing, with the expectation that children then apply them in their own independent writing. Grammatical terminology can be introduced and explained during the discussion of shared texts. Vocabulary is also best taught in the context of shared texts – whole class in shared reading and with groups in guided reading. However, there is value in lively, interactive games and activities, with a focus on these aspects of English, used as lesson starters.

Case study: fronting adverbials

The focus of Tom's writing lesson in Year 3 was to be varying sentence openings. He started with a human sentence activity which demonstrated how elements of the sentence can be moved around – in particular, the fronting of adverbials.

Tom gave four children large cards on which the separate elements of a sentence had been written:

- a little dragon (the subject)
- lived (verb)
- deep in the forest (adverbial)
- all alone (adverbial)

He asked the children to stand at the front and make a sentence. Normal word order in English has the subject first, followed by the verb, followed by any other elements, and this was how the children arranged themselves. Tom then asked the rest of the class how the sentence could be rearranged. Adverbials are highly mobile elements, and the class produced several versions, including: 'Deep in the forest, all alone, lived a little dragon.'

This sounded more like writing than speech, with the fronted adverbials building up tension, and the subject following the verb, a reversal of normal word order. Tom then modelled the use of fronted adverbials in shared writing and the children were encouraged to think about varying sentence openings as they wrote, and during redrafting.

Planning cross-curricular links

Links between English and subjects such as history, geography and science are obvious. English lessons, particularly when the focus is non-fiction reading and writing, may make use of topics being studied in other subjects. Alternatively, skills learned in English lessons may be applied in other subjects. For example, children may have been learning about birds in science, and then in English use that knowledge as the basis for writing a non-chronological report, with a focus on organising the content into sections and writing an introduction and conclusion. Children may have been studying the conventions of debate in English, and then hold a debate on mining in a geography lesson. While thematic approaches to curriculum planning may suggest that several subjects can be taught at once, it is often helpful in any lesson to have one primary focus; trying to teach concepts, skills or knowledge from two or more subjects within the space of an hour or so can be challenging for the teacher and overwhelming for pupils.

Learning outcomes review

You should now know:

- why schools need to plan their English curriculum;
- the different levels of planning involved;
- the factors that need to be considered when developing long-term, medium-term and short-term plans for English.

Self-assessment questions

1. What key documents are you likely to base your English planning on?
2. Which aspects of English teaching are likely to fall outside the main English lessons?
3. Which main text types should children become familiar with during the primary years?
4. In choosing texts to study, what key issues need to be considered?

Answers to activities

Activity: aims of the English curriculum

You may have included points such as the following:

The English curriculum should ensure that all pupils:

- become competent and confident users of spoken language;
- read accurately and effortlessly, and understand and appreciate what they read;
- communicate effectively in writing;
- have a wide vocabulary and an interest in language and literature;
- use both spoken and written language to support their learning across the curriculum.

Activity: constructing a medium-term plan

This example shows a possible approach, balancing text types in units varying in length from one to four weeks.

Term 1					
Stories from other cultures	Explanations	Film narratives	Significant author	Instructions (making Christmas decorations)	Classic poetry ('The Night Before Christmas')
2 weeks	1 week	3 weeks	4 weeks	1 week	1 week
Term 2					
Non-chronological reports	Older literature	Choral poetry	Persuasive writing: letters	Myths and legends	
2 weeks	3 weeks	1 week	2 weeks	4 weeks	
Term 3					
Classic narrative poetry	Dramatic conventions	Persuasive writing: adverts	Reports	Significant author	Performance poetry
2 weeks	2 weeks	2 weeks	3 weeks	2 weeks	1 week

Further reading

For clear and helpful guidance on planning for progress in English, read:

Brien, J (2012) *Teaching Primary English*. London: SAGE.

For an exploration of the theory and practice of English teaching, along with practical advice on planning, read:

Cox, R (ed.) (2011) *Primary English Teaching: An Introduction to Language, Literacy and Learning*. London: Sage/United Kingdom Literacy Association.

For approaches to creative planning for a range of genres, try:

Lambirth, A (ed.) (2005) *Planning Creative Literacy Lessons*. London: David Fulton.

For an outline of key principles in planning for English, along with useful advice on practice, read:

Waugh, D and Jolliffe, W (2013) *English 5–11: A Guide for Teachers*. Abingdon: Routledge.

References

Department for Education (DfE) (2013) *The National Curriculum in England: Key Stages 1 and 2 Framework Document*. London: DfE.

Department for Education and Employment (DfEE) (1998) *The National Literacy Strategy: Literacy Training Pack*. London: DfEE.

Department for Education and Skills (DfES) (2006) *Primary National Strategy: Primary Framework for Literacy and Mathematics*. Norwich: OPSI. Available at: www.educationengland. org.uk/documents/pdfs/2006-primary-national-strategy.pdf (accessed 2 January 2014).

DfES (2007) *Letters and Sounds: Principles and Practice of High Quality Phonics*. London: DfES Publications.

Ofsted (2012) *Moving English Forward: Action to Raise Standards in English.* Manchester: Ofsted. Available at: **www.ofsted.gov.uk/resources/moving-english-forward** (accessed 2 January 2014).

Powell, R, McIntyre, E and Rightmyer, E (2006) Johnnie won't read, and Susie won't either: reading instruction and student resistance. *Journal of Early Childhood Literacy*, 6(1): 5–31.

QCA (1999) *Target Setting and Assessment in the National Literacy Strategy*. London: QCA Publications.

14 Assessment: An Invaluable Classroom Resource

Kirsty Anderson

Learning outcomes

By reading this chapter you will develop your understanding of:

- why assessing children is important: its impact and use;
- how to assess different skills and knowledge of the National Curriculum in English;
- how we can effectively link planning, teaching and assessing pupils;
- different approaches to assessment in school: summative and formative.

Teachers' Standards
1. Make accurate and productive use of assessment:

- know and understand how to assess the relevant subject and curriculum areas, including statutory assessment requirements;
- make use of formative and summative assessment to secure pupils' progress;
- use relevant data to monitor progress, set targets, and plan subsequent lessons;
- give pupils regular feedback, both orally and through accurate marking, and encourage pupils to respond to the feedback.

Introduction

Ed, a trainee teacher on his final placement, listens intently as Karen, the class teacher, describes the class. He starts to worry: How can he gather as much information as the teacher has? Karen shares information about the language needs of the pupils in her class. There's Ruby who loves sharing stories when the teacher reads, especially when she is in a smaller group, because she gets the chance to ask questions. And Daniel who is starting to think aloud when planning his writing, and often acts out his story using puppets in the role-play area. He talks to his partner about what he likes in his own writing.

What does Ed need to do in order to make a formative or a summative assessment of the children's progress and needs? How is this essential information collected and used?

Assessment can take different forms, including *testing, marking, feedback, questioning*. This list is by no means exhaustive. It is the intention of this chapter first to explain why teachers assess and then to give examples and suggestions for both formative and summative assessments. Assessment examples of the Programmes of Study for English are given in the following order: speaking and listening, reading, writing. Formative assessment looks at understanding during teaching which is understood as assessment *for* learning (AfL), in contrast to summative assessment which is assessment *of* learning. Summative assessments take place at the end of a taught sequence to sum up pupil learning. It is useful to outline briefly the history of assessment of English in order to understand previous assessment practices.

Assessment in schools: a brief history

Summative assessments (testing) were used to assess pupil learning at the end of a Key Stage (in Years 2 and 6). Standardised Assessment Tests (SATs) were introduced for 7-year-olds (Year 2) in 1991, and for 11-year-olds (Year 6) in 1995 to summarise learning up to this point. In English pupils were tested on word reading (Key Stage 1 only) and comprehension, writing composition, spelling and handwriting. SATs scores equated to a 'level' for pupils. In primary schools levels ranged from level 1 to 5, though in some cases higher achieving pupils might achieve level 6. Each level was split into A, B and C. Nationally, data was analysed for key strengths and areas for development. This data was published in league tables and comparisons between schools and local authorities made. Schools used this information to prioritise needs in future teaching and learning. In 2009, Assessing Pupil Progress (APP) grids were introduced which showed pupil achievement and gaps which became next steps in learning. APP was designed to support teachers' **continuous** assessment of and planning for pupils, so was **formative** rather than **summative**. APP grids described pupils as low, secure or high within a particular level rather than C, B or A.

The 2014 National Curriculum removed the use of levels to judge pupils' attainment. The DfE has stated that the previous focus on levels of attainment was *complicated and difficult to understand, especially for parents. It also encourages teachers to focus on a pupil's current level, rather than consider more broadly what the pupil can actually do* (DfE, 2013a). Schools are required to focus on formative assessment and to track pupils' attainment and whether they are meeting expectations.

What is the purpose of assessment?

To teach successfully, Ed must ensure he is competent with both formative and summative assessment. The timing of assessments is also important. Teachers need to plan to assess pupils before, during and after teaching and learning take place. These timings will be explored more fully later in the chapter. The purposes of formative and summative assessments can be explained under five different headings:

- to recognise prior knowledge (formative);
- to identify and plan for next steps in learning (formative and summative);
- to diagnose particular difficulties (formative);
- to check learning (summative);
- to evaluate the impact of teaching and teachers (formative and summative).

Prior knowledge

Children bring much to a learning opportunity, which is not always fully explored. This includes talking and playing with family and friends, reading, using digital media, watching TV and films. All of these experiences contribute to and influence children's learning and interests. Teachers will know pupils' prior teaching and learning experiences because they talk to colleagues and review previous planning. Assessment records passed from class to class show teachers what children have already achieved. This must be done in conjunction with assessing the pupils as they are at that moment of learning. Pupils in Year 2 will have some knowledge of traditional tales, for example, but planning records only show part of the picture. Asking children what they know and remember about traditional tales – characters, settings, and events – can tell a teacher much more *at the time* of the lesson. This is not to dismiss information gathered from a previous teacher; rather, it is to remind teachers that they should never assume pupils will remember all previous learning and that for each session reviews can help match learning to needs.

Identifying next steps

Teachers can assess readiness to move from one objective to the next based on several factors as they teach. Did children answer questions? Could they complete the tasks? When marking, if teachers find that children are unable to apply their learning, then planning can be annotated and adapted to give further opportunities to develop understanding. Summative assessments, such as a spelling test, or a 'cold' piece of writing might also be used to identify planning needs. The closeness of a test to the direct teaching determines whether it is 'hot' or 'cold'. Asking pupils to write a narrative at the end of a sequence of learning about a particular genre can summarise what they have learned and would be considered a 'hot' assessment as pupils are tested on what they have just learned. Such writing tasks can also be used as a means of assessing *prior knowledge* if set before teaching and learning, which would make the task a 'cold' assessment which checks what pupils recall from previous learning. 'Cold' assessments must be detached from the taught skills being assessed.

Diagnosing difficulties

Listening to individual readers, scrutinising written work, or observing role play and drama can all support teachers to assess particular difficulties some children may be experiencing. Knowing what a specific area for development or gap is, such as not punctuating sentences with full stops, can facilitate teaching which closes specific gaps. It is important to recognise too that diagnostic assessment in schools is used to identify specific needs of pupils who have special educational needs. Specialised diagnostic materials are most likely to be used with some rather than all pupils in school, and are most often used by specialised practitioners such as SENCOs (special educational needs coordinators) or educational psychologists.

Checking learning

Although formative assessments are essential to meet the needs of pupils, it is useful at times to check learning through summative assessments. Testing to summarise what has been learned would take place at the end of a sequence of lessons, or possibly at the end of term. Spelling tests, comprehension questions, independent timed writing tasks and formal presentations all offer opportunities to review learning. This summative assessment can also, of course, be used formatively. Checking understanding of previous learning before starting a new theme can prioritise need and identify next steps; the success of a strategy used or a teacher's style can be evaluated and adapted or continued and any specific needs would be easily recognised.

Evaluating teaching

Reflective teachers use assessment evidence like marking to evaluate the success of the teaching strategies used. Teachers can also consider how much the children enjoy what they are learning. Learning should be enjoyable and engaging; use of AfL strategies can explore this. If Ed considers the information shared by the class teacher about Daniel who learns well with his partner and Ruby who enjoys discussing texts in guided reading he can continue to use and develop peer assessment and small-group teaching opportunities. Ed can extend learning by teaching pupils to ask questions: about books they read and their own work. By becoming skilled with questions themselves, children begin to learn to self-assess, which is important when developing deep understanding in any learners.

Research focus: formative assessment

Some of the most widely recognised research into assessment is that of Paul Black and Dylan Wiliam (1998), who argue that tests are restrictive forms of assessment. They examine the 'weak link' between assessments and teaching and learning. Teachers need to ensure that teaching is not limited by the content of the summative test. Ofsted's 2012 report *Moving English Forward* recognises that although preparation for tests is important, this needs to be appropriate and not begun too early to avoid limiting the range of the curriculum. Schools should remember there is no such thing as a 'perfect test' and it would be impossible for one test to examine pupils on all aspects of learning. So a summative assessment covering a half term of 30 lessons might show some of the learning achieved, but is unlikely to show everything pupils have learned in those 30 hours. The influential research of Black and Wiliam (1998) raised the status of formative assessment. It is not without some problems as Bennett (2011) indicates that implementation of AfL varies widely. Ofsted acknowledges the need for systematic use of formative assessment to be developed as long as it does not interrupt learning. It is important to get a balance: for pupils to complete a task before they review their learning using peer or self-assessment. The UKLA and NATE further emphasised the importance of formative assessment in the 2016 Final Report of the Commission on Assessment Without Levels. Usefully for schools, this report highlights the importance of in-school and formative assessments, recognising that it is individual schools and teachers who can and do use relevant information to support pupil progress.

Effective assessment of the curriculum

Teachers need to be secure and confident that they can make use of good practice in assessing to understand pupil needs and development. Within the English Curriculum, assessment will include objectives for speaking and listening, reading and writing. By the end of each Key Stage, pupils should know and apply the skills learned from the objectives. These are the *attainment targets*. In this section, examples to assess before, during and after learning are given, along with a summary of overall expectations for the different dimensions of English.

Activity: effective questioning

Teachers use a range of different question types. It is important to use open questions which lead to further discussion and challenge pupils to explain their answer. Consider the English objective in the table below, then using the descriptions as a guide, complete the table of AfL questions to support a topic about books versus films. Questions may be about the topic, or debating skills.

Pupils should be taught to understand what they read by:

- Explaining and discussing their understanding of what they have read, including through formal debates, maintaining a focus on the topic and using notes where necessary (Years 5 and 6)

Type of question	Before	During	After
Questions which yield a range of answers	*Which of these features would you include in a formal presentation?* *Standard English, wide vocabulary, talking to your friend, expression, diagrams, shouting*	*If you can explain why it is useful, I will give you vocabulary and phrases useful for a debate.*	*Can you explain which of these features made your presentation a success?* *Information, notes, listening to each other*
Questions posed as a statement	*Books are better than films, do you agree or disagree?*		*Why are some books more popular than others?*
Questions which ask for a different point of view	*Will all people think films are better than books?*	*Will using notes help you to present?*	*After listening to the debate should we only agree with one person?*

(Possible answers can be found at the end of the chapter.)

Speaking and listening

Before considering how to assess speaking and listening, it is useful to decide what competency in this aspect of English looks like (see also Chapter 2). How would a Year 2 pupil with good listening skills differ from a successful pupil in Year 4? A trainee teacher like Ed should look closely at the objectives and guidance and non-statutory notes in the National Curriculum, then picture these competencies as a progression of skills.

The speaking and listening aspects of the curriculum are: turn taking, listening, participation in discussion, presentations and reading aloud. Through this learning language skills develop, including vocabulary extension and formalised speech. Assessment of speaking and listening learning can be illustrated by using the following objective from Lower Key Stage 2 comprehension:

Pupils should be taught to:

Participate in discussion about both books that are read to them and those they can read for themselves, taking turns and listening to what others say.

(DfE, 2013b, p18)

Practical opportunities to check turn-taking and listening skills *before* teaching are through observations. Do the pupils shout out, dominate or interrupt others? Are responses repetitions of those from other pupils? Activities to develop turn taking and listening such as role play or puppet shows can then be planned if needed. *During* these activities further assessment can be made through use of success criteria: a checklist of the taught skills used to achieve the objective. Pupils learn to refer to success criteria, which can establish and enhance peer and self-assessment. Success criteria are sometimes given and sometimes generated with pupils. If pupils can identify success criteria they understand what they are trying to achieve. *After* learning turn-taking and listening skills, pupils could give a presentation. Teachers can again observe the use of turn taking and compare this with pupil starting points. If recordings have been used, then sharing these can help pupils to see their own progress, self-assessing learning.

Reading

The aim is for children to develop into confident and fluent readers acquiring a wide vocabulary and understanding of grammar (see also Chapter 6). The National Curriculum is designed to cultivate reading for pleasure and for information, and expects that teachers will support children to find their interests, and to appreciate English literary heritage. In the National Curriculum, reading objectives are helpfully organised into two dimensions: word reading and comprehension. Good teaching aims to ensure that children contextualise word-reading skills rather than isolating these from whole texts, but as different kinds of teaching are required for each of these dimensions, it is sensible to consider different ways to assess.

Research focus: word reading and comprehension

The interdependence of word reading and comprehension was highlighted by the Rose Report (Rose, 2006). Standards of English had improved since the introduction of the National Literacy Strategy (NLS) in 1998, which engaged schools with phonics and how to teach it. HMI reviews of the NLS found that teaching of reading and spelling would further improve if phonic knowledge and skills were taught thoroughly. Rose examined early reading and recommended teaching a programme of systematic synthetic phonics to ensure rapid progression of word reading. This recommendation has been criticised because it may lead to a separation of word reading from comprehension. Cremin et al. (2008) suggest further that teachers might focus on word reading rather than literature. They explored teachers' knowledge of children's literature, and concluded that this too needs to be enhanced as teachers rely heavily on a few well-known authors. Knowledge of literary heritage is an expectation in the National Curriculum. Rose counters criticism by explaining that since development of word-reading

→

skills (phonics) is time limited, it will not detract from the importance of comprehension as this continues throughout life. The two dimensions are shown in the Simple View of Reading Model featured in Chapter 6.

Teachers can quickly assess the needs of pupils if use is made of this model during reading sessions. Pupils may have good word recognition skills but poor comprehension, or vice versa.

Assessing word reading

Word-reading skills need to be secure to ensure that pupils can decode unfamiliar words with speed, and quickly recognise familiar words. Schools will follow a phonics programme which supports development of decoding skills. Phonic programmes facilitate assessment as there are daily opportunities to review previous learning and practise new skills. Teachers may use a record of pupil progress listing the taught phonemes which can be highlighted when achieved. When phonics skills are secure, teachers like trainee Ed should consider ways to assess knowledge of etymology and morphology as word-reading skills grow. The following objective from Lower Key Stage 2 is used to illustrate ways to approach assessment before, during and after learning.

Pupils should be taught to:

Apply their growing knowledge of root words, prefixes and suffixes as listed in Appendix 1, to both read aloud and understand the meaning of new words they meet.

(DfE, 2013b, p25)

Questioning *before* teaching can review what pupils recall from previous years about adding prefixes and suffixes to words. Pupils can be asked to identify the odd one out from a range of suffixes and prefixes, or to discuss a statement like 'all words can have prefixes added' which would reveal misconceptions and understanding. *During* the lesson, missing words or cloze procedure shows understanding and correct application. For example pupils could be asked for appropriate words with prefixes for this sentence: *The cars raced at _____ speed. Unbelievable, irresponsible, supersonic* and *illegal* would all fit. *After* teaching, listening to pupils read and ensuring they make good, sensible attempts at pronunciation would show how well word-reading skills are developing. Use of a growing vocabulary, both in oral and written work, also demonstrates this.

Case study: a trainee teacher

Helena was a trainee teacher on placement in Year 1. She taught phonics daily to a group. The teacher explained that pupils were making progress in phonics but made mistakes when working independently. This was expected but the teacher and Helena wanted

→

to encourage pupils to develop self-help strategies. Together, they planned to observe the pupils blending for reading and segmenting for spelling in independent writing. They decided to plan opportunities to observe pupils transferring phonics skills to different tasks. Observations gave Helena the chance to see pupils applying skills and indicated that pupils needed support to recall the phonics they had learned to apply it independently. They provided children with a phonics mat separated into three sections: *words I know, words I am learning, practising space*. The mats were laminated and pupils were able to write on them to add the words they were learning and try out a spelling independently. Pupils were encouraged to use these in all lessons. The benefit was twofold: pupil confidence grew as they progressed and when Helena reviewed the mats she could see which words she needed to include in planning.

Curriculum link

Helena is very sensible to encourage pupils to make use of their phonics mats in other lessons. The National Curriculum highlights English as a medium providing access to other subjects. Pupils in Year 1 might learn about green plants, for example, and should be learning investigative skills which include 'asking simple questions and recognising that they can be answered in different ways' (DfE, 2013b, Science Programme of Study, p6). Having their phonics mats available to remind pupils of phonemes and words they know can help to make sense of their reading.

Assessing comprehension

Comprehension is about pupils learning to understand what they are reading and this can be at both literal and non-literal levels. It is essential to ensure that comprehension strategies are taught to support this. Reading a text followed by answering questions about it is not teaching comprehension. If the intention is to assess pupil needs, then gathering a range of information is necessary. If children are to develop comprehension skills which can be assessed, then understanding vocabulary, asking questions, making predictions, drawing inferences, recalling key events, knowing language and layout features must all be taught. Some examples of comprehension assessments are illustrated with the following objective from Lower Key Stage 2.

Pupils should be taught to understand what they read, in books they can read independently by:

Drawing inferences such as inferring characters' feelings, thoughts and motives from their actions, and justifying inferences with evidence predicting what might happen from details stated and implied.

(DfE, 2013b, p26)

Asking for predictions about a text from sharing the front cover and title is commonly used *before* reading and developing comprehension. The potential assessment opportunities could be developed further by sharing images linked to a text in the week before reading, placed around the classroom with little explanation. A teacher would be able to assess pupils' interests, the questions which arise about the pictures, and any background knowledge they already have and what might be needed to understand the text fully. *During* reading, asking pupils to draw characters and annotate their drawing with a list of emotions would further show which pupils are learning to consider characters' actions or dialogue as an indication of feelings. *After* teaching, the plenary can be used to review learning, focusing on asking pupils what they have learned which is new alongside specific questions linked to the success criteria.

Activity: miscue analysis

Miscue analysis is one method of analysis of the errors that a child makes when reading, in order to identify particular aspects that require further teaching. Read the example below to identify the needs of this child.

A six-year-old pupil, Maya, was asked by a trainee teacher to read aloud from *Owl Babies* by Martin Waddell. The teacher recorded any errors using the following codes:

// = pausing

<u>mother</u> = blending to read

C = self-correction

~~woke~~ = word omitted

/ = addition of words

~~asked~~ said = substitution

---

upon a time

Once / there were three baby owls: Sarah, Percy and Bill. They lived in a hole in the trunk of a tree with their owl <u>mother</u>. The hole had twigs and // ~~leaves~~ and owl feathers C in it. It was their house. One night they ~~woke~~ wok up and their Owl Mother was GONE. 'Where's Mummy?' ~~asked~~ said Sarah.

'Oh my goodness!' said Percy.

'I <u>want</u> my ~~mummy~~!' said Bill. 'I want my mummy!' said Bill.'

(Continued)

(Continued)

Write a brief analysis and assessment of Maya's abilities and needs, using the National Curriculum and looking at both word reading and comprehension skills.

(Possible answers can be found at the end of the chapter.)

Writing

Through teaching the National Curriculum pupils should be supported in their command of written English and be able to write clearly, accurately and coherently. Pupils should be given opportunities to write in a range of forms, for different audiences. As Chapter 10 explained, writing skills are divided into two dimensions: transcription and composition. It is useful for assessment to consider the progression of these separate skills, and to decide which particular aspect will be assessed. It is not always useful and it is time consuming to attempt to assess everything in a written text. Purposeful marking and feedback will link to the use of the learned objective which may be from transcription or composition. So, if pupils in Year 3 have been learning to extend sentences with conjunctions within a composition, marking should focus on the use of these.

Assessing transcription skills

In order to be able to write fluently, pupils need to have well-developed, speedy handwriting and have skills and knowledge they can draw on for spelling. Without these, the flow of writing, from drafting ideas to composition, can be slowed. The following indicates how one objective might be assessed:

Pupils should be taught to:

Use the diagonal and horizontal strokes that are needed to join letters and understand which letters, when adjacent to one another are best left unjoined.

(DfE, 2013b, p28)

Assessment *before* teaching in this case can be from ongoing marking of written work. Handwriting skills can be practised discretely but pupils should be expected to apply these in everyday work. *During* teaching, peer assessment could be used, with pupils supporting each other to check joins. Some ICT software would also be useful at this point, especially if several pupils are practising together, so that teachers can be assured that pupils are not left without support. Animated programmes can support pupils to see the correct joins. Checking independent writing *after* in the ongoing marking of work will show how secure pupils are and will continue to show which joins need further revision.

Assessing composition

To communicate ideas through writing, pupils need to learn to articulate clearly and to organise ideas. Considering and understanding the needs of the reader through knowledge of audience and purpose is also important. Reading pupil work and giving feedback are without doubt useful AfL strategies but, as Ed has discovered, supporting pupils to self-assess will allow pupils to consider the reader as they plan, draft and edit their work independently. Possible ways to assess at different points are given to support the following objective:

> Pupils should be taught to evaluate and edit by:
>
> Proposing changes to grammar, vocabulary and punctuation to enhance effects and clarify meaning.
>
> (DfE, 2013b, p38)

Sharing the learning objective with children can be useful to assess understanding *before* teaching. With this particular objective, asking pupils to explain how they understand 'enhance effects and clarify meaning' can guide the direction of the lesson. A good teacher will have examples to illustrate the meaning ready, and will ask for these from pupils. *During* the process of composition, asking children to read their writing aloud, listening to make sure their writing makes sense and is effective, can support teachers to check the objective is understood, and help pupils to evaluate the impact their writing might have on readers especially if other pupils are encouraged to ask questions about the writer's intention. It should in turn encourage careful and close listening skills. Reading and commenting on pupils' writing *after* is the most obvious assessment strategy to use. However, it can also be useful to have small group or one-to-one conferences with pupils to discuss how writing can be improved, looking at particular elements like the effect of vocabulary choices.

Case study: what we can learn about this pupil from the National Curriculum?

Kayleigh was a pupil in Year 6. Her Year 6 teachers made use of different writing opportunities to develop a full picture of attainment and progress: timed assessed writing tasks, cross-curricular writing, opportunities to write in own preferred styles, genres or own choice of audience. Feedback was used carefully with children, ensuring they understood what the areas for development were in their writing, and how they could learn to improve their writing to address these. The teachers used the National Curriculum carefully to identify which objectives would represent progress and targets for Kayleigh. The teachers looked closely at composition, grammar and punctuation. Kayleigh planned well, considering the audience of

→

her writing, but her teachers identified that after drafting, Kayleigh lacked effective skills in evaluating and editing. In particular, work was needed to understand the effectiveness of her own writing. Kayleigh was taught to plan carefully for a particular audience, and to understand and talk about the purpose of her writing, which then supported decisions on vocabulary and sentence structure. Kayleigh learned to talk through and explain her ideas to a partner as she was checking her writing. Partners used questions to help focus on the intended effect the writing would have.

Curriculum link

Showing pupils how to reread and redraft their writing is important in all curriculum areas. Kayleigh might apply these skills if writing a non-chronological report to describe different types of settlement and land use in geography.

Activity: next steps in writing

Look at this writing extract. Pupils were asked to write a mystery story. The key teaching focused on describing settings, characters and atmosphere. Using the National Curriculum as a guide, identify two aspects completed well and one next step which should be taught.

> It was just an ordinary day. Andrew went to school the same as he did every day. Late. He walked quite slowly along New Street, the street just before his school. He went past the old biscuit factory. Nobody worked there anymore. It closed 50 years ago after an accident. He wasn't alone on the street. That doesn't sound that unusual. But New Street was always empty. Someone else was there. Someone was behind him.

(Possible answers can be found at the end of the chapter.)

Formative and summative assessments guide teachers in planning for pupil need, and support children in learning to reflect on what they know and how they might move forward. Although at first it may seem that assessment is separate from learning, and may consume much of a teacher's time, this chapter has shown that the opposite is true. When teachers ask questions, mark writing, make observations or annotate planning, they are assessing. Evidence of assessments are found in teachers' marking, their planning and in any records which are collected according to the decisions made by an individual school. Assessment should be recognised as an invaluable tool to support effective teaching and learning and, something which trainees like Ed can quickly realise, can be made productive use of every day.

Learning outcomes review

You should now know:

- how children can show their understanding of English;
- what we need to know as primary teachers about assessing English;
- some of the challenges identifying steps in learning;
- different approaches to assessing English.

Self-assessment questions

1. What is the difference between summative and formative assessment?
2. How do schools make use of assessment to evaluate a teaching strategy?
3. Marking is the only way to give feedback on pupil writing. Do you agree or disagree?
4. What different ways do you know to assess reading comprehension?

Activity answers

Effective questioning

Suggested questions

Pupils should be taught to understand what they read by:			
• Explaining and discussing their understanding of what they have read, including through formal debates, maintaining a focus on the topic and using notes where necessary. (Years 5 and 6) (DfE, 2013b, p35)			
Type of question	**Before**	**During**	**After**
Questions which yield a range of answers	*Which of these features would you include in a formal presentation?* *Standard English, wide vocabulary, talking to your friend, expression, diagrams, shouting*		

(Continued)

(Continued)

Type of question	Before	During	After
Questions posed as a statement		*You use more imagination reading a book than watching a film. Do you agree or disagree?*	
Questions which ask for a different point of view			*After listening to the debate should we only agree with one person?*

Miscue analysis

Word reading: phonic awareness is generally good. Reading *woke* as *wok* indicates that pupils have not yet learned split digraphs. Omitting *leaves* also suggests this is the case. There may be some over-reliance on sounding out and blending shown by *want*, which is a high-frequency word, so should be read more speedily.

Comprehension: the addition of *upon a time* shows an awareness of traditional story openings. Some self-correction is evident – *feathers* – which means there is a growing ability to contextualise word reading. Substitution of *asked* for *said* retains the meaning, so this pupil is reading with understanding.

It is important to note that miscue analysis can support detailed assessment of reading, but teachers would only use this with some individuals or at certain points of a year as it is time-consuming.

Next steps in writing

A possible assessment of pupil success and need has been supported using this objective – *pupils should be taught to draft and write by: in narratives, describing settings, characters and atmosphere and integrating* dialogue to convey character and advance the action (DfE, 2013b, p38).

> It was just an ordinary day. Andrew went to school the same as he did every day. Late. He walked quite slowly along New Street, the street just before his school. He went past the old biscuit factory. <u>Nobody</u> worked there anymore. It closed 50 years ago after an accident. He wasn't alone on the street. That doesn't sound that unusual. But New Street was always empty. <u>Someone</u> else was there. <u>Someone</u> was behind him.

Possible positive comments.

- 'Empty' words (underlined) are used well to create a mysterious atmosphere.
- The pupil is beginning to create atmosphere with the setting. Readers might wonder what is inside the old biscuit factory.

Possible next step.

- Describe Andrew further so the reader discovers more about why he is late and gets a picture of the sort of boy he is.

Further reading

The texts below will broaden your understanding of different forms of assessment.

The following is written by education researchers widely recognised for their analysis of assessment in schools:

Black, P and Wiliam, D (1998) *Inside the Black Box: Raising Standards through Classroom Assessment.* London: Granada Learning.

Shirley Clarke has written a wide range of accessible texts within which well-developed strategies for formative assessments are outlined:

Clarke, S (2001) *Unlocking Formative Assessment.* London: Hodder & Stoughton.

A useful publication with guidance for good practice is:

Ofsted (2012) *Moving English Forward: Action to Raise Standards in English.* Manchester: Ofsted.

References

Bennett, RE (2011) Formative assessment: a critical review. *Assessment in Education: Principles, Policy & Practice*, 18(1): 5–25.

Black, P and Wiliam, D (1998) *Inside the Black Box: Raising Standards through Classroom Assessment.* London: Granada Learning.

Cremin, T, Mottram, M, Bearne, E and Goodwin, P (2008) Exploring teachers' knowledge of children's literature. *Cambridge Journal of Education*, 38(4): 449–64.

Department for Education (DfE) (2013a) Assessing without levels, 14 June. Available at: **http://webarchive.nationalarchives.gov.uk/20130904084116/https://www.education. gov.uk/schools/teachingandlearning/curriculum/nationalcurriculum2014/a00225864/ assessing-without-levels** (accessed 27 June 2016).

DfE (2013b) *The National Curriculum in England: Key Stages 1 and 2 Framework Document.* London: DfE.

Ofsted (2012) *Moving English Forward: Action to Raise Standards in English.* Manchester: Ofsted. Available at: **http://webarchive.nationalarchives.gov.uk/20141124154759/http://www. ofsted.gov.uk/resources/moving-english-forward** (accessed 27 June 2016).

Rose, J (2006) *Independent Review of the Teaching of Early Reading: Final Report.* London: DfE.

United Kingdom Literary Association (UKLA) (2016) *Curriculum and Assessment in English 3 to 19: A Better Plan.* London: UKLA.

15 Mastery in English

Kate Allott

Learning outcomes

By reading this chapter you will develop your understanding of:

- what is meant by the term 'mastery learning';
- how mastery learning might apply to English;
- some of the challenges of using the approach in English teaching.

Teachers' Standards
1. A teacher must set high expectations which inspire, motivate and challenge pupils:

- Set goals that stretch and challenge pupils of all backgrounds, abilities and dispositions.

2. Demonstrate good subject and curriculum knowledge:

- Have a secure knowledge of the relevant subject and curriculum area, foster and maintain pupils' interest in the subject, and address misunderstandings.

Introduction

The concept of mastery learning has come to the fore in recent years, almost half a century since it was introduced by Bloom (1968), and it has been linked with an interest in England in high-achieving East Asian education systems. Mastery learning is currently being discussed largely in terms of mathematics, and an evaluation of the Mathematics Mastery programme in English schools showed children in the programme making one month's additional progress in a year (Education Endowment Foundation 2015). This chapter will begin with a brief consideration of Bloom's original work and also of what may be learned from approaches used in countries such as Singapore. However, mathematics and English are very different subjects, and if the mastery learning approach is to be applied to English, there needs to be consideration first of what mastery in that subject might look like, and second whether the teaching approach associated with the concept is appropriate to English. This chapter will address both questions. It will also emphasise the importance of teacher subject knowledge in both teaching for mastery and assessment of mastery.

Bloom (1968) was concerned that many pupils moved through their education scoring badly on tests, with an assumption being made by teachers and eventually the students themselves that they were not capable of fully grasping what they were taught. He considered that students needed to master content before moving on to something new. Bloom advocated an approach in which curriculum content was broken down into units and the learning within each unit was carefully sequenced, with early formative assessment indicating to teachers and students how much content had been mastered. For those students who needed it, additional support was then provided: this might consist of small group work, peer support, the use of alternative approaches or resources, or feedback which motivated the learner to persevere. Further assessment then took place, to check that those pupils had now achieved mastery within the unit. Students who did well on the first test were provided with enrichment and extension activities to deepen and broaden their understanding of the topic. In a sense this might seem to match the differentiation that has been the prevalent approach in English education for many years, but there is an important difference. Bloom felt that most students were capable of mastery, but some needed more time to achieve it. The British system, with its sorting of children into high-, medium- and low- 'ability' groups, often from Reception on, and sometimes with the same groupings for all curriculum areas, suggests that some children will never reach the same finishing point as others. There is a danger that those lowered expectations become a self-fulfilling prophecy, with 'low-ability' children offered over-simplified tasks, a slower pace and a narrower curriculum.

Research focus

The interest in East Asian approaches stems from the impressive performance of, for example, Singapore, Shanghai, Hong Kong and South Korea in the international PISA tests; typically, they outperform countries such as the United States, Britain and Australia by more than a year of schooling (Jerrim, 2015). It should be noted first that questions have been raised about underlying methodological problems with the PISA study (Prais, 2003). Beyond this, however, it is not easy to identify a clear 'East Asian' teaching approach, and Jerrim's study of children of East Asian descent born and educated in Australia showed that they too scored highly on the PISA maths test, outperforming other children by 100 points, equivalent to two and a half years of progress. This throws into question whether it is actually the education systems in those countries which are leading to high attainment, or whether other factors might be at play. Jerrim suggests that these other factors might include parents' choice of schools, the value families place on education, their willingness to pay for out of school tuition, their work ethic and their high aspirations. He comments that widespread cultural change might be needed for Britain to be able to catch up with high-performing countries.

In attempting to learn lessons from those successful East Asian education systems and the mastery learning approach, several possible factors have been identified. These include:

- believing that all pupils are capable of achieving high standards;
- planning for all children to move through curriculum units at the same pace, while providing individual support for those who might otherwise not master the content;
- a very carefully planned curriculum, with well-focused lessons and resources;
- studying fewer topics but in more depth;
- practice and consolidation of new learning;
- careful questioning to assess learning, and regular assessment;
- high quality textbooks.

(NCETM, 2014)

None of these, apart perhaps from the last, looks particularly different from what many schools in this country might consider to be their own practice. How useful, then, is the concept of mastery learning, and in particular in relation to English? Mastery, depending on exactly what is to be mastered, can be seen as involving secure understanding of concepts, strong subject knowledge and very good skills, and the ability to apply all of these in meaningful contexts. Mastery does, of course, depend very much on the age and stage of the child, and the aspect of English being considered. Mastery in relation to speaking and listening will not look the same at four and eleven. It can only be judged in relation to the curriculum and age-related expectations. In terms of aspects of English, mastery of word reading is very different from mastery of language comprehension; as the Simple View of Reading (Rose, 2006) suggests, it is possible to have mastery of one of those two dimensions of reading without the other. A reader may be able to decode texts quickly and accurately but not gain a clear picture of what they mean; another reader may read slowly and inaccurately, and yet be able to gain a deep understanding of texts. The ultimate challenge of application is seen very clearly in writing, where children use their knowledge of text types and both compositional and transcriptional skills to produce successful pieces.

Having considered these general issues, we will now consider each aspect of English in turn. For speaking and listening, the National Curriculum programme of study states the following:

> Pupils should be taught to speak clearly and convey ideas confidently using Standard English. They should learn to justify ideas with reasons; ask questions to check understanding; develop vocabulary and build knowledge; negotiate; evaluate and build on the ideas of others; and select the appropriate register

for effective communication. They should be taught to give well-structured descriptions and explanations and develop their understanding through speculating, hypothesising and exploring ideas.

(DfE, 2013, p10)

The programme of study goes on to say that the statements apply to all ages, so it is left to teachers to decide what is appropriate to each age group. Immediately, the importance of teacher subject knowledge becomes apparent. Without a secure understanding of language development, it is very difficult to know at what age children might have the discourse skills to recognise what another child has said and then build on or contradict the original view. Even with an aspect of language which may appear relatively straightforward – vocabulary – where development is often judged by numbers of words known, there are questions about the difference between words understood and words used appropriately in context, and also depth of vocabulary – in other words, understanding that some words have a range of meanings – for example, that an atmosphere can be chilly in different ways. Judgements about what is a 'good' vocabulary at different ages need to take all of this into account. The programme of study does introduce two very important concepts which are central to the idea of mastery: *competence* and *confidence*. However, the two do not necessarily go together. Some children may be competent in something, but do not believe themselves to be so; probably less often children may have a misplaced confidence in their own competence.

It was stated earlier that mastery of the two dimensions of reading, word reading and language comprehension, would look very different. Word reading is relatively simple to assess. At the end of the Early Years Foundation Stage children are expected to be able to read simple words accurately, using the grapheme–phoneme correspondences they have been taught and sounding out and blending as necessary, and also recognising a small number of common exception words. To show mastery of these skills we would expect children to apply these skills confidently and successfully to unknown words. It has sometimes been argued that the Year 1 phonics screening check in some way disadvantages children who are considered to be 'good readers' because they try to turn non-words such as 'yed', 'emp' and 'sheb' into words they know, and therefore misread them. However, children need to learn to read words as they are; all readers are faced with words they do not know, such as names of people and places, and good readers read what the words actually say.

Mastery of word reading at later stages is also relatively easy to recognise: it involves fast and accurate decoding of longer words and words including more complex spelling patterns. It will involve knowing that there may be different possible ways of pronouncing an unknown word, first because graphemes may represent different phonemes. A child who did not know the word 'chasm' might pronounce it with a /ch/ or /k/ at the beginning, for example. Mastery would be demonstrated if the child tried out the alternatives to see if any produced a recognisable word. In addition, pronunciation might vary depending on which syllables are stressed and which are unstressed. For example, in the word 'antonymy' the first and third syllables might be stressed, or possibly the first and second. Readers who have mastery of word reading will try out alternatives, listening in case they hear a word which is part of their oral vocabulary but which they have not seen written down before. Older children, whose vocabulary development increasingly comes from their reading, are likely to use plausible but incorrect pronunciations of words they have only seen written down, such as stressing the first syllable of 'awry' (making it rhyme with 'story') rather than the second syllable. Such mispronunciations are not signs of poor word-reading skills but almost the opposite, as the reader has selected and internalised what seems the most likely pronunciation.

Mastery of language comprehension is far more complex, depending as it does on not only understanding of vocabulary and grammatical structures, but also knowledge of different text types and, significantly, knowledge and understanding of the world. It involves grasping what is read at different levels – the simple retrieval of facts, or literal understanding; the ability to go beyond that level to make inferences, either connecting different pieces of information (bridging inferences) or building a bigger picture from one piece of information (elaborative inferences). Beyond that is the level of response to and evaluation of texts, and consideration of, for example, authorial intent: why did the writer do this and does it work? Mastery of comprehension also involves metacognition: good readers monitor their own understanding of what they read, and actively interrogate texts and consider reading strategies. It tends to be assumed that older, well-educated readers will naturally do these things, but Dartmouth College's Harvard Report (2001) is an interesting example of highly educated college students who still did not read in this way. Given a text to read in twenty minutes, only 15 of the 1,500 were able to write a short statement about the main theme of the text; these were the ones who had read the summary and subheadings, while the rest simply started reading from the beginning. Reading for mastery therefore needs to address these aspects.

It is important to note that while progression in comprehension in part depends on applying skills to longer and more complex texts, there is also progression in terms of the sophistication of readers' responses to texts. A six-year-old and an adult reviewer of children's books might read the same book, and their responses would be vastly different, with the reviewer perhaps identifying underlying themes and comparing the book to others by the same writer or of the same genre while the child might retell the story, link the book to her own experiences and make simple inferences. For example, a young child reading Eric Carle's *The Very Hungry Caterpillar* might recall the stages of the caterpillar's development in order, and infer that the caterpillar's stomach-ache resulted not only from the amount he ate, but also that he was eating inappropriate foods. An adult reader (perhaps not entirely seriously) might interpret the story as a commentary on waste and over-consumption in consumer societies. With another classic children's story, Julia Donaldson's *The Gruffalo,* child readers may make the expected inferences when the predators – the fox, owl and snake – invite the mouse for a meal. They are unlikely, however, to notice the puzzle at the heart of the book: since the mouse says repeatedly, in asides to the reader, that gruffaloes do not exist, how is he able to describe so accurately the creature which does then appear at the midpoint of the story? Indeed, not all adult readers notice this conundrum and not all readers will have a wider knowledge of traditional stories to note that *The Gruffalo* is a modern example of stories such as *The Brave Little Tailor,* where the hero outwits strong and dangerous enemies.

There are, of course, many parallels between reading and writing when considering mastery of writing. Mastery of transcriptional aspects of writing are probably simpler to assess than compositional aspects. By the end of the Reception year many children have mastered writing in the sense that they can segment words into their constituent phonemes and know at least one grapheme to represent each phoneme they use in their spoken language. This is perhaps the most dramatic development in English – that in the course of a year children have mastered encoding; others can now read what they have written. Mastery of the English spelling system is a much more prolonged process. It is possible, of course, to devise a spelling programme, with units covering different spelling rules and patterns, and test pupils' mastery of those rules. However, real mastery should involve children then applying that learning in their own writing, and that can be much harder to assess as they may simply not use words containing the pattern often or even occasionally, or may avoid using more unusual words because of anxieties about spelling. It might be useful to supplement assessment linked to a spelling programme with assessment of the proportion of the words in children's independent writing which are spelled correctly: Bloom suggested that pupils should score at least 80–90 per cent on end of unit tests before the class moved on, and this could be a helpful rule of thumb here.

Handwriting is another relatively straightforward aspect of writing in terms of mastery. Both individual letter formation and a cursive script can be taught in a planned sequence broken down into units – for example, the anti-clockwise letters such as c, a, d, g, o, e and q, or diagonal joins. Carefully planned and supported practice is key to mastery of a controlled, legible, fluent style. With individual interventions to support children with difficulties in fine motor skills, almost all children should be able to develop such a style and also be able to vary the standard of their writing depending on the writing task (DfE, 2013, p47). Research by Medwell and Wray (2014) suggests that handwriting is important not simply in terms of presentation, but also because automaticity in handwriting frees up attention for other aspects of writing, and they suggest that this could explain the link between handwriting fluency and successful writing composition.

Punctuation is rather more complicated. While some aspects, such as the use of apostrophes, are quite straightforward, sentence punctuation is more problematic because it depends on being able to recognise what a sentence is, and that is difficult, even for some highly educated adults. Other aspects are a question of style and choice rather than correctness, as the National Curriculum (2013, p48) indicates by offering alternative ways of marking parenthesis and clause boundaries. Mastery here would include not only 'correct' punctuation, but also choices which actively enhance the quality of the writing, and a confidence in making those choices – for example, deciding to use dashes rather than brackets or parenthetical commas.

As Chapter 10 suggests, compositional aspects of learning to write are much more complex than transcriptional aspects. At what point can we say that writers have 'mastered' story writing? Once they have been short-listed for a short story competition? When they have met all the success criteria displayed on the whiteboard? When their story has a beginning, middle and end? While writing is a craft, in which skills and techniques can be mastered, it is also an art, and successful writers may break all the rules which are so painstakingly taught to young writers. On the other hand, those young writers may demonstrate all the 'key performance indicators' for their age group (NAHT, 2014) but still produce writing which is clumsy and dull.

However, despite the inevitability of a certain level of subjectivity when assessing writing, there are meaningful indicators of mastery. First, it is important that the writer can produce texts independently. This may sound obvious, but students often move through their education being given so much support in structuring their written work and planning what to include that they do not feel competent to make those decisions for themselves. Writing frames and planning templates should be seen as crutches which are thrown away as soon as possible. That is not to say that writers do not plan, but that they should be in control of the planning process. Another element of mastery is conscious control of the writing process. This does not mean consciously trying to include subordinate clauses or fronted adverbials, which can inhibit writing, but regularly reviewing what is being written, considering and rejecting alternative phrases and words, checking for clumsy expression or repetition, always asking 'What am I trying to say?' and 'Does it read well?' and writing with a reader's eye.

Case study: redrafting a poem

The following short poem by Beth, a Year 2 pupil, shows this process at work. Beth chose to write a poem in her own time, and immediately redrafted her first version.

Version 1

By the fire

By the fire,

Its keeps me warm.

I watch the flames leap higher,

I stroke the cat,

On the mat.

Version 2

By The Fire

I sit by the fire,

And watch the flames leap higher.

I stroke the cat,

Asleep on the mat.

→

Beth has chosen to leave out a line which added little to the meaning of the poem, and has thereby reduced it to two rhyming couplets. At the same time she has made other changes which improve the rhythm of the piece. She demonstrates confidence, first by choosing to write, and second by showing that she felt that she herself could improve her first draft without support and advice from others. While she could not have explained the changes she made in technical terms, she has that sense of what sounds right, which is fundamental to good writing, and the writing of poetry in particular.

Mastery of writing involves not only mastery of the writing process, but also knowledge of a range of text types. Even young writers often demonstrate understanding of the organisation and stylistic features of different text types such as information books, letters or instructions. By Upper Key Stage 2, some writers will have mastered different fiction genres such as historical fiction or mystery stories, and may even be able to produce parodies of text types. This is the 'deep understanding' referred to in maths mastery. It goes beyond an ability to reproduce a text type to understanding of the possibilities as well as the constraints of the genre, and an understanding of how its rules may be bent or even broken for effect. It also involves a constant monitoring while writing of the intended purpose and audience.

It is important that teachers have a clear view of what mastery of reading, writing, speaking and listening looks like at different ages. This is what they are aiming at. Every lesson should be a step on the way to that goal. But it is also important to consider whether the teaching approach associated with mastery learning works for English. The strategies of breaking learning down into small steps, keeping the class together, and not moving on until the learning is secure might seem most relevant to phonics, and indeed the Primary National Strategy's Communication, Language and Literacy Development programme (2006) advocated exactly that approach, with catch-up interventions for children in danger of falling behind. Oddly enough, this is precisely the area where many schools have chosen instead to teach children in separate groups working at very different paces, with the gap between the groups often growing wider as time goes on. Of course, the danger of some children becoming thoroughly disengaged because the pace of learning is too slow for them is obvious, and this is why Bloom recognised that enrichment and extension within the whole-class teaching is essential. For example, in a Year 1 class, learning the 'ea' grapheme, while some children might sort simple CVC words such as bead, head, mean, deaf, beak and dead, others might also have words with adjacent consonants such as bread and dream, or two syllable words such as header, reader, feather and breathing (and, indeed, might also explore the challenges of great and bread, or read and lead).

In writing, classes are much more likely to work together on units focusing on a particular text type. This, though, is where Bloom's picture of the constantly unsuccessful student may be seen, with some children at the end of each unit producing a weak piece of writing, and then moving on to a new unit. What mastery learning would indicate is that such children need more regular practice of the writing task, with early formative feedback and focused feedback on what aspects of the text type they have mastered and what still needs to be achieved. This does not necessarily mean writing several stories, or recounts, or discussions, but could also involve time spent discussing their writing and redrafting. The formative assessment should also be used to inform intervention. For example, if some children have not organised the information in a non-chronological report effectively, rather than provide a list of subheadings which does the organising for them, they need to practise grouping pieces of information logically.

Reading comprehension is perhaps the most difficult aspect of English to link to mastery learning. While a unit on traditional stories could be assessed in terms of the children's knowledge of the characteristics of the genre, or skills such as skimming and scanning can be taught and assessed, it is difficult to imagine a unit on making complex inferences, with assessment at the beginning and end to check whether the children have learned to make such inferences. On the other hand, there is a danger in simply saying that reading comprehension is addressed in a wide range of contexts over a very long time-scale, which is that it is not addressed effectively at all. The University of York's Reading for Meaning project (Clarke *et al.* 2010) demonstrated that carefully planned interventions delivered by well-trained teaching assistants could result in significant long-term improvement in children's comprehension. Topping (2016) suggests that peer tutoring in reading can have a significant impact on the tutor as well as the tutee.

Careful assessment is crucial to well-focused teaching. While analysis of end of Key Stage reading tests can give valuable information as to which aspects of comprehension both a cohort as a whole and individual children find difficult, regular formative assessment through noting children's responses to texts during guided reading are more important in planning teaching. Children need to be aware what the goal is: they should be familiar with metalanguage such as inference, for example, and need clear teaching, including modelling, of how good readers make both simple and complex inferences. Perhaps the most important message from mastery learning for teachers of reading is that of high expectations of all pupils. The links with mindset theory (Dweck, 2012) are clear. Young readers need to know that some texts are difficult to understand and require effort, and that it is good to challenge ourselves with such texts sometimes.

Case study: private reading

Ellie, a 10-year-old in a Year 5/6 class, picked up *Jane Eyre* to read. Her teacher had intended the book to be a more challenging read for 'good' readers in the class, but Ellie had been extremely late in learning to read, and was still a very slow and inaccurate decoder. Her teacher suggested tactfully that she might find it a little difficult, but this only made Ellie more determined to read it. At the end she seemed, somewhat to her teacher's surprise, to have a good grasp of the story and to be keen to talk about it. She also asked if Charlotte Brontë

→

had written anything else, and over the course of a few months she worked her way through a number of Brontë titles. In a discussion about the Brontë sisters, her teacher mentioned *Wuthering Heights* but said it was only suitable for older readers. Ellie acquired a copy and read it. Her image of herself as a reader had become one of a grown-up reader who persisted with difficult texts and was able to enjoy them. Her teacher was able to reflect on how her own judgements of her pupils might be limiting their learning.

The mastery learning approach is unlikely to revolutionise primary schools. In their evaluation of the Mathematics Mastery programme for the Education Endowment Foundation mentioned earlier, Jerrim and Vignoles (2015) weighed its modest impact of a month's additional progress against possible costs, such as increased preparation time and the need for professional development for teachers. The Foundation suggested that it might be better to consider it as one strategy among a number, possibly to be used for particularly difficult topics rather than for all lessons, and there was also a concern over longer term use, as it appeared to become less effective over time.

Perhaps rather than attempting to import the approach from Shanghai to this country, and from mathematics to English, the concept of mastery is of most value in reinforcing our understanding of some key factors in effective teaching, and also in raising some important questions. First, as the Carter review of initial teacher training (2015) pointed out, good teaching is dependent on strong subject knowledge. Teachers also need to have a good grasp of subject specific pedagogy, knowing what mastery looks like, how to break down learning into small steps where appropriate, and how to assess that learning. They need to be able to draw on a range of strategies to support any children who are taking longer to grasp a concept, and also be able to plan challenging enrichment and extension activities for any children who grasp a concept very quickly. This raises an important question about the expectation in many schools that all learning tasks should be differentiated for learners of different 'abilities'. Mastery learning does indicate that teachers need to recognise and plan for individual needs, but that this needs to be based on assessment evidence rather than on assumptions about groups of children. Beyond this is the key question of whether we do genuinely believe that the vast majority of children are capable of achieving high standards in English.

Learning outcomes review

You should now have developed your understanding of:

- What is meant by the term 'mastery learning'.
- How mastery learning might apply to English.
- Some of the challenges of using the approach in English teaching.

Questions for reflection

- Do you consider that most children are capable of achieving high standards in English?
- How important do you think confidence is in achieving mastery?
- What do you think are the implications of the mastery learning approach for high-attaining pupils?

References

Bloom, BS (1968) Learning for mastery. *Evaluation Comment*, 1(2): 112.

Carter, A (2015) *Carter Review of Initial Teacher Training (ITT)*. London: DfE.

Clarke, PJ, Snowling, MJ, Truelove, E and Hulme, C (2010) Ameliorating children's reading difficulties: a randomised controlled trial. *Psychological Science*, 21(8): 1106–16.

Dartmouth College Academic Skills Centre (2001) *Harvard Report*. Available at: *www.dartmouth.edu/~acskills/docs/harvard_reading_report.doc* (accessed 21 June 2016).

Department for Education (DfE) (2013) *The 2014 Primary National Curriculum in England*. Romsey: Shurville Publishing.

Dweck, CS (2012) *Mindset: How You Can Fulfil Your Potential*. London: Robinson.

Education Endowment Foundation (EEF) (2015) *Mathematics Mastery: Overarching Summary Report*. London: EEF.

Jerrim, J (2015) Why do East Asian children perform so well in PISA? An investigation of Western-born children of East Asian descent. *Oxford Review of Education*, 41(3): 310–33, DOI: 1080/03054985.2015.1028525.

Jerrim, J and Vignoles, A (2015) The link between East Asian 'mastery' teaching methods and English children's mathematical skills. *Economics of Education Review*, 50 (2016): 29–44.

Medwell, J and Wray, D (2014) Handwriting automaticity: the search for performance thresholds. *Language and Education*, 28(1): 34–51.

NAHT (2014) NAHT assessment framework materials. Available at: **www.naht.org.uk/welcome/news-and-media/key-topics/assessment/naht-assessment-framework-materials/** (accessed 21 June 2016).

National Centre for Excellence in the Teaching of Mathematics (NCETM) (2014) Mastery approaches to mathematics and the new National Curriculum. Available at: **www.ncetm.org.uk/public/files/19990433/Developing_mastery_in_mathematics_october_2014.pdf** (accessed 21 June 2016).

Prais, SJ (2003) Cautions on OECD's Recent Educational Survey (PISA), *Oxford Review of Education*, 29(2): 139–63.

Primary National Strategy (2006) Communication, Language and Literacy Programme. Available at: http://webarchive.nationalarchives.gov.uk/20110809091832/ teachingandlearningresources.org.uk/collection/34987

Rose, J (2006) Independent review of the teaching of early reading: final report. London: Department for Education and Skills.

Topping, K, Duran, D and Van Keer, H (2016) *Using Peer Tutoring to Improve Reading Skills: A Practical Framework for Teachers.* London: Routledge.

Conclusion

We hope that reading this book has helped you to understand the content of the National Curriculum for English. We hope, too, that it has alerted you to a wide range of texts and resources which will support you in the classroom and help to develop your thinking about primary English.

The 2014 curriculum makes considerable demands on teachers' subject knowledge, but if you take up the challenge of developing your knowledge and understanding of English, you will find that the children you teach will gain enthusiasm and a fascination with language, which should enable them to become confident and competent communicators.

David Waugh, Kate Allott, Wendy Jolliffe

January 2017

Appendix 1 Glossary

adverbial	Any single word, phrase or even clause used as an adverb.
affix	An addition to a word to form a new word e.g. do, undo, doing.
alliteration	A sequence of words beginning with the same sound, e.g. Ruthless Rovers ran riot at Rotherham.
antagonist	An opponent or enemy, who causes a conflict for the main character in a story.
binary opposition	Two terms or concepts which are opposite in meaning, e.g. good and evil, light and dark.
digraph	Two letters which combine to make a new sound, e.g. ch, sh, ai, ou in chip, shop, rain, out.
etymology	The study of words' origins and how they may have changed meaning or usage over time, e.g. nice originally meant something more like 'foolish', and silly meant 'simple'.
fronted adverbial	Sometimes we place words, phrases or clauses at the beginning of a sentence when they could equally well be placed after the verb, e.g. Mike ran a marathon, despite having sore feet. Despite having sore feet, Mike ran a marathon. When we do this with an adverbial, this is known as a fronted adverbial e.g. Quickly, he opened the door. Without a sound, she hid behind the sofa.
genre	Specific type of, for example, fiction, such as science fiction, historical fiction, traditional tales.
grapheme	A letter, or combination of letters, that represent a phoneme.
idiom	A group of words with a figurative rather than a literal meaning, e.g. I'm trying to keep my head above water. Idioms can be confusing for people for whom English is a second language. Other languages have their own idiomatic phrases, for example the French equivalent of It's raining cats and dogs is Il pleut comme une vache qui pisse.
imagery	Language which creates pictures in the mind of the reader, or helps them to imagine what the thing being described sounds, smells, tastes or feels like.
inference	A conclusion which is not actually stated but which is worked out from evidence in the text.
intertextuality	The relationship between texts, which may reflect or influence each other and as a result have additional layers of meaning.
'magpie'	A term used often in the 'Talk for Writing' approaches to show that writers can 'steal' or take ideas from each other.
metalanguage	The language we use to discuss language, e.g. the terms in this glossary.
metaphor	Giving a name or description to something which is imaginative but not literal, e.g. her car was a tiger in sheep's clothing; John was the pillar which supported the whole organisation.
metre	A form of poetic rhythm.
mnemonic	A device for remembering something, such as Richard of York gave battle in vain to remember the colours of the rainbow (red, orange, yellow, green, blue, indigo, violet).

morpheme	A morpheme is the smallest unit of language that can convey meaning. It cannot be broken down into anything smaller that has a meaning. A word may consist of one morpheme (need), two morphemes (need/less, need/ing) or three or more morphemes (un/happi/ness). Suffixes and prefixes are morphemes.
morphology	Morphology is the study of the forms of words.
orthography	Standardised spelling – the sounds of a language represented by written or printed symbols, i.e. the ways in which graphemes and phonemes relate to each other. The English orthographic system is more complex than many languages, since most phonemes can be represented by more than one grapheme.
phoneme	A speech sound. In writing, words are made up of letters and in speech they are made up of phonemes. There are roughly 44 phonemes in standard English, 20 vowels and 24 consonants. Phonemes can be represented by a single letter, pairs of letters (digraphs) such as sh, ea and ll, three letters (trigraphs) such as tch, and even four letters (ough in though).
prefix	Prefixes are morphemes which are placed at the beginning of a word to modify or change its meaning, e.g. dis/like, micro/scope, tri/cycle.
protagonist	A main character in a story or play.
pun	A type of word play where two or more meanings are suggested, by using multiple meanings of words, or of similar-sounding words, for humorous effect, e.g. I put rabbits on my head because from a distance they look like hares (hairs).
readers' theatre	A dramatic reading of a text in play-script form; this could be drawn from fiction with a significant amount of dialogue. Parts are allocated to different readers and the reading is rehearsed.
root word	A root word is a word which contains only one idea or unit of meaning and cannot be split into smaller units, e.g. need, walk, penguin.
semiotic	The study of how signs and symbols of all kinds convey meaning – for example 'thumbs up' can mean Everything's all right or Please give me a lift.
simile	A figure of speech in which we compare something with something else of a different type, e.g. he was as swift as a cheetah; the sun was like a golden ball.
split digraph	Two letters, making one sound, which are separated by a consonant, e.g. a-e as in take; i-e in mine, o-e in hope.
stanza	A unit in a poem consisting of a recurring group of lines. The stanza in poetry is like a paragraph in prose; related thoughts are grouped together.
suffix	Suffixes are morphemes added to the ends of words to modify their meanings, e.g. use and useful or useless; look and looking, looks or looked.
synonym	Synonyms are words with the same or similar meanings, such as big and large, quick and rapid, tall and high.
transcription	Aspects of writing including spelling, punctuation and handwriting.
word-cline	A vocabulary development activity in which a set of words is arranged in order e.g. irritated, cross, angry, livid, furious.
writing frame	Proformas which help children structure their writing of different text types, providing section headings and/or sentence starters.

Appendix 2 Self-assessment Model Answers

Chapter 1

1. **Which types of school do not have to implement the new National Curriculum?**

Free schools, academies and independent schools.

2. **How does the new National Curriculum differ from the National Literacy Framework in its approach to text genres?**

The new National Curriculum devotes much less attention to different text genres.

3. **Do children have to work at the appropriate stage of the curriculum for their age?**

Some children's needs will be better met if they work from Programmes of Study from earlier or later Key Stages and the National Curriculum states that teachers are 'only required to teach the relevant programme of study by the end of the key stage'.

Chapter 2

1. **What are the major ways in which spoken language supports learning?**

Spoken language supports learning by encouraging an interactive approach, where dialogue helps in sharing and developing knowledge. By talking through ideas, children develop and consolidate their understanding. In addition the use of a more competent peer or adult to work with can scaffold, or support, the learning process.

2. **How does spoken language support reading and writing skills?**

Spoken language, and particularly high quality discussion, supports reading skills by developing understanding of what is read and extending a child's vocabulary. Writing skills are also enhanced by talk as is identified in the 'Talk for Writing' project which put an emphasis on oral rehearsal of what is to be written. Discussion involving reflection during and after writing can also improve the final quality.

3. **How can teachers provide authentic opportunities for spoken language?**

Some of the ways in which teachers can provide authentic opportunities for spoken language include using drama with a meaningful stimulus; using carefully planned cooperative group work; encouraging enquiry and problem-solving and considering the types of questions used to encourage maximum participation.

Chapter 3

1. What is meant by a language-rich classroom environment?

A language-rich classroom is one that promotes and facilitates communication, promotes an interest in language and supports vocabulary development. This can be achieved through both the physical arrangement and appearance of the classroom e.g. providing spaces where children can share books; arrangements that support group and guided work; interactive displays that encourage engagement and discussion and the ethos developed e.g. curiosity about language encouraged, book-talk. Re-read the section titled 'Vocabulary development to support communication and language development' for further ideas.

2. What is the link between reading comprehension and vocabulary development?

Reading comprehension is about understanding meaning and understanding individual words is part of this process. After all, if you don't understand the vocabulary in a text you will not comprehend the text as a whole! A key skill of comprehension is inference and we use inference to help comprehend the meaning of vocabulary in a text; we do this by reading on and back, by referring to the context including where appropriate the picture or diagram in the text and by making connections to prior knowledge. See the section titled 'Vocabulary development to support reading comprehension' for further detail.

3. Why are the spelling objectives in the National Curriculum important as part of vocabulary teaching?

Understanding how and why words are spelt in the way they are is an important element of vocabulary teaching and is also a feature of the National Curriculum. Fostering a curiosity about the origins of words and their meanings enables children to engage with vocabulary learning. See the section titled 'Vocabulary development to support spelling – morphology and etymology'.

Chapter 4

1. Can you now summarise what children need to learn to become good spellers?

Children need:

- good phonic skills and knowledge;
- good knowledge of spelling patterns and rules, and morphology;
- good strategies for learning spellings and for tackling unknown words;
- an interest in words;
- good teaching.

2. **Can you explain how you would teach a spelling pattern?**

- Identify words the children are likely to know and use which contain the pattern.

- Teach/explain how the pattern works.

- Give children time to practise through e.g. look cover write check.

- Check whether the children have learned the pattern through an assessment such as a short dictation, and through monitoring their independent writing.

3. **Can you describe what you would be looking for when using children's writing to assess their spelling?**

- Which spelling patterns and 'tricky' words the children can spell.

- Which common spelling patterns and high-frequency words are not secure.

- Whether spelling errors are based on a phonic strategy (i.e. spelling the word the way it sounds).

Chapter 5

You can check your answers in the 'Glossary for the programmes of study for English' in the National Curriculum, pp.84–102: https://www.gov.uk/government/uploads/system/uploads/attachment_data/file/260388/MASTER_final_national_curriculum_11_9_13_2.pdf (accessed 22 June 2014).

Chapter 6

1. **Why is it important to develop reading for pleasure, from the very start, alongside teaching word reading and comprehension?**

Children need to develop a willingness to want to read along with the skills associated with being able to read in order to develop as life-long readers.

2. **Why is providing opportunities for children to discuss their reading, focusing on language development, important?**

This will not only develop children's motivation, it will also develop their vocabulary and grammatical understanding. Reading comprehension depends on language comprehension.

3. **Why is phonics needed to develop pupils' word reading?**

The complex orthographic system used in the English language means that phonemes can be represented by multiple graphemes. Phonics provides children with the knowledge (alphabetic code: knowledge of grapheme-phoneme correspondences) and skills (segmenting and blending) to be able to work out (decode) words.

4. **If pupils in Key Stage 2 are struggling with word reading, what should you do?**

These pupils should be provided with a systematic phonics programme to enable them to catch up with their peers.

Chapter 7

1. **Why is it important to introduce children to a range of literary genres?**

Teachers should introduce children to a wide variety of literary genres to show them that there are many different ways and formats through which to represent human experiences.

2. **What is the value of picturebooks?**

- Picturebooks can stimulate children's curiosity and imaginative thinking by connecting them emotionally to a range of intriguing characters that overcome a variety of challenges in recognisable and unfamiliar settings.

- Picturebooks help pupils to construct new, integrated meanings and understanding of the world from words and pictures.

3. **What is the place of new literacies in the primary classroom?**

- The use of new literacies in the primary classroom enables teachers to draw on a range of communication tools to support the development of collaborative learning networks through which learners can co-construct knowledge and understanding.

- The use of new literacy practices supports inquiry-based learning, enabling children to collect, analyse, manipulate and present information and data in multi-modal formats requiring the integration of text, images, numbers and symbols.

Chapter 8

1. **In which Key Stage are children expected to appreciate rhymes and poems, and recite some by heart?**

Key Stage 1.

2. **What is free verse?**

Free verse is a form of poetry which has no set metre to it. It can be rhyming or non-rhyming. Free verse does not necessarily have to have a particular structure, although many poems written in this form have a structure of some kind.

3. **What is narrative poetry?**

Narrative poems tell a story and can often be very long. They often employ the use of different voices and include different characters.

Chapter 9

1. **What is the difference between learning to read and reading to learn?**

Learning to read involves decoding words into phonemes and blending these to read the words. Reading to learn means using a text to find further information.

2. **Why do pupils need a focus before attempting to retrieve information from a non-fiction text?**

Having a distinct focus can ensure that pupils know what they are looking for in a text.

3. **When do children learn some of the organisational devices associated with non-fiction (such as bullet points and parenthesis)?**

The objectives which include organisational devices are introduced in Upper Key Stage 2. It should be noted that children may use these earlier so teaching may need to accommodate this.

4. **Why is non-fiction useful across the curriculum?**

Skills in non-fiction are useful to enable children to locate further information on other curriculum subjects and to write or present information effectively about these.

Chapter 10

1. **Can you now explain the difference between transcription and composition?**

- Transcription involves spelling and handwriting.

- Composition involves forming, articulating and communicating ideas; organising them coherently for a reader; clarity, and awareness of the audience, purpose and context; and an increasingly wide knowledge of vocabulary and grammar.

2. **What are the key elements of the teaching sequence for writing?**

- familiarisation with the genre or text type;

- capturing ideas for the children's own writing;

- scaffolded writing experiences, leading to independent written outcomes.

3. **Why do you think that reading is so important for writing?**

Your answer may include some or all of the following:

- Good writers are almost always good readers.

- Reading can provide young writers with ideas for their own writing.

- Hearing texts read aloud and reading them for themselves allows children to become familiar with the overall shape of the text and how it is constructed.

- Reading as a writer helps to deepen understanding of how language has been used to create different effects.

- Texts can offer a stimulus for writing and offer authentic contexts to write about.

Chapter 11

1. How can drama be used to teach reading comprehension?

Read the section on 'Drama and Reading'. This section describes how simple techniques such as hot seating can allow the children to develop higher order reading skills such as predicting and projecting.

2. Can drama be used in different areas of the curriculum?

Look at the section on 'Drama across the curriculum'. Here it was shown that drama needs content and that content can be drawn from any area of the curriculum. The case study in this section describes how drama can be very useful for enhancing children's understanding of aspects of history.

3. Is drama a useful activity for working with children who have special educational needs?

Look at the work of Peter (1994) described in the section entitled 'Drama and Inclusion'. The case study demonstrates how effective drama can be for pupils with special educational needs.

Chapter 12

What key documents are you likely to base your English planning on?

- National Curriculum Framework.

- The school's long-term plan and any relevant policy documents.

- Any unit plans which the school already has in place.

Which aspects of English teaching are likely to fall outside the main English lessons?

- Phonics, spelling, handwriting, guided reading, reading stories to the class, drama.

Which main text types should children become familiar with during the primary years?

- Fiction, including traditional tales and fairytales, stories from other cultures, historical fiction, fantasy and science fiction.

- Poetry in a range of forms including free verse.

- Play-scripts.

- Non-fiction texts including recounts, instructions, non-chronological reports, persuasive and discursive writing.

In choosing texts to study, what key issues need to be considered?

- Is the text likely to extend children's knowledge of literature?

- Will the children be able to read the text independently or with some support?

- Is the text a rich, multi-layered text with interesting themes, which will provide much to think and talk about?

- Is the language of high quality?

- Are any illustrations of high quality?

- Could the text provide a good model for the children's own writing?

Chapter 13

1. What is the difference between summative and formative assessment?

Summative assessment is assessment of learning, summarising what is recalled. Formative assessment is ongoing assessment for learning, helping pupils to move forward.

2. How do schools make use of assessment to evaluate a teaching strategy?

Schools can use pupil feedback from questioning and marking to evaluate the success of a teaching strategy.

3. Marking is the only way to give feedback on pupil writing. Do you agree or disagree?

Marking is an important way to give feedback on writing, but there are others including 1:1 conferences and peer assessment.

4. What different ways do you know to assess reading comprehension?

To assess reading comprehension questions can be used, as can discussion, annotated drawings and miscue analysis.

English programmes of study: key stages 1 and 2

National curriculum in England

September 2013

Contents

Purpose of study

English has a pre-eminent place in education and in society. A high-quality education in English will teach pupils to speak and write fluently so that they can communicate their ideas and emotions to others and through their reading and listening, others can communicate with them. Through reading in particular, pupils have a chance to develop culturally, emotionally, intellectually, socially and spiritually. Literature, especially, plays a key role in such development. Reading also enables pupils both to acquire knowledge and to build on what they already know. All the skills of language are essential to participating fully as a member of society; pupils, therefore, who do not learn to speak, read and write fluently and confidently are effectively disenfranchised.

Aims

The overarching aim for English in the national curriculum is to promote high standards of language and literacy by equipping pupils with a strong command of the spoken and written word, and to develop their love of literature through widespread reading for enjoyment. The national curriculum for English aims to ensure that all pupils:

- read easily, fluently and with good understanding
- develop the habit of reading widely and often, for both pleasure and information
- acquire a wide vocabulary, an understanding of grammar and knowledge of linguistic conventions for reading, writing and spoken language
- appreciate our rich and varied literary heritage
- write clearly, accurately and coherently, adapting their language and style in and for a range of contexts, purposes and audiences
- use discussion in order to learn; they should be able to elaborate and explain clearly their understanding and ideas
- are competent in the arts of speaking and listening, making formal presentations, demonstrating to others and participating in debate.

Spoken language

The national curriculum for English reflects the importance of spoken language in pupils' development across the whole curriculum – cognitively, socially and linguistically. Spoken language underpins the development of reading and writing. The quality and variety of language that pupils hear and speak are vital for developing their vocabulary and grammar and their understanding for reading and writing. Teachers should therefore ensure the continual development of pupils' confidence and competence in spoken language and listening skills. Pupils should develop a capacity to explain their understanding of books and other reading, and to prepare their ideas before they write. They must be assisted in making their thinking clear to themselves as well as to others and teachers should ensure that pupils build secure foundations by using discussion to probe and remedy their misconceptions. Pupils should also be taught to understand and use the conventions for discussion and debate.

All pupils should be enabled to participate in and gain knowledge, skills and understanding associated with the artistic practice of drama. Pupils should be able to adopt, create and sustain a range of roles, responding appropriately to others in role. They should have opportunities to improvise, devise and script drama for one another and a range of audiences, as well as to rehearse, refine, share and respond thoughtfully to drama and theatre performances.

Statutory requirements which underpin all aspects of spoken language across the six years of primary education form part of the national curriculum. These are reflected and contextualised within the reading and writing domains which follow.

Reading

The programmes of study for reading at key stages 1 and 2 consist of two dimensions:

- word reading
- comprehension (both listening and reading).

It is essential that teaching focuses on developing pupils' competence in both dimensions; different kinds of teaching are needed for each.

Skilled word reading involves both the speedy working out of the pronunciation of unfamiliar printed words (decoding) and the speedy recognition of familiar printed words. Underpinning both is the understanding that the letters on the page represent the sounds in spoken words. This is why phonics should be emphasised in the early teaching of reading to beginners (i.e. unskilled readers) when they start school.

Good comprehension draws from linguistic knowledge (in particular of vocabulary and grammar) and on knowledge of the world. Comprehension skills develop through pupils' experience of high-quality discussion with the teacher, as well as from reading and discussing a range of stories, poems and non-fiction. All pupils must be encouraged to read widely across both fiction and non-fiction to develop their knowledge of themselves and the world in which they live, to establish an appreciation and love of reading, and to gain knowledge across the curriculum. Reading widely and often increases pupils' vocabulary because they encounter words they would rarely hear or use in everyday speech. Reading also feeds pupils' imagination and opens up a treasure-house of wonder and joy for curious young minds.

It is essential that, by the end of their primary education, all pupils are able to read fluently, and with confidence, in any subject in their forthcoming secondary education.

Writing

The programmes of study for writing at key stages 1 and 2 are constructed similarly to those for reading:

- transcription (spelling and handwriting)
- composition (articulating ideas and structuring them in speech and writing).

It is essential that teaching develops pupils' competence in these two dimensions. In addition, pupils should be taught how to plan, revise and evaluate their writing. These aspects of writing have been incorporated into the programmes of study for composition.

Writing down ideas fluently depends on effective transcription: that is, on spelling quickly and accurately through knowing the relationship between sounds and letters (phonics) and understanding the morphology (word structure) and orthography (spelling structure) of words. Effective composition involves forming, articulating and communicating ideas, and then organising them coherently for a reader. This requires clarity, awareness of the audience, purpose and context, and an increasingly wide knowledge of vocabulary and grammar. Writing also depends on fluent, legible and, eventually, speedy handwriting.

Spelling, vocabulary, grammar, punctuation and glossary

The two statutory appendices – on spelling and on vocabulary, grammar and punctuation – give an overview of the specific features that should be included in teaching the programmes of study.

Opportunities for teachers to enhance pupils' vocabulary arise naturally from their reading and writing. As vocabulary increases, teachers should show pupils how to understand the relationships between words, how to understand nuances in meaning, and how to develop their understanding of, and ability to use, figurative language. They should also teach pupils how to work out and clarify the meanings of unknown words and words with more than one meaning. References to developing pupils' vocabulary are also included within the appendices.

Pupils should be taught to control their speaking and writing consciously and to use Standard English. They should be taught to use the elements of spelling, grammar, punctuation and 'language about language' listed. This is not intended to constrain or restrict teachers' creativity, but simply to provide the structure on which they can construct exciting lessons. A non-statutory Glossary is provided for teachers.

Throughout the programmes of study, teachers should teach pupils the vocabulary they need to discuss their reading, writing and spoken language. It is important that pupils learn the correct grammatical terms in English and that these terms are integrated within teaching.

School curriculum

The programmes of study for English are set out year-by-year for key stage 1 and two-yearly for key stage 2. The single year blocks at key stage 1 reflect the rapid pace of development in word reading during these two years. Schools are, however, only required to teach the relevant programme of study by the end of the key stage. Within each key stage, schools therefore have the flexibility to introduce content earlier or later than set out in the programme of study. In addition, schools can introduce key stage content during an earlier key stage if appropriate. All schools are also required to set out their school curriculum for English on a year-by-year basis and make this information available online.

Attainment targets

By the end of each key stage, pupils are expected to know, apply and understand the matters, skills and processes specified in the relevant programme of study.

Schools are not required by law to teach the example content in [square brackets] or the content indicated as being 'non-statutory'.

Spoken language – years 1 to 6

Spoken language

Statutory requirements

Pupils should be taught to:

- listen and respond appropriately to adults and their peers

- ask relevant questions to extend their understanding and knowledge

- use relevant strategies to build their vocabulary

- articulate and justify answers, arguments and opinions

- give well-structured descriptions, explanations and narratives for different purposes, including for expressing feelings

- maintain attention and participate actively in collaborative conversations, staying on topic and initiating and responding to comments

- use spoken language to develop understanding through speculating, hypothesising, imagining and exploring ideas

- speak audibly and fluently with an increasing command of Standard English

- participate in discussions, presentations, performances, role play, improvisations and debates

- gain, maintain and monitor the interest of the listener(s)

- consider and evaluate different viewpoints, attending to and building on the contributions of others

- select and use appropriate registers for effective communication.

Notes and guidance (non-statutory)

These statements apply to all years. The content should be taught at a level appropriate to the age of the pupils. Pupils should build on the oral language skills that have been taught in preceding years.

Pupils should be taught to develop their competence in spoken language and listening to enhance the effectiveness with which they are able to communicate across a range of contexts and to a range of audiences. They should therefore have opportunities to work in groups of different sizes – in pairs, small groups, large groups and as a whole class. Pupils should understand how to take turns and when and how to participate constructively in conversations and debates.

Attention should also be paid to increasing pupils' vocabulary, ranging from describing

Notes and guidance (non-statutory)

their immediate world and feelings to developing a broader, deeper and richer vocabulary to discuss abstract concepts and a wider range of topics, and to enhancing their knowledge about language as a whole.

Pupils should receive constructive feedback on their spoken language and listening, not only to improve their knowledge and skills but also to establish secure foundations for effective spoken language in their studies at primary school, helping them to achieve in secondary education and beyond.

Key stage 1 – year 1

During year 1, teachers should build on work from the Early Years Foundation Stage, making sure that pupils can sound and blend unfamiliar printed words quickly and accurately using the phonic knowledge and skills that they have already learnt. Teachers should also ensure that pupils continue to learn new grapheme-phoneme correspondences (GPCs) and revise and consolidate those learnt earlier. The understanding that the letter(s) on the page represent the sounds in spoken words should underpin pupils' reading and spelling of all words. This includes common words containing unusual GPCs. The term 'common exception words' is used throughout the programmes of study for such words.

Alongside this knowledge of GPCs, pupils need to develop the skill of blending the sounds into words for reading and establish the habit of applying this skill whenever they encounter new words. This will be supported by practice in reading books consistent with their developing phonic knowledge and skill and their knowledge of common exception words. At the same time they will need to hear, share and discuss a wide range of high-quality books to develop a love of reading and broaden their vocabulary.

Pupils should be helped to read words without overt sounding and blending after a few encounters. Those who are slow to develop this skill should have extra practice.

Pupils' writing during year 1 will generally develop at a slower pace than their reading. This is because they need to encode the sounds they hear in words (spelling skills), develop the physical skill needed for handwriting, and learn how to organise their ideas in writing.

Pupils entering year 1 who have not yet met the early learning goals for literacy should continue to follow their school's curriculum for the Early Years Foundation Stage to develop their word reading, spelling and language skills. However, these pupils should follow the year 1 programme of study in terms of the books they listen to and discuss, so that they develop their vocabulary and understanding of grammar, as well as their knowledge more generally across the curriculum. If they are still struggling to decode and spell, they need to be taught to do this urgently through a rigorous and systematic phonics programme so that they catch up rapidly.

Teachers should ensure that their teaching develops pupils' oral vocabulary as well as their ability to understand and use a variety of grammatical structures, giving particular support to pupils whose oral language skills are insufficiently developed.

Year 1 programme of study

Reading – word reading

Statutory requirements

Pupils should be taught to:

- apply phonic knowledge and skills as the route to decode words

- respond speedily with the correct sound to graphemes (letters or groups of letters) for all 40+ phonemes, including, where applicable, alternative sounds for graphemes

- read accurately by blending sounds in unfamiliar words containing GPCs that have been taught

- read common exception words, noting unusual correspondences between spelling and sound and where these occur in the word

- read words containing taught GPCs and –s, –es, –ing, –ed, –er and –est endings

- read other words of more than one syllable that contain taught GPCs

- read words with contractions [for example, I'm, I'll, we'll], and understand that the apostrophe represents the omitted letter(s)

- read aloud accurately books that are consistent with their developing phonic knowledge and that do not require them to use other strategies to work out words

- re-read these books to build up their fluency and confidence in word reading.

Notes and guidance (non-statutory)

Pupils should revise and consolidate the GPCs and the common exception words taught in Reception. As soon as they can read words comprising the year 1 GPCs accurately and speedily, they should move on to the year 2 programme of study for word reading.

The number, order and choice of exception words taught will vary according to the phonics programme being used. Ensuring that pupils are aware of the GPCs they contain, however unusual these are, supports spelling later.

Young readers encounter words that they have not seen before much more frequently than experienced readers do, and they may not know the meaning of some of these. Practice at reading such words by sounding and blending can provide opportunities not only for pupils to develop confidence in their decoding skills, but also for teachers to explain the meaning and thus develop pupils' vocabulary.

Notes and guidance (non-statutory)

Pupils should be taught how to read words with suffixes by being helped to build on the root words that they can read already. Pupils' reading and re-reading of books that are closely matched to their developing phonic knowledge and knowledge of common exception words supports their fluency, as well as increasing their confidence in their reading skills. Fluent word reading greatly assists comprehension, especially when pupils come to read longer books.

Reading – comprehension

Statutory requirements

Pupils should be taught to:

- develop pleasure in reading, motivation to read, vocabulary and understanding by:
    - listening to and discussing a wide range of poems, stories and non-fiction at a level beyond that at which they can read independently
    - being encouraged to link what they read or hear read to their own experiences
    - becoming very familiar with key stories, fairy stories and traditional tales, retelling them and considering their particular characteristics
    - recognising and joining in with predictable phrases
    - learning to appreciate rhymes and poems, and to recite some by heart
    - discussing word meanings, linking new meanings to those already known
- understand both the books they can already read accurately and fluently and those they listen to by:
    - drawing on what they already know or on background information and vocabulary provided by the teacher
    - checking that the text makes sense to them as they read and correcting inaccurate reading
    - discussing the significance of the title and events
    - making inferences on the basis of what is being said and done
    - predicting what might happen on the basis of what has been read so far
- participate in discussion about what is read to them, taking turns and listening to what others say
- explain clearly their understanding of what is read to them.

Notes and guidance (non-statutory)

Pupils should have extensive experience of listening to, sharing and discussing a wide range of high-quality books with the teacher, other adults and each other to engender a love of reading at the same time as they are reading independently.

Pupils' vocabulary should be developed when they listen to books read aloud and when they discuss what they have heard. Such vocabulary can also feed into their writing. Knowing the meaning of more words increases pupils' chances of understanding when they read by themselves. The meaning of some new words should be introduced to pupils before they start to read on their own, so that these unknown words do not hold up their comprehension.

However, once pupils have already decoded words successfully, the meaning of those that are new to them can be discussed with them, so contributing to developing their early skills of inference. By listening frequently to stories, poems and non-fiction that they cannot yet read for themselves, pupils begin to understand how written language can be structured in order, for example, to build surprise in narratives or to present facts in non-fiction. Listening to and discussing information books and other non-fiction establishes the foundations for their learning in other subjects. Pupils should be shown some of the processes for finding out information.

Through listening, pupils also start to learn how language sounds and increase their vocabulary and awareness of grammatical structures. In due course, they will be able to draw on such grammar in their own writing.

Rules for effective discussions should be agreed with and demonstrated for pupils. They should help to develop and evaluate them, with the expectation that everyone takes part. Pupils should be helped to consider the opinions of others.

Role-play can help pupils to identify with and explore characters and to try out the language they have listened to.

Writing – transcription

Statutory requirements

Spelling (see English Appendix 1)

Pupils should be taught to:

- spell:
  - words containing each of the 40+ phonemes already taught
  - common exception words
  - the days of the week

Statutory requirements

- name the letters of the alphabet:
  - naming the letters of the alphabet in order
  - using letter names to distinguish between alternative spellings of the same sound
- add prefixes and suffixes:
  - using the spelling rule for adding –s or –es as the plural marker for nouns and the third person singular marker for verbs
  - using the prefix un–
  - using –ing, –ed, –er and –est where no change is needed in the spelling of root words [for example, helping, helped, helper, eating, quicker, quickest]
- apply simple spelling rules and guidance, as listed in English Appendix 1
- write from memory simple sentences dictated by the teacher that include words using the GPCs and common exception words taught so far.

Notes and guidance (non-statutory)

Reading should be taught alongside spelling, so that pupils understand that they can read back words they have spelt.

Pupils should be shown how to segment spoken words into individual phonemes and then how to represent the phonemes by the appropriate grapheme(s). It is important to recognise that phoneme-grapheme correspondences (which underpin spelling) are more variable than grapheme-phoneme correspondences (which underpin reading). For this reason, pupils need to do much more word-specific rehearsal for spelling than for reading.

At this stage pupils will be spelling some words in a phonically plausible way, even if sometimes incorrectly. Misspellings of words that pupils have been taught to spell should be corrected; other misspelt words should be used to teach pupils about alternative ways of representing those sounds.

Writing simple dictated sentences that include words taught so far gives pupils opportunities to apply and practise their spelling.

Statutory requirements

Handwriting

Pupils should be taught to:

- sit correctly at a table, holding a pencil comfortably and correctly
- begin to form lower-case letters in the correct direction, starting and finishing in the right place
- form capital letters
- form digits 0-9
- understand which letters belong to which handwriting 'families' (i.e. letters that are formed in similar ways) and to practise these.

Notes and guidance (non-statutory)

Handwriting requires frequent and discrete, direct teaching. Pupils should be able to form letters correctly and confidently. The size of the writing implement (pencil, pen) should not be too large for a young pupil's hand. Whatever is being used should allow the pupil to hold it easily and correctly so that bad habits are avoided.

Left-handed pupils should receive specific teaching to meet their needs.

Writing – composition

Statutory requirements

Pupils should be taught to:

- write sentences by:
  - saying out loud what they are going to write about
  - composing a sentence orally before writing it
  - sequencing sentences to form short narratives
  - re-reading what they have written to check that it makes sense
- discuss what they have written with the teacher or other pupils
- read aloud their writing clearly enough to be heard by their peers and the teacher.

Notes and guidance (non-statutory)

At the beginning of year 1, not all pupils will have the spelling and handwriting skills they need to write down everything that they can compose out loud.

Pupils should understand, through demonstration, the skills and processes essential to writing: that is, thinking aloud as they collect ideas, drafting, and re-reading to check their meaning is clear.

Writing – vocabulary, grammar and punctuation

Statutory requirements

Pupils should be taught to:

- develop their understanding of the concepts set out in English Appendix 2 by:
  - leaving spaces between words
  - joining words and joining clauses using and
  - beginning to punctuate sentences using a capital letter and a full stop, question mark or exclamation mark
  - using a capital letter for names of people, places, the days of the week, and the personal pronoun 'I'
  - learning the grammar for year 1 in English Appendix 2
- use the grammatical terminology in English Appendix 2 in discussing their writing.

Notes and guidance (non-statutory)

Pupils should be taught to recognise sentence boundaries in spoken sentences and to use the vocabulary listed in English Appendix 2 ('Terminology for pupils') when their writing is discussed.

Pupils should begin to use some of the distinctive features of Standard English in their writing. 'Standard English' is defined in the Glossary.

Key stage 1 – year 2

By the beginning of year 2, pupils should be able to read all common graphemes. They should be able to read unfamiliar words containing these graphemes, accurately and without undue hesitation, by sounding them out in books that are matched closely to each pupil's level of word reading knowledge. They should also be able to read many common words containing GPCs taught so far [for example, shout, hand, stop, or dream], without needing to blend the sounds out loud first. Pupils' reading of common exception words [for example, you, could, many, or people], should be secure. Pupils will increase their fluency by being able to read these words easily and automatically. Finally, pupils should be able to retell some familiar stories that have been read to and discussed with them or that they have acted out during year 1.

During year 2, teachers should continue to focus on establishing pupils' accurate and speedy word reading skills. They should also make sure that pupils listen to and discuss a wide range of stories, poems, plays and information books; this should include whole books. The sooner that pupils can read well and do so frequently, the sooner they will be able to increase their vocabulary, comprehension and their knowledge across the wider curriculum.

In writing, pupils at the beginning of year 2 should be able to compose individual sentences orally and then write them down. They should be able to spell correctly many of the words covered in year 1 (see English Appendix 1). They should also be able to make phonically plausible attempts to spell words they have not yet learnt. Finally, they should be able to form individual letters correctly, so establishing good handwriting habits from the beginning.

It is important to recognise that pupils begin to meet extra challenges in terms of spelling during year 2. Increasingly, they should learn that there is not always an obvious connection between the way a word is said and the way it is spelt. Variations include different ways of spelling the same sound, the use of so-called silent letters and groups of letters in some words and, sometimes, spelling that has become separated from the way that words are now pronounced, such as the 'le' ending in table. Pupils' motor skills also need to be sufficiently advanced for them to write down ideas that they may be able to compose orally. In addition, writing is intrinsically harder than reading: pupils are likely to be able to read and understand more complex writing (in terms of its vocabulary and structure) than they are capable of producing themselves.

For pupils who do not have the phonic knowledge and skills they need for year 2, teachers should use the year 1 programmes of study for word reading and spelling so that pupils' word reading skills catch up. However, teachers should use the year 2 programme of study for comprehension so that these pupils hear and talk about new books, poems, other writing, and vocabulary with the rest of the class.

Year 2 programme of study

Reading – word reading

Statutory requirements

Pupils should be taught to:

- continue to apply phonic knowledge and skills as the route to decode words until automatic decoding has become embedded and reading is fluent

- read accurately by blending the sounds in words that contain the graphemes taught so far, especially recognising alternative sounds for graphemes

- read accurately words of two or more syllables that contain the same graphemes as above

- read words containing common suffixes

- read further common exception words, noting unusual correspondences between spelling and sound and where these occur in the word

- read most words quickly and accurately, without overt sounding and blending, when they have been frequently encountered

- read aloud books closely matched to their improving phonic knowledge, sounding out unfamiliar words accurately, automatically and without undue hesitation

- re-read these books to build up their fluency and confidence in word reading.

Notes and guidance (non-statutory)

Pupils should revise and consolidate the GPCs and the common exception words taught in year 1. The exception words taught will vary slightly, depending on the phonics programme being used. As soon as pupils can read words comprising the year 2 GPCs accurately and speedily, they should move on to the years 3 and 4 programme of study for word reading.

When pupils are taught how to read longer words, they should be shown syllable boundaries and how to read each syllable separately before they combine them to read the word.

Pupils should be taught how to read suffixes by building on the root words that they have already learnt. The whole suffix should be taught as well as the letters that make it up.

Pupils who are still at the early stages of learning to read should have ample practice in reading books that are closely matched to their developing phonic knowledge and knowledge of common exception words. As soon as the decoding of most regular words and common exception words is embedded fully, the range of books that pupils can read independently will expand rapidly. Pupils should have opportunities to exercise choice in selecting books and be taught how to do so.

Reading – comprehension

Statutory requirements

Pupils should be taught to:

- develop pleasure in reading, motivation to read, vocabulary and understanding by:
    - listening to, discussing and expressing views about a wide range of contemporary and classic poetry, stories and non-fiction at a level beyond that at which they can read independently
    - discussing the sequence of events in books and how items of information are related
    - becoming increasingly familiar with and retelling a wider range of stories, fairy stories and traditional tales
    - being introduced to non-fiction books that are structured in different ways
    - recognising simple recurring literary language in stories and poetry
    - discussing and clarifying the meanings of words, linking new meanings to known vocabulary
    - discussing their favourite words and phrases
    - continuing to build up a repertoire of poems learnt by heart, appreciating these and reciting some, with appropriate intonation to make the meaning clear
- understand both the books that they can already read accurately and fluently and those that they listen to by:
    - drawing on what they already know or on background information and vocabulary provided by the teacher
    - checking that the text makes sense to them as they read and correcting inaccurate reading
    - making inferences on the basis of what is being said and done
    - answering and asking questions
    - predicting what might happen on the basis of what has been read so far
- participate in discussion about books, poems and other works that are read to them and those that they can read for themselves, taking turns and listening to what others say
- explain and discuss their understanding of books, poems and other material, both those that they listen to and those that they read for themselves.

Notes and guidance (non-statutory)

Pupils should be encouraged to read all the words in a sentence and to do this accurately, so that their understanding of what they read is not hindered by imprecise decoding (for example, by reading 'place' instead of 'palace').

Notes and guidance (non-statutory)

Pupils should monitor what they read, checking that the word they have decoded fits in with what else they have read and makes sense in the context of what they already know about the topic.

The meaning of new words should be explained to pupils within the context of what they are reading, and they should be encouraged to use morphology (such as prefixes) to work out unknown words.

Pupils should learn about cause and effect in both narrative and non-fiction (for example, what has prompted a character's behaviour in a story; why certain dates are commemorated annually). 'Thinking aloud' when reading to pupils may help them to understand what skilled readers do.

Deliberate steps should be taken to increase pupils' vocabulary and their awareness of grammar so that they continue to understand the differences between spoken and written language.

Discussion should be demonstrated to pupils. They should be guided to participate in it and they should be helped to consider the opinions of others. They should receive feedback on their discussions.

Role-play and other drama techniques can help pupils to identify with and explore characters. In these ways, they extend their understanding of what they read and have opportunities to try out the language they have listened to.

Writing – transcription

Statutory requirements

Spelling (see English Appendix 1)
Pupils should be taught to:

- spell by:
    - segmenting spoken words into phonemes and representing these by graphemes, spelling many correctly
    - learning new ways of spelling phonemes for which one or more spellings are already known, and learn some words with each spelling, including a few common homophones
    - learning to spell common exception words
    - learning to spell more words with contracted forms
    - learning the possessive apostrophe (singular) [for example, the girl's book]
    - distinguishing between homophones and near-homophones
- add suffixes to spell longer words, including –ment, –ness, –ful, –less, –ly

Statutory requirements

- apply spelling rules and guidance, as listed in <u>English Appendix 1</u>
- write from memory simple sentences dictated by the teacher that include words using the GPCs, common exception words and punctuation taught so far.

Notes and guidance (non-statutory)

In year 2, pupils move towards more word-specific knowledge of spelling, including homophones. The process of spelling should be emphasised: that is, that spelling involves segmenting spoken words into phonemes and then representing all the phonemes by graphemes in the right order. Pupils should do this both for single-syllable and multi-syllabic words.

At this stage children's spelling should be phonically plausible, even if not always correct. Misspellings of words that pupils have been taught to spell should be corrected; other misspelt words can be used as an opportunity to teach pupils about alternative ways of representing those sounds.

Pupils should be encouraged to apply their knowledge of suffixes from their word reading to their spelling. They should also draw from and apply their growing knowledge of word and spelling structure, as well as their knowledge of root words.

Statutory requirements

Handwriting

Pupils should be taught to:

- form lower-case letters of the correct size relative to one another
- start using some of the diagonal and horizontal strokes needed to join letters and understand which letters, when adjacent to one another, are best left unjoined
- write capital letters and digits of the correct size, orientation and relationship to one another and to lower case letters
- use spacing between words that reflects the size of the letters.

Notes and guidance (non-statutory)

Pupils should revise and practise correct letter formation frequently. They should be taught to write with a joined style as soon as they can form letters securely with the correct orientation.

Writing – composition

Statutory requirements

Pupils should be taught to:

- develop positive attitudes towards and stamina for writing by:
  - writing narratives about personal experiences and those of others (real and fictional)
  - writing about real events
  - writing poetry
  - writing for different purposes
- consider what they are going to write before beginning by:
  - planning or saying out loud what they are going to write about
  - writing down ideas and/or key words, including new vocabulary
  - encapsulating what they want to say, sentence by sentence
- make simple additions, revisions and corrections to their own writing by:
  - evaluating their writing with the teacher and other pupils
  - re-reading to check that their writing makes sense and that verbs to indicate time are used correctly and consistently, including verbs in the continuous form
  - proof-reading to check for errors in spelling, grammar and punctuation [for example, ends of sentences punctuated correctly]
- read aloud what they have written with appropriate intonation to make the meaning clear.

Notes and guidance (non-statutory)

Reading and listening to whole books, not simply extracts, helps pupils to increase their vocabulary and grammatical knowledge, including their knowledge of the vocabulary and grammar of Standard English. These activities also help them to understand how different types of writing, including narratives, are structured. All these can be drawn on for their writing.

Pupils should understand, through being shown these, the skills and processes essential to writing: that is, thinking aloud as they collect ideas, drafting, and re-reading to check their meaning is clear.

Drama and role-play can contribute to the quality of pupils' writing by providing opportunities for pupils to develop and order their ideas through playing roles and improvising scenes in various settings.

Pupils might draw on and use new vocabulary from their reading, their discussions about it (one-to-one and as a whole class) and from their wider experiences.

Writing – vocabulary, grammar and punctuation

Statutory requirements

Pupils should be taught to:

- develop their understanding of the concepts set out in <u>English Appendix 2</u> by:
    - learning how to use both familiar and new punctuation correctly (see English Appendix 2), including full stops, capital letters, exclamation marks, question marks, commas for lists and apostrophes for contracted forms and the possessive (singular)

- learn how to use:
    - sentences with different forms: statement, question, exclamation, command
    - expanded noun phrases to describe and specify [for example, the blue butterfly]
    - the present and past tenses correctly and consistently including the progressive form
    - subordination (using when, if, that, or because) and co-ordination (using or, and, or but)
    - the grammar for year 2 in English Appendix 2
    - some features of written Standard English

- use and understand the grammatical terminology in English Appendix 2 in discussing their writing.

Notes and guidance (non-statutory)

The terms for discussing language should be embedded for pupils in the course of discussing their writing with them. Their attention should be drawn to the technical terms they need to learn.

Lower key stage 2 – years 3 and 4

By the beginning of year 3, pupils should be able to read books written at an age-appropriate interest level. They should be able to read them accurately and at a speed that is sufficient for them to focus on understanding what they read rather than on decoding individual words. They should be able to decode most new words outside their spoken vocabulary, making a good approximation to the word's pronunciation. As their decoding skills become increasingly secure, teaching should be directed more towards developing their vocabulary and the breadth and depth of their reading, making sure that they become independent, fluent and enthusiastic readers who read widely and frequently. They should be developing their understanding and enjoyment of stories, poetry, plays and non-fiction, and learning to read silently. They should also be developing their knowledge and skills in reading non-fiction about a wide range of subjects. They should be learning to justify their views about what they have read: with support at the start of year 3 and increasingly independently by the end of year 4.

Pupils should be able to write down their ideas with a reasonable degree of accuracy and with good sentence punctuation. Teachers should therefore be consolidating pupils' writing skills, their vocabulary, their grasp of sentence structure and their knowledge of linguistic terminology. Teaching them to develop as writers involves teaching them to enhance the effectiveness of what they write as well as increasing their competence. Teachers should make sure that pupils build on what they have learnt, particularly in terms of the range of their writing and the more varied grammar, vocabulary and narrative structures from which they can draw to express their ideas. Pupils should be beginning to understand how writing can be different from speech. Joined handwriting should be the norm; pupils should be able to use it fast enough to keep pace with what they want to say.

Pupils' spelling of common words should be correct, including common exception words and other words that they have learnt (see English Appendix 1). Pupils should spell words as accurately as possible using their phonic knowledge and other knowledge of spelling, such as morphology and etymology.

Most pupils will not need further direct teaching of word reading skills: they are able to decode unfamiliar words accurately, and need very few repeated experiences of this before the word is stored in such a way that they can read it without overt sound-blending. They should demonstrate understanding of figurative language, distinguish shades of meaning among related words and use age-appropriate, academic vocabulary.

As in key stage 1, however, pupils who are still struggling to decode need to be taught to do this urgently through a rigorous and systematic phonics programme so that they catch up rapidly with their peers. If they cannot decode independently and fluently, they will find it increasingly difficult to understand what they read and to write down what they want to say. As far as possible, however, these pupils should follow the year 3 and 4 programme of study in terms of listening to new books, hearing and learning new vocabulary and grammatical structures, and discussing these.

Specific requirements for pupils to discuss what they are learning and to develop their wider skills in spoken language form part of this programme of study. In years 3 and 4, pupils should become more familiar with and confident in using language in a greater variety of situations, for a variety of audiences and purposes, including through drama, formal presentations and debate.

Years 3 and 4 programme of study

Reading – word reading

Statutory requirements

Pupils should be taught to:

- apply their growing knowledge of root words, prefixes and suffixes (etymology and morphology) as listed in English Appendix 1, both to read aloud and to understand the meaning of new words they meet

- read further exception words, noting the unusual correspondences between spelling and sound, and where these occur in the word.

Notes and guidance (non-statutory)

At this stage, teaching comprehension should be taking precedence over teaching word reading directly. Any focus on word reading should support the development of vocabulary.

When pupils are taught to read longer words, they should be supported to test out different pronunciations. They will attempt to match what they decode to words they may have already heard but may not have seen in print [for example, in reading 'technical', the pronunciation /tɛtʃnɪkəl/ ('tetchnical') might not sound familiar, but /tɛknɪkəl/ ('teknical') should].

Reading – comprehension

Statutory requirements

Pupils should be taught to:
- develop positive attitudes to reading and understanding of what they read by:
    - listening to and discussing a wide range of fiction, poetry, plays, non-fiction and reference books or textbooks
    - reading books that are structured in different ways and reading for a range of purposes
    - using dictionaries to check the meaning of words that they have read
    - increasing their familiarity with a wide range of books, including fairy stories, myths and legends, and retelling some of these orally
    - identifying themes and conventions in a wide range of books

Statutory requirements

- preparing poems and play scripts to read aloud and to perform, showing understanding through intonation, tone, volume and action
- discussing words and phrases that capture the reader's interest and imagination
- recognising some different forms of poetry [for example, free verse, narrative poetry]

- understand what they read, in books they can read independently, by:
  - checking that the text makes sense to them, discussing their understanding and explaining the meaning of words in context
  - asking questions to improve their understanding of a text
  - drawing inferences such as inferring characters' feelings, thoughts and motives from their actions, and justifying inferences with evidence
  - predicting what might happen from details stated and implied
  - identifying main ideas drawn from more than one paragraph and summarising these
  - identifying how language, structure, and presentation contribute to meaning

- retrieve and record information from non-fiction

- participate in discussion about both books that are read to them and those they can read for themselves, taking turns and listening to what others say.

Notes and guidance (non-statutory)

The focus should continue to be on pupils' comprehension as a primary element in reading. The knowledge and skills that pupils need in order to comprehend are very similar at different ages. This is why the programmes of study for comprehension in years 3 and 4 and years 5 and 6 are similar: the complexity of the writing increases the level of challenge.

Pupils should be taught to recognise themes in what they read, such as the triumph of good over evil or the use of magical devices in fairy stories and folk tales.

They should also learn the conventions of different types of writing (for example, the greeting in letters, a diary written in the first person or the use of presentational devices such as numbering and headings in instructions).

Pupils should be taught to use the skills they have learnt earlier and continue to apply these skills to read for different reasons, including for pleasure, or to find out information and the meaning of new words.

Notes and guidance (non-statutory)

Pupils should continue to have opportunities to listen frequently to stories, poems, non-fiction and other writing, including whole books and not just extracts, so that they build on what was taught previously. In this way, they also meet books and authors that they might not choose themselves. Pupils should also have opportunities to exercise choice in selecting books and be taught how to do so, with teachers making use of any library services and expertise to support this.

Reading, re-reading, and rehearsing poems and plays for presentation and performance give pupils opportunities to discuss language, including vocabulary, extending their interest in the meaning and origin of words. Pupils should be encouraged to use drama approaches to understand how to perform plays and poems to support their understanding of the meaning. These activities also provide them with an incentive to find out what expression is required, so feeding into comprehension.

In using non-fiction, pupils should know what information they need to look for before they begin and be clear about the task. They should be shown how to use contents pages and indexes to locate information.

Pupils should have guidance about the kinds of explanations and questions that are expected from them. They should help to develop, agree on, and evaluate rules for effective discussion. The expectation should be that all pupils take part.

Writing – transcription

Statutory requirements

Spelling (see English Appendix 1)

Pupils should be taught to:

- use further prefixes and suffixes and understand how to add them (English Appendix 1)

- spell further homophones

- spell words that are often misspelt (English Appendix 1)

- place the possessive apostrophe accurately in words with regular plurals [for example, girls', boys'] and in words with irregular plurals [for example, children's]

- use the first two or three letters of a word to check its spelling in a dictionary

- write from memory simple sentences, dictated by the teacher, that include words and punctuation taught so far.

Notes and guidance (non-statutory)

Pupils should learn to spell new words correctly and have plenty of practice in spelling them.

As in years 1 and 2, pupils should continue to be supported in understanding and applying the concepts of word structure (see English Appendix 2).

Pupils need sufficient knowledge of spelling in order to use dictionaries efficiently.

Statutory requirements

Handwriting

Pupils should be taught to:

- use the diagonal and horizontal strokes that are needed to join letters and understand which letters, when adjacent to one another, are best left unjoined

- increase the legibility, consistency and quality of their handwriting [for example, by ensuring that the downstrokes of letters are parallel and equidistant; that lines of writing are spaced sufficiently so that the ascenders and descenders of letters do not touch].

Notes and guidance (non-statutory)

Pupils should be using joined handwriting throughout their independent writing. Handwriting should continue to be taught, with the aim of increasing the fluency with which pupils are able to write down what they want to say. This, in turn, will support their composition and spelling.

Writing – composition

Statutory requirements

Pupils should be taught to:

- plan their writing by:
  - discussing writing similar to that which they are planning to write in order to understand and learn from its structure, vocabulary and grammar
  - discussing and recording ideas
- draft and write by:
  - composing and rehearsing sentences orally (including dialogue), progressively building a varied and rich vocabulary and an increasing range of sentence structures (English Appendix 2)
  - organising paragraphs around a theme
  - in narratives, creating settings, characters and plot
  - in non-narrative material, using simple organisational devices [for example, headings and sub-headings]
- evaluate and edit by:
  - assessing the effectiveness of their own and others' writing and suggesting improvements
  - proposing changes to grammar and vocabulary to improve consistency, including the accurate use of pronouns in sentences
- proof-read for spelling and punctuation errors
- read aloud their own writing, to a group or the whole class, using appropriate intonation and controlling the tone and volume so that the meaning is clear.

Notes and guidance (non-statutory)

Pupils should continue to have opportunities to write for a range of real purposes and audiences as part of their work across the curriculum. These purposes and audiences should underpin the decisions about the form the writing should take, such as a narrative, an explanation or a description.

Pupils should understand, through being shown these, the skills and processes that are essential for writing: that is, thinking aloud to explore and collect ideas, drafting, and re-reading to check their meaning is clear, including doing so as the writing develops. Pupils should be taught to monitor whether their own writing makes sense in the same way that they monitor their reading, checking at different levels.

Writing – vocabulary, grammar and punctuation

Statutory requirements

Pupils should be taught to:

- develop their understanding of the concepts set out in <u>English Appendix 2</u> by:
    - extending the range of sentences with more than one clause by using a wider range of conjunctions, including when, if, because, although
    - using the present perfect form of verbs in contrast to the past tense
    - choosing nouns or pronouns appropriately for clarity and cohesion and to avoid repetition
    - using conjunctions, adverbs and prepositions to express time and cause
    - using fronted adverbials
    - learning the grammar for years 3 and 4 in English Appendix 2
- indicate grammatical and other features by:
    - using commas after fronted adverbials
    - indicating possession by using the possessive apostrophe with plural nouns
    - using and punctuating direct speech
- use and understand the grammatical terminology in English Appendix 2 accurately and appropriately when discussing their writing and reading.

Notes and guidance (non-statutory)

Grammar should be taught explicitly: pupils should be taught the terminology and concepts set out in English Appendix 2, and be able to apply them correctly to examples of real language, such as their own writing or books that they have read.

At this stage, pupils should start to learn about some of the differences between Standard English and non-Standard English and begin to apply what they have learnt [for example, in writing dialogue for characters].

Upper key stage 2 – years 5 and 6

By the beginning of year 5, pupils should be able to read aloud a wider range of poetry and books written at an age-appropriate interest level with accuracy and at a reasonable speaking pace. They should be able to read most words effortlessly and to work out how to pronounce unfamiliar written words with increasing automaticity. If the pronunciation sounds unfamiliar, they should ask for help in determining both the meaning of the word and how to pronounce it correctly.

They should be able to prepare readings, with appropriate intonation to show their understanding, and should be able to summarise and present a familiar story in their own words. They should be reading widely and frequently, outside as well as in school, for pleasure and information. They should be able to read silently, with good understanding, inferring the meanings of unfamiliar words, and then discuss what they have read.

Pupils should be able to write down their ideas quickly. Their grammar and punctuation should be broadly accurate. Pupils' spelling of most words taught so far should be accurate and they should be able to spell words that they have not yet been taught by using what they have learnt about how spelling works in English.

During years 5 and 6, teachers should continue to emphasise pupils' enjoyment and understanding of language, especially vocabulary, to support their reading and writing. Pupils' knowledge of language, gained from stories, plays, poetry, non-fiction and textbooks, will support their increasing fluency as readers, their facility as writers, and their comprehension. As in years 3 and 4, pupils should be taught to enhance the effectiveness of their writing as well as their competence.

It is essential that pupils whose decoding skills are poor are taught through a rigorous and systematic phonics programme so that they catch up rapidly with their peers in terms of their decoding and spelling. However, as far as possible, these pupils should follow the upper key stage 2 programme of study in terms of listening to books and other writing that they have not come across before, hearing and learning new vocabulary and grammatical structures, and having a chance to talk about all of these.

By the end of year 6, pupils' reading and writing should be sufficiently fluent and effortless for them to manage the general demands of the curriculum in year 7, across all subjects and not just in English, but there will continue to be a need for pupils to learn subject-specific vocabulary. They should be able to reflect their understanding of the audience for and purpose of their writing by selecting appropriate vocabulary and grammar. Teachers should prepare pupils for secondary education by ensuring that they can consciously control sentence structure in their writing and understand why sentences are constructed as they are. Pupils should understand nuances in vocabulary choice and age-appropriate, academic vocabulary. This involves consolidation, practice and discussion of language.

Specific requirements for pupils to discuss what they are learning and to develop their wider skills in spoken language form part of this programme of study. In years 5 and 6, pupils' confidence, enjoyment and mastery of language should be extended through public speaking, performance and debate.

Years 5 and 6 programme of study

Reading – word reading

Statutory requirements

Pupils should be taught to:

- apply their growing knowledge of root words, prefixes and suffixes (morphology and etymology), as listed in English Appendix 1, both to read aloud and to understand the meaning of new words that they meet.

Notes and guidance (non-statutory)

At this stage, there should be no need for further direct teaching of word reading skills for almost all pupils. If pupils are struggling or failing in this, the reasons for this should be investigated. It is imperative that pupils are taught to read during their last two years at primary school if they enter year 5 not being able to do so.

Pupils should be encouraged to work out any unfamiliar word. They should focus on all the letters in a word so that they do not, for example, read 'invitation' for 'imitation' simply because they might be more familiar with the first word. Accurate reading of individual words, which might be key to the meaning of a sentence or paragraph, improves comprehension.

When teachers are reading with or to pupils, attention should be paid to new vocabulary – both a word's meaning(s) and its correct pronunciation.

Reading – comprehension

Statutory requirements

Pupils should be taught to:

- maintain positive attitudes to reading and understanding of what they read by:
  - continuing to read and discuss an increasingly wide range of fiction, poetry, plays, non-fiction and reference books or textbooks
  - reading books that are structured in different ways and reading for a range of purposes
  - increasing their familiarity with a wide range of books, including myths, legends and traditional stories, modern fiction, fiction from our literary heritage, and books from other cultures and traditions

Statutory requirements

- recommending books that they have read to their peers, giving reasons for their choices
- identifying and discussing themes and conventions in and across a wide range of writing
- making comparisons within and across books
- learning a wider range of poetry by heart
- preparing poems and plays to read aloud and to perform, showing understanding through intonation, tone and volume so that the meaning is clear to an audience

- understand what they read by:
  - checking that the book makes sense to them, discussing their understanding and exploring the meaning of words in context
  - asking questions to improve their understanding
  - drawing inferences such as inferring characters' feelings, thoughts and motives from their actions, and justifying inferences with evidence
  - predicting what might happen from details stated and implied
  - summarising the main ideas drawn from more than one paragraph, identifying key details that support the main ideas
  - identifying how language, structure and presentation contribute to meaning
- discuss and evaluate how authors use language, including figurative language, considering the impact on the reader
- distinguish between statements of fact and opinion
- retrieve, record and present information from non-fiction
- participate in discussions about books that are read to them and those they can read for themselves, building on their own and others' ideas and challenging views courteously
- explain and discuss their understanding of what they have read, including through formal presentations and debates, maintaining a focus on the topic and using notes where necessary
- provide reasoned justifications for their views.

Notes and guidance (non-statutory)

Even though pupils can now read independently, reading aloud to them should include whole books so that they meet books and authors that they might not choose to read themselves.

The knowledge and skills that pupils need in order to comprehend are very similar at different ages. Pupils should continue to apply what they have already learnt to more complex writing.

Pupils should be taught to recognise themes in what they read, such as loss or heroism. They should have opportunities to compare characters, consider different accounts of the same event and discuss viewpoints (both of authors and of fictional characters), within a text and across more than one text.

They should continue to learn the conventions of different types of writing, such as the use of the first person in writing diaries and autobiographies.

Pupils should be taught the technical and other terms needed for discussing what they hear and read, such as metaphor, simile, analogy, imagery, style and effect.

In using reference books, pupils need to know what information they need to look for before they begin and need to understand the task. They should be shown how to use contents pages and indexes to locate information.

The skills of information retrieval that are taught should be applied, for example, in reading history, geography and science textbooks, and in contexts where pupils are genuinely motivated to find out information, for example, reading information leaflets before a gallery or museum visit or reading a theatre programme or review. Teachers should consider making use of any library services and expertise to support this.

Pupils should have guidance about and feedback on the quality of their explanations and contributions to discussions.

Pupils should be shown how to compare characters, settings, themes and other aspects of what they read.

Writing – transcription

Statutory requirements

Spelling (see <u>English Appendix 1</u>)

Pupils should be taught to:

- use further prefixes and suffixes and understand the guidance for adding them
- spell some words with 'silent' letters [for example, knight, psalm, solemn]
- continue to distinguish between homophones and other words which are often confused
- use knowledge of morphology and etymology in spelling and understand that the spelling of some words needs to be learnt specifically, as listed in English Appendix 1
- use dictionaries to check the spelling and meaning of words
- use the first three or four letters of a word to check spelling, meaning or both of these in a dictionary
- use a thesaurus.

Notes and guidance (non-statutory)

As in earlier years, pupils should continue to be taught to understand and apply the concepts of word structure so that they can draw on their knowledge of morphology and etymology to spell correctly.

Statutory requirements

Handwriting and presentation

Pupils should be taught to:

- write legibly, fluently and with increasing speed by:
  - choosing which shape of a letter to use when given choices and deciding whether or not to join specific letters
  - choosing the writing implement that is best suited for a task.

Notes and guidance (non-statutory)

Pupils should continue to practise handwriting and be encouraged to increase the speed of it, so that problems with forming letters do not get in the way of their writing down what they want to say. They should be clear about what standard of handwriting is appropriate for a particular task, for example, quick notes or a final handwritten version. They should also be taught to use an unjoined style, for example, for labelling a diagram or data, writing an email address, or for algebra and capital letters, for example, for filling in a form.

Writing – composition

Statutory requirements

Pupils should be taught to:

- plan their writing by:
    - identifying the audience for and purpose of the writing, selecting the appropriate form and using other similar writing as models for their own
    - noting and developing initial ideas, drawing on reading and research where necessary
    - in writing narratives, considering how authors have developed characters and settings in what pupils have read, listened to or seen performed
- draft and write by:
    - selecting appropriate grammar and vocabulary, understanding how such choices can change and enhance meaning
    - in narratives, describing settings, characters and atmosphere and integrating dialogue to convey character and advance the action
    - précising longer passages
    - using a wide range of devices to build cohesion within and across paragraphs
    - using further organisational and presentational devices to structure text and to guide the reader [for example, headings, bullet points, underlining]
- evaluate and edit by:
    - assessing the effectiveness of their own and others' writing
    - proposing changes to vocabulary, grammar and punctuation to enhance effects and clarify meaning
    - ensuring the consistent and correct use of tense throughout a piece of writing
    - ensuring correct subject and verb agreement when using singular and plural, distinguishing between the language of speech and writing and choosing the appropriate register
- proof-read for spelling and punctuation errors

Statutory requirements

- perform their own compositions, using appropriate intonation, volume, and movement so that meaning is clear.

Notes and guidance (non-statutory)

Pupils should understand, through being shown, the skills and processes essential for writing: that is, thinking aloud to generate ideas, drafting, and re-reading to check that the meaning is clear.

Writing – vocabulary, grammar and punctuation

Statutory requirements

Pupils should be taught to:

- develop their understanding of the concepts set out in English Appendix 2 by:
    - recognising vocabulary and structures that are appropriate for formal speech and writing, including subjunctive forms
    - using passive verbs to affect the presentation of information in a sentence
    - using the perfect form of verbs to mark relationships of time and cause
    - using expanded noun phrases to convey complicated information concisely
    - using modal verbs or adverbs to indicate degrees of possibility
    - using relative clauses beginning with who, which, where, when, whose, that or with an implied (i.e. omitted) relative pronoun
    - learning the grammar for years 5 and 6 in English Appendix 2
- indicate grammatical and other features by:
    - using commas to clarify meaning or avoid ambiguity in writing
    - using hyphens to avoid ambiguity
    - using brackets, dashes or commas to indicate parenthesis
    - using semi-colons, colons or dashes to mark boundaries between independent clauses
    - using a colon to introduce a list
    - punctuating bullet points consistently
- use and understand the grammatical terminology in English Appendix 2 accurately and appropriately in discussing their writing and reading.

Notes and guidance (non-statutory)

Pupils should continue to add to their knowledge of linguistic terms, including those to describe grammar, so that they can discuss their writing and reading.

Index

Page numbers in **bold** denote Programmes of Study. Page numbers followed by 'g' denote glossary entries.